Social Policy, Ageing and Voluntary Action

SOCIAL POLICY, AGEING AND VOLUNTARY ACTION

Nicholas Acheson and Brian Harvey
Centre for Voluntary Action Studies
University of Ulster

IPA
INSTITUTE OF PUBLIC
ADMINISTRATION

First published 2008
by the Institute of Public Administration
57–61 Lansdowne Road
Dublin 4
Ireland

ISBN: 978-1-904541-73-8

British Library Cataloguing in Publication Data
A catalogue record for this book is available from the British Library.

Cover design by Alice Campbell, Dublin
Typeset by Carole Lynch, Sligo
Printed in Ireland by ColourBooks Ltd, Dublin

Contents

Acknowledgements   **ix**

Foreword   **xiii**
    Terms of reference   *xiii*
    Method   *xiv*
    Definitions   *xiv*

Chapter 1   Common Contexts   **1**
    Introduction and overview   *1*
    Welfare regimes and global trends in welfare   *4*
    Older people: the broader European context   *6*
    Voluntary action in Europe   *9*
    Voluntary action for older people in Europe   *10*
    Conclusions   *14*

Chapter 2   Older People and Public Policy: Northern Ireland   **16**
    Introduction   *16*
    Demographic trends   *17*
    Social situation of older people   *18*
    Public policies for older people   *22*
    Differences between Northern Ireland and the
      rest of the UK   *29*
    Conclusions   *36*

Chapter 3   Older People and Public Policy: Ireland   **38**
    Demographic trends   *38*
    Social situation of older people   *40*
    Policies for older people   *45*
    Critique of policies   *60*
    Conclusions   *63*

Chapter 4   **Community and Voluntary Action:**
              Northern Ireland   **66**
              Introduction   *66*
              Public policy and voluntary action in Northern Ireland *67*
              Voluntary and community action: a profile   *75*
              Voluntary and community organisations   *86*
              Regional bodies   *87*
              Subregional network organisations   *99*
              Building the independent voice of older people in
              Northern Ireland   *101*
              Conclusions   *103*

Chapter 5   **Community and Voluntary Action: Ireland**   **106**
              Policy for voluntary and community action   *106*
              Policy for voluntary and community action for
                older people   *112*
              Voluntary and community action for older people:
                emergence   *120*
              Voluntary and community action for older people:
                map   *130*
              Voluntary and community action for older people:
                profiles   *132*
              Case studies   *138*
              Conclusions   *141*

Chapter 6   **Older People's Organisations and Policy-making**   **145**
              Policy-making: Northern Ireland   *148*
              The experience of participation in policy-making   *158*
              Policy-making: Ireland   *161*
              The experience of participation in policy-making   *168*
              Conclusions: reaching a tipping point?   *171*

Chapter 7   **The Comparison and Some Conclusions**   **177**

Methodological Note   **187**

Appendices **189**
A.1   *Profile of Organisations Working with Older People,*
          Northern Ireland   *189*
A.2   *Profile of Organisations Working with Older People,*
          Ireland   *197*
A.3   *Voluntary and Community Action for Older People:*
          Profiles   *220*

Bibliography and References **230**

Index **249**

Acknowledgements

The authors wish to acknowledge and thank all those who assisted in the research. In the first instance, we wish to thank the Royal Irish Academy for making available the funding that made the research possible. We acknowledge in particular the role of Professor Arthur Williamson, Professor of Non-Profit Research and Director of the Centre of Voluntary Action Studies at the University of Ulster, who conceived of the project and guided it through to completion. He also contributed the profiles of organisations in Appendix A.1.

We wish to thank those who advised on the project for contributing to meetings and for reading and commenting on the draft texts, and we wish to thank those who co-operated by giving us time through personal interviews (* indicates that they gave interviews by telephone).

In Ireland, these were:

Louise Richardson, Older Women's Network
Dónal McManus, Irish Council for Social Housing
Pat Lane, ALONE
Niamh Macken, Friends of the Elderly
Catherine Rose, Age & Opportunity
Sheila Simmonds, Irish Association for Older People
Brian Judd, Federation of Active Retirement Associations
David Strattan, Paul Murray and Robin Webster, Age Action Ireland
Bob Carroll, National Council on Ageing and Older People
Dolores Moran, Department of Health and Children
Michael O'Halloran, Irish Senior Citizens Parliament
Gráinne McGettrick, Alzheimer's Society
Laura Mahoney, Head of Research Programmes, The Royal Irish Academy
Jean Manahan, Atlantic Philanthropies
Mo Flynn and Janet Convery, Health Service Executive
Eugene Murray, Hospice Foundation
Columba Faulkner, Society of St Vincent de Paul
Monica-Ann Dunne, National Federation of Pensioners' Associations

David Silke, Housing Unit, formerly National Economic and Social Forum*
Michael Browne, independent researcher*
Frank Goodwin, Carers Association
Noel Byrne, Westgate Foundation
Prof. Eamonn O'Shea, National University of Ireland, Galway
Orlaith McHugh, Carlow EQUAL*
Brian Holland, Sligo Alzheimer*
Frances Callaghan, Positive Age, Cavan*
Petronella Martin, Sisters of Our Lady of Charity
John Kincaid, Midland Health Board (retired)
Charles McDonald, Sue Ryder Foundation*
David Lee, Dublin Central Mission
Seamas Devine, Mind the Gap, Donegal*
David Wilkinson, Dublin Central Mission
Ethel McKenna, St Francis Hospice, Raheny, Dublin

In Northern Ireland these were:

Zoë Anderson and Gordon McCullough, Northern Ireland Council for
    Voluntary Action
Seamus Lynch and Grace Henry, Help the Aged, Northern Ireland
Una Lynch, Prof. Sally Wheeler and Nathan Emmerich, Institute of
    Governance, Queen's University, Belfast
Anne O'Reilly and David McConnell, Age Concern, Northern Ireland
Ryan Sampson, Age Concern, England
Alison Forbes and Paddy Joe McClean, Sperrin Lakeland Senior
    Citizens Forum
Denise McBride and Phil Evans, Newry and Mourne Senior Citizens
    Consortium
Colm Fitzpatrick, independent consultant
Majella McCluskey, Association of Chief Officers of Voluntary
    Organisations
Marie Gribbon, Engage with Age
John Ley, Northern Ireland Pensioners' Convention
Ken Logue, Atlantic Philanthropies
Pat Newe, Northern Ireland Social Services Inspectorate
Ray Martin, DHSSPS
Avril Clarke, Voluntary and Community Unit, Department for Social
    Development
Gerry Mulligan, Jim Breen and Michael Pollock, Office of the First
    Minister and Deputy First Minister
Helen Ferguson, Carers Northern Ireland

We wish to thank those who responded to requests for information or who provided assistance in other ways: Margaret Roe, Age & Opportunity; Robin George, Protestant Aid; Cathy Lanigan, Respond! Dublin; Anne Connolly, consultant; Catherine Power, Waterford Partnership; Natasha O'Keefe, An Siol; Brenda Farrelly, Volunteer Coordinator, St Francis Hospice, Raheny, Dublin; Mary Upton TD and Alissa McCarty Zimmerman, Comhrá na nAosach. We wish to thank Carol Ivory in the Health Service Executive for her assistance in obtaining lists of voluntary and community organisations working with older people and funded by the executive.

The authors are deeply grateful to Professor Sally Wheeler and Dr Una Lynch of the Institute of Governance at Queen's University Belfast for enabling access to survey data. We are particularly indebted to Nathan Emmerich, also of the Institute, for data entry and the conduct of preliminary analysis. We wish to acknowledge Age Concern NI and Help the Aged for permission to use their data.

The authors were assisted, for their research in the Republic, by an advisory group comprising Dr Freda Donoghue, Dublin University (Trinity College); Deirdre Garvey, Chief Executive Officer, The Wheel; Dr Fergus O'Ferrall, the Adelaide Hospital Society; and Dr Joe Larragy, National University of Ireland (Maynooth). The authors are most grateful to them for their good advice, assistance, comments and information.

We would like to thank colleagues at the University of Ulster, in particular Ms Liz McNeill at the Centre for Voluntary Action Studies who administered the questionnaire in Northern Ireland and who provided data input and data analysis among a multitude of other tasks. Dr Anne Marie Gray kindly read and commented on Chapter 2. We would also like to acknowledge the help of Ms Hazel Boyd at the University of Ulster's Social and Policy Research Institute.

Foreword

Terms of reference

The project on which this book is based was the first north–south comparative study of older people and the voluntary and community sector on the island of Ireland. As a result of demographic change, longer life expectancy and other factors, the coming decades will see a significant growth in the numbers of older people. The social policy dimension is important, for studies in both parts of the island have highlighted the risk to poverty of many older people.

This study comes at a time of growing awareness of older people in society and of the increasingly important role of the voluntary and community sector and civic action. Although voluntary and community organisations have long played a role in providing welfare services for older people, there are substantial information deficits in our knowledge. Only limited work appears to have been done to examine the relationship between the sector and the policy-making process concerning older people — and how that could develop in the future.

The research:

- Mapped the origin, extent and scope of voluntary action on ageing: numbers, types of organisations, scale, origins, pathways of development
- Assessed the functions and capacity of voluntary action: activities, services, structures, strengths, weaknesses, leadership, capacity for innovation and change
- Examined the relationships with policy: funding, interfaces with government (local to departmental), structures, contribution to policy, levels of influence, differences and commonalities in policy perspectives.

In all these areas, a comparative dimension was examined: what were the key similarities and differences between the two parts of the island? How can we explain them? What can we learn from these different experiences, lines of development, structures and systems? Can good models be applied from one to the other?

The research was intended to add to existing knowledge; to make a comparison between Northern Ireland and the Republic that sheds light on broader social policies; and to present insights that will be useful to policy-makers for future development in the field of older people and voluntary action.

Method

The following methods were used in this research:

- Literature review of the field
- Desk research of information, research and policy reports
- Assembly of information on organisations working with or providing services for older people
- Survey of a sample of these organisations
- In-depth case studies of a number of organisations
- Interviews with leaders of voluntary and community-sector organisations; officials in government and statutory agencies and bodies; experts on policies for older people, and the community and voluntary sector.

An advisory committee assisted in guiding the research in Ireland. This comprised Dr Fergus O'Ferrall, Director of the Adelaide Hospital Society; Dr Freda Donoghue of Dublin University (Trinity College); Deirdre Garvey, Chief Executive Officer, The Wheel; and Dr Joe Larragy, National University of Ireland, Maynooth. Additional advice was given by Geraldine Prizeman of Dublin University (Trinity College).

The research took place over 2005–06 and concluded in 2007. A seminar was held on 29 August 2006 in the Royal Irish Academy to present the first results of the research in Ireland, and comments were invited and received from the participants. The outcome of the survey was also sent to survey participants for comment. The descriptions of the individual organisations working with older people were sent to the organisations concerned, for checking and accuracy, and comments were duly received.

Definitions

The term 'older people' presents difficulties. Historically, the term applied to persons of pensionable age (currently sixty-six years in Ireland; sixty in Northern Ireland for women, and sixty-five for men). The term 'old' is often popularly now applied to sixty years. In some cases, the term 'old' has been defined even further downward: in the terminology of the European Union, older workers are those aged fifty years and over, and the Equality Authority in Ireland uses the age fifty, since that is the age at which affirmative action is authorised under the Employment Equality Act, 1998. In this research, the term 'old' will generally apply to those aged sixty or over, but we are conscious that under certain circumstances it may apply to people of fifty and over, in which case this will be stated.

In dealing with the member states of the European Union, the term 'EU12' refers to the twelve member states in the early 1990s; 'EU15' refers to the fifteen member states in 2003; 'EU25' refers to the members for 2004–06 after the great enlargement; and 'EU27' refers to the member states in 2007.

We have endeavoured to adopt the formal names of the two Irish jurisdictions throughout. 'Ireland' thus refers to the state of that name, and 'Northern Ireland' to the region in the northeast of the island that remains part of the United Kingdom. From time to time, the term 'Republic of Ireland' will be used, which, although it has no constitutional standing, is in widespread use and is well understood. The term 'island of Ireland' will be used as a geographical, non-political one to refer to the whole island. 'The Irish state' will refer to Ireland.

The term 'voluntary action' creates some definitional issues. There is no universally agreed definition of 'voluntary action' in Europe, and the problem is compounded by the use of a variety of overlapping terms, each with somewhat different connotations, such as 'nongovernmental organisations', the 'third sector', 'non-profit sector', 'charities', 'associations' and the broader term, 'civil society'.

Any study of voluntary action must struggle with questions of definition, limits, contours, self-consciousness and self-identity. The earlier work by these authors (Acheson, Harvey, Kearney, Williamson, 2004) discussed these issues and, for both suitability and convenience, used a definition adapted from the Northern Ireland Council for Voluntary Action's *State of the Sector III* (NICVA, 2002), which in turn was based on an amended version of the classification used by three bodies: the Charity Commission, the Office for National Statistics and the International Classification for Non-Profit Organisations (ICNPO) developed for international comparative purposes by the Johns Hopkins University in Baltimore, Maryland. Between them, they mean that voluntary action is understood to comprise bodies that:

- Are self-governing
- Are independent (thereby excluding governmental and non-departmental public bodies)

- Are non-profit
- Benefit from a meaningful degree of philanthropy, given financially or in time
- Have a wider public benefit and purpose (thereby excluding bodies that exist solely for their own members)
- Are non-sacramental (but including activities of public benefit performed by religious organisations, for example in the area of social services).

This definition, which has a number of advantages, does not distinguish voluntary and community organisations by size (large and small); geography (local, regional and national); nature (those that provide services to those that campaign for a wider public good); or finance (those that benefit from public funding — provided they retain their independent and self-governing nature — and those that do not). In the case of older people, it does not necessarily distinguish between those that are *of* the elderly, *for* the elderly, mutualist, religious, civil, or political, although these distinctions are important. At the edges of this territory, there are inevitably some grey areas and we include:

- Organisations that provide services for people other than older people, provided that older people are their main, primary focus and concern. This would include, for example, dementia services which are used primarily, though not exclusively, by older people.
- Voluntary action that is not directly for older people but has a strong bearing on the situation in which older people find themselves. This would include, for example, carers' groups that deal with the older age group.
- Institutional services for older people with a clear voluntary base, fulfilling the requirements above. This would take in, for example, hospice services and religious-based homes for older people.

1

Common Contexts

Introduction and overview

This book is an examination of the relationship between voluntary action and the development of social policy on ageing in contemporary welfare states. It is based on the first attempt to describe, analyse and compare voluntary action in both jurisdictions in Ireland as it relates to policies and programmes that address the challenge of an ageing population. The so-called crisis of an ageing society, together with pressures exerted on welfare states by globalisation, has generated a wide-ranging debate on the competencies and the extent of state interventions and the role of voluntary organisations in meeting social needs and sustaining social solidarity. The case of Ireland's two jurisdictions provides an intriguing window into how this debate is shaping developments in the forms and functions of voluntary action in the field of ageing.

Whilst both Irish jurisdictions share a broad welfare regime type, differences in history, politics and institutional development all point to a useful entry to an examination of the forces that are shaping the development of voluntary action in the contemporary world. Accordingly, the book provides information on the respective voluntary sectors in the field of ageing in both Northern Ireland and the Republic of Ireland. It provides a comparative analysis and discusses the degree to which voluntary action provides access to political decision-making for older people in general.

The core question that this book addresses is the relationship between voluntary action among and on behalf of older people and political influence over the crucial resource allocation decisions that determine access to health, social care and other social goods. The evidence we uncover in this book shows a pattern of a massive expansion of voluntary action among older people and the existence of structures facilitating joint discussion between governments and organisations that represent the interests of older people. However, these are coupled with an actual absence of political influence evident in both Irish jurisdictions. The lack of a relationship between activism and influence is a puzzle that deserves to be addressed, particularly in the light of a long-standing, albeit contested, view that extols the virtue of civic engagement for the efficient working of democracy (Dahl, 1961; Almond and Verba, 1963; Putnam, 1993, 2000).

Theoretical approach

In our earlier comparative work (Acheson et al., 2004), an institutional approach was adopted to explain the divergence and convergence of the voluntary sectors in the two parts of Ireland, looking to contrasting narratives in the developments of the two welfare states as an explanatory framework. The 'social origins' approach was used, and this suggested that national differences in the shape, size and disposition of national voluntary sectors could be explained by differences in welfare regimes (Salamon and Anheier, 1998; Anheier, 2005). Using historical reconstruction as well as contemporary evidence, we were able to show how diverse patterns of voluntary action developed alongside divergence in political and economic contexts in the two Irish jurisdictions.

However, the analysis remained rather crude, reflecting unsatisfactory elements in the schema adopted by Salamon and Anheier to carry out their international comparisons (Salamon and Anheier, 1994; Donoghue et al., 1999) and its reliance on the concept of welfare regimes (Esping-Andersen, 1990). A particular problem of this approach is that its level of analysis is confined to the nation state, leading to a lack of precision and an inability to specify either the impact of supranational bodies, especially (in the European context) the European Union, or the conditions within specific jurisdictions that might underpin the emergence of differing forms of voluntary action. Additionally, it presents problems in comparative north–south studies as Northern Ireland, as a self-governing region of the UK, is not equivalent to the Republic, an independent state (Rottman, 1999).

As a result, whilst retaining a broad institutionalist approach to the analysis, we extend our conceptual framework to facilitate a more nuanced understanding of the dynamic interplay between welfare and voluntary action. We believe this to be necessary to understand the respective places of solidarity among older people, welfare service delivery and political influence within the broader category of voluntary action that our evidence in Ireland uncovers.

By adopting an 'institutional approach' we mean that the voluntary sector is 'embedded in, indeed inseparable from, the political economy' (Smith and Gronbjerg, 2006, p. 222). Government activity and policies and the way in which the economy is structured are all central, as is the role of welfare ideology (how a society views its priorities and values such as equality, opportunity and fairness). Ideology and economic structure will generate social needs and determine the welfare mix between the state, market and family in meeting needs. These processes will, in turn, structure both the shape and the roles of the voluntary sector itself (ibid, p. 222). We tease this out with reference to the discussion by Evers and Laville (2004) of embeddedness. They argue that the concept of 'sector' can be misleading if it is taken to refer to an entirely separate sphere parallel to the state and the market. Rather, using the European idea of the welfare mix (Johnson, 1998), they suggest that the voluntary sector is embedded in a tri-polar system of welfare distribution made up of the market, state and informal economies like the family, and that organisations in the voluntary sector 'act as a kind of tension field', simultaneously influenced by all three (Evers and Laville, 2004, pp. 14, 15).

They suggest that in contemporary discussion of mixed economies of welfare there is a hierarchy among the three, with the market economy considered primary, the non-market economy of state-led redistribution as supplementary and the informal economy as residual.

Organisational forms within the voluntary sector are embedded in the interplay of these factors, accounting for the forms of solidarity that emerge, as well as the range and types of service-providing organisations. In the field of older people, with which we are concerned here, the way old age is culturally constructed, the welfare regime and the relative openness of the political system will all affect the kinds and range of organisations. Conversely, evidence of the disposition of organisation forms will provide insights into the nature of the political economy as it affects older people.

The kinds of voluntary organisation that have developed can also usefully be assessed by examining the extent to which they operate in a purely private sphere of activity, a civic or philanthropic sphere, or what has been termed the public sphere. Whilst private activity and civic activity are focused on the immediate needs of those involved or of others, activity in the public sphere 'consists in voicing issues for public debate about what ought to be done, what principles and priorities should guide social life, what policies should be adopted, how the powerful should be held accountable, and what responsibility citizenship carries' (Young, 2000, p. 162–3). In this view, it is only through operating in the public sphere that voluntary action can influence government institutions and hold them accountable. Private action and civic voluntary action, whilst they have their place and value, have no specific bearing on political processes of this kind.

The question we ask is whether, and to what extent, the particular way in which voluntary organisations addressing the needs of and issues about older people are embedded in the system of welfare distribution in Ireland, north and south, simultaneously encourages private and discourages public action.

Structure

This book is structured so as to apply our conceptual framework to our comparisons of the two jurisdictions in Ireland. In each case, analysis of the older people's voluntary sector will be preceded by a chapter discussing the relevant political economy of welfare as it affects older people. Chapter 1 will start by discussing the changing context of welfare from a European perspective, considering how global trends are impacting on developments in both parts of the island of Ireland and identifying common issues and themes. Using the concept of welfare regimes we will discuss the extent to which the Irish approach to welfare shares features that contrast with other welfare regimes in Europe. Suggestions will be made of some broad features of the older people's voluntary sector that we would expect to find in both parts of Ireland.

Chapter 1 will continue with a comparative historical account of older people's policy in Europe and the treatment of the issue by the supra-national policies of the European Union. It will be completed by a similar discussion of the development of voluntary action in Europe to provide some points of comparison with the situation in Ireland.

Chapters 2 and 3 will continue the contextual discussion and consider the situation of older people and the development of public policy on ageing in Northern Ireland and the Republic of Ireland respectively. Chapters 4 and 5 will discuss the development of voluntary action and ageing in each of the two jurisdictions and provide detailed evidence on the shape, size and diversity of the sector in Ireland, north and south. Chapter 6 will consider the role of the voluntary and community sector in policy-making in both parts of Ireland, setting out the similarities and differences in policy architecture and the ways in which this has shaped the development of a 'voice' of older people in government. Chapter 7 will summarise the similarities and differences in the picture in each jurisdiction and will discuss some of the implications of these for the theoretical model we have developed.

Welfare regimes and global trends in welfare

There is widespread agreement in the literature that governments have been re-engineering welfare state institutions as a response to globalisation (Lewis, 2004; Surender, 2004). The impact of the growth of flexible labour markets, the free movement of capital and the outsourcing of jobs to other jurisdictions, linked to an ageing population, are the central trends to which governments have had to respond. In Western welfare states, there has been some convergence in policy towards active rather than passive welfare and a stress on an enabling role for the state and a renewed focus on the role of welfare in securing greater social cohesion (Lewis, 2004, p. 179; Pierson, 1998).

At the same time, the processes of governance have been reformed through a 'hollowing out of the state' (Rhodes, 1994), in which power has moved downwards from the national to the local, sideways to alternative institutions particularly in the private sector and quasi-nongovernmental organisations, and upwards to supranational institutions such as (in the European context) the European Commission. Public administration is conducted by means of a plethora of partnership arrangements involving different tiers of government, different agencies within government and voluntary and private organisations. Some of these are standing arrangements, others assembled to address time-limited problems. Some are area based, others issue based.

This 'recalibration' (Pierson, 2001) has been accompanied by a reconceptualisation of third sector organisations as partners with governments in the production of welfare goods, rather than as alternative, and more market-sensitive, providers of services on behalf of government (Lewis, 2004). The underpinning assumption that voluntary agencies 'can be both agents of efficient and effective service delivery and institutions in civil society enforcing civic virtue, social cohesion and participation' applies across many different political ideologies and national circumstances (Anheier, 2004, pp. 118–19).

In his influential discussion of welfare regimes, Esping-Andersen (1990) distinguished between social democratic, corporatist and liberal regimes, each of which reflects differing political settlements on the levels of taxation and the universality of social benefits that should be underpinned by the state. From this perspective, both the Republic of Ireland and Northern Ireland, as part of the UK, share more similarities than differences. Together they are the only examples of developed liberal regimes in Europe. Both tax less than in either social democratic and corporatist regimes such as Sweden and Germany, and both rely more heavily on targeting social benefits rather than on universal provision. Social goods are to a greater extent distributed through market mechanisms and there tends to be a greater rhetorical commitment to informal welfare. These trends are accompanied by greater levels of inequality in income distribution. The evidence shows that Ireland, north and south, is among the most unequal places in Europe with the greatest differences between the richest and the poorest. In both the UK and Ireland, the challenges of globalisation and an ageing population have been met by an increased emphasis on personal responsibility and the potential of voluntary organisations as a replacement source of social solidarity

CSPS (AND) D.

The impact of this welfare regime on the structuring of voluntary action is elucidated in the model we discussed. Dependency in old age is created in the context of the extent of state redistribution between younger and older generations and the consequent extent to which social needs are met through the informal economy of the family. Greater use of the market to distribute welfare goods means greater differentials between rich and poor in access to these goods. In both parts of Ireland, the welfare regime emphasises the priority of the market in the distribution of welfare goods, with the state and informal welfare in subsidiary and residual roles as identified by Evers and Laville (2004). A residual rather than a universal welfare state creates and maintains space for private philanthropy and the market. The drive for solidarity among older people themselves is sustained by the pressures created for informal systems of welfare in meeting human need for contact at a time when the capacity of informal welfare is undermined by changes in the labour market.

We argue that this type of welfare regime will tend to sustain a field of voluntary action that has a focus on private philanthropy in various states of tension with state agencies and a large solidarity sector that is nevertheless to a great extent focused on private concerns, rather than public campaigning. The reasons this might be so are complex, but may be said to be broadly reflective of the extent to which participants in solidarity organisations can assume that their basic needs will be met whatever happens. Trust in universal state services seems an important factor, indicating belief that collective action can lead to policy change. The extent to which this is the case will be influenced by the relative openness of the political system and this, in turn, will be influenced by the extent to which the structure of the welfare regime acknowledges and provides for the expression of group rights.

Older people: the broader European context

Both Northern Ireland, through the United Kingdom, and Ireland are part of the European Union and thus share a common contemporary backdrop to voluntary action for older people, a common policy environment, participation in the political project for European integration and a common demographic context. For all these reasons, the situation of both jurisdictions within the European Union merits a brief scene-setting for the areas of interest of this study.

The ageing of the European population is its most striking demographic feature (European Commission, 2005a). Ageing is, of course, not a trend that can happen in isolation but is connected to other population variables, such as fertility, inward and outward migration and life expectancy. In the end quarter of the twentieth century, three distinct trends emerged in the pattern of population ageing in the European Union. First, older people began to live longer, because of improved health leading to longer life expectancy. Second, the postwar generation began to approach retirement age. Third, birth rates fell and families opted to have fewer children. European populations were less able to replace themselves and their numbers were sustained only by immigration from outside the Union. From the point of view of older people, these trends had two main consequences. First, the numbers of older people in the population began to grow, both in absolute and relative terms; and second, the larger numbers of older people became dependent on a smaller working age population to sustain their living standards (this is called a higher 'dependency ratio'). Because of a number of particular features of its economic situation, the Republic of Ireland was slow to follow the European pattern, but all indications are that it will do so, albeit 'behind the curve' of the others.

Average life expectancy across Europe is expected to rise by five years between now and 2050. So far, the population of older people in the European Union has risen slowly, from 10 per cent of the total to 16 per cent of the total, from 1960 to 2003. It is projected that the proportion of the population in Europe (EU25) aged over sixty-five years will rise from 16 per cent in 2000 to 25 per cent in 2030 and 31 per cent in 2050. The proportion aged eighty years and over will rise from 4 per cent in 2000 to 7 per cent in 2030 and 12 per cent in 2050, from 18.8 million in 2000 to 34.7 million in 2030 and 50 million in 2051. The European dependency ratio will rise from 49 per cent in 2005 to 66 per cent in 2030.

Table 1.1 illustrates the projection for population increase for 2004–50 for older people:

Table 1.1: Projection of population of older people in the EU(25), Ireland and the United Kingdom

	2004	2010	2030	2050
EU25	75.284m	81.598m	115.848m	134.541m
Rep. Ireland	0.449m	0.509m	0.928m	1.435m
UK	9.543m	10.142m	14.754m	17.123m

Source: Giampaolo Lanzieri, Long-term population projections at national level. Eurostat: Statistics in focus, *Population and Social Conditions* series, 3/2006, Luxembourg. 'Older' is defined as sixty or over.

This will lead to a significant increase in the proportion of older people dependent, for their welfare, on those of working age (the dependency ratio). Table 1.2 illustrates the projected rise in the dependency ratio:

Table 1.2: Projected increase in 'dependency ratio', EU(25), Ireland and the United Kingdom

	2010	2030	2050
EU25	26.3 per cent	40.3 per cent	52.8 per cent
Rep. Ireland	17.5 per cent	28.3 per cent	45.3 per cent
UK	24.3 per cent	37.4 per cent	45.3 per cent

Source: Eurostat: *Old-age dependency ratios*. Luxembourg, 2006.

Turning from demographic to policy issues, from the 1990s, as it developed its social policies, the European Union interested itself ever more in the situation of older people. This was necessary, both as a tool for economic and social planning at European and member state level and because the situation of older people became increasingly emblematic of the situation and future of the European social model.

 The ageing of the European population had already impacted on pensions policies, for such policies had historically been formulated in a postwar period when workforces were expanding, economic growth was high and older people were a smaller proportion of the population. The demographic changes outlined above first became apparent in the 1990s, both within national states and at European level, forcing a reconsideration of policies for older people in general and pensions in particular (European Commission, 2003). Many member states have already retrenched their pension policies through such means as raising retirement age, changing the pension formula and altering the balance of funding of pensions for the state to the private sector. Pessimism that the value of pensions will fall in the future has been evident for some time (Walker, 1999). Issues around the affordability and sustainability of pensions are already familiar features in the policy discourse concerning older people in both the UK and the Republic of Ireland.

The Treaty of Maastricht (1992) empowered the European Union to act in the area of public health, while the Treaty of Amsterdam (1997) gave the European Union the authority to act against discrimination against older people. The Treaty of Nice (2001) gave the European Union competence in the area of the coordination of pensions, health and long-term care. Following this, pensions and long-term care were drawn into the system known as the Open Method of Coordination (OMC) whereby member states share, with due respect for national and regional policies, their policies for pensions, health, long-term care and social inclusion. In 2006, each member state was required to draw up three-year national strategies for inclusion, pensions, health and long-term care according to a common European template, a process designed to promote a convergence of such policies across the Union.

While bringing the welfare of older people into the European policy-making community, many organisations working with the elderly have great reservations about old people being seen largely in the context of their need for health care, social services and pensions (which implies that they are a problem), rather than as citizens (which implies that they have rights) (Murray, 2005).

Voluntary action in Europe

In addition, we look briefly at the broad common political context for voluntary action in which both the Republic and Northern Ireland operate, namely the European Union. From the 1990s, the European Union began to develop an agreed view of the desirability and nature of voluntary action. Under the presidency of Jacques Delors, the European Union pitched for a broader range of policy-making, with the white paper, *Growth, Competitiveness and Work* (1993), and its companion in social policy, *European Social Policy — A Way Forward for the Union* (1994). A successful implementation of these social policies necessarily involved an engagement with civil society in general and the world of associations in particular. This was formalised when the Treaty of Maastricht (1992) adopted, in declaration 23, a phrase recognising the importance of 'charitable associations and foundations as institutions responsible for welfare establishments and services'. The Commission established a Comité des Sages who issued a report, *For a Europe of Civic, Social and Political Rights* (1996), which proposed the intensifying of the relationship between government and nongovernmental organisations.

Coinciding with the completion of the single market, the European Commission announced in 1992 that it would prepare a policy paper on the role of the voluntary sector in the Union. That year, it published a draft common statute for European associations, one designed to ensure that a voluntary organisation registered in one state could legally function automatically in another, matching legislation for co-operatives and mutual societies. Preparation of the policy paper took much longer than anticipated, five years. It was eventually published as the Commission

Communication, *On Promoting the Role of Voluntary Organisations and Foundations in Europe* (1997). This acknowledged the role that voluntary organisations played in employment creation, active citizenship, democracy, social inclusion, representing civic interests to the public authorities and in promoting human rights and global development.

A landmark in the process of European engagement with civic society was the European white paper on governance (2001). Preparatory documents for the white paper visualised a crucial role for mass social movements in European politics in the future. The white paper endorsed and put forward the principle that Europe should be governed on common lines of openness, participation and subsidiarity. According to the white paper, civil society organisations — which the Commission defined to include the social partners, non-government organisations, professional associations, charities, grass-roots organisations, organisations that involved citizens in local and municipal life (including churches and religious communities) — must have platforms to change policy and society, with structured channels for feedback, criticism and protest. Article 47 of the draft European constitution (2003) committed the Union to 'open, transparent and regular dialogue with representative associations and civil society'. Article 11 of the structural fund general regulation for 2007–13 defined, as partners of government in economic, environment and social policy, nongovernmental and civil society organisations.

The European Union attempted to promote the nongovernmental sector in Europe concerned with older people, funding projects to mark *1993: European Year of older people and solidarity between the generations*. This came to an abrupt but temporary halt following a legal challenge by Britain, which led to the European Court of Justice declaring the welfare of older people to be without the competence of the treaties. Some of this ground was recovered when in 1997 article 13 of the Treaty of Amsterdam permitted the European Union to take action against discrimination against older people; and article 39 permitted the European Union to take measures to promote social inclusion. NGOs were funded for both such purposes from 2000.

Voluntary action for older people in Europe

National organisations working with older people are now an important part of the European landscape of nongovernmental organisations. Pratt (1995) made the case that organisations for older people came into existence at key stages of social and political organisation, namely:

• The campaign for pensions in the nineteenth century.

- The development of welfare services for older people in the mid-twentieth century. The organisations associated with this were often broad based and had large memberships.
- More recently, as part of new social movements. These were characteristically small and militant.

In the first stage, during the second half of the nineteenth century, there were several organisations committed to the concept of a pension for older people and, by the twentieth century, ten western European nations had pensions, Germany having one of the most developed systems and providing the model for others.

In the second stage, organisations came into existence to build the welfare of older people. Germany was the leading country in this wave. The year 1917 saw the formation of the Reichsbund (its full title was the Reichsbund der Kriegsopfer, Behinderten, Sozialrentner und Hinterbliebenen). This was, in effect, an organisation of pensioners and war veterans and it soon attracted hundreds of thousands of members. Unlike some of its predecessors, it was interested in shaping a broader range of policies for the welfare of older people. The Reichsbund made an early political impact on the Weimar Republic and is credited with a landmark in German social policy, the Social Assistance Act, 1923. Reorganised after the Second World War as the Bund der Ruhestandbeamten, Rentner und Hinterbliebenen, it shaped postwar welfare legislation in the federal republic through a mixture of parliamentary and street action and continues to have over a million members. It was joined by confessional and other groups for older people (for example, Bundesarbeitsgemeinschaft Katholisches Alterwerk, 1958), eventually leading to a federal coalition of all older people's organisations, the German Seniors Organisation or Bundesarbeitsgemeinschaft Senioren Organisation.

Comparable voluntary organisations may be found in other European countries (Walker, 1999; Walker and Naegele, 1993). Associations of older people were established in the Netherlands, according to the three pillars of Dutch society (Protestant, Catholic, humanist); likewise in Austria in the 1950s, the social democratic Pensions Organisation and the conservative Seniors Federation. In Italy, each of the three main unions had retired members associations embracing 20 per cent of all the older people in the country. In Germany and the Netherlands, retiring people are expected to continue their trade union membership, and in these countries 13 to 14 per cent of trade union members are no longer in the workforce.

The third stage comprised generally smaller, often more militant groups which arose to reflect the new social movements of the 1960s and worked on themes of rights and empowerment. Again, Germany was in the vanguard, with the Senior Protection Association (1975), which within twenty years had built up 200 local groups with 15,000 members. Comparable groups in other European countries were the C team (Denmark, 1990) and, in Britain, the National Pensioners Convention (1979). Some groups, while adopting a vanguard style of politics, sought a broad membership base, perhaps the most successful being the Landesforeningen Aeldre Sagen in Denmark, operating under the more popular title of DaneAge. It was set up in 1986, and within ten years a quarter of older people in Denmark had joined up as individual members. Apart from its advocacy, political participation and antidiscrimination work, DaneAge provides a range of direct services for its members, such as telephone advice (for example, finance), training and the organisation of social visiting. Some organisations for older people chose a role in electoral politics, with representatives being successfully elected in 1990 (Portugal, the Pensioner Party) and 1992 (Rome and the Dutch Parliament).

The political system responded by trying to incorporate the aspirations of older people within party structures. Again, Germany was in the forefront, where the Christian Democrats established the Seniorenunion der CDU in 1988, open to members and non-members over sixty. The Social Democratic Party set up senior circles (Seniorenkreise) at district and local level and senior representatives at Land and federal levels (SPD60+, 1994).

Not all European states followed this pattern. In many southern European states, Italy excepted, older people were politically passive, inactive, acquiescent, family-oriented and uninterested in political participation. Indeed, Cumming and Henry (1961) articulated a paradigm of old age called 'disengagement', which modelled the manner in which older people progressively disengaged from society and politics. There is evidence that retirement can induce a level of depoliticisation and disengagement, especially in a political culture in which values of empowerment are weak. Indeed, Hodgins and Greve (2004a) would consider the approach to older people by the Republic of Ireland's health and social services as falling well within this model.

The mobilisation, indeed radicalisation, of older people and voluntary organisations for them might lead one to expect identifiable political and policy outcomes. Walker (1998) warns us against coming to such a conclusion, suggesting that despite their large numbers, their influence has been comparatively small. They have, nevertheless, challenged the acquiescence and condescension that hitherto characterised the politics of old age throughout these countries. Despite small numbers, these new social movements had high visibility and an abundance of energy, being peopled by 'younger' older people encouraged to make an early exit from the labour force in their fifties.

Governments responded in several ways to the appearance of representative and, later, advocacy organisations for older people. At national level, improved levels of pensions made substantial inroads on the postwar poverty of some older people (European Commission, 1981). Institutionally, greater prominence was given to issues affecting older people. In Germany, for example, a federal ministry specifically addressed the needs of older people. National advisory boards for the welfare of older people were first established in Belgium and followed in France, the Netherlands, Ireland, Luxembourg and Austria. At local level, these developments were even more significant and, granted Ireland's small size and centralised government, it is important not to overlook the significance of such developments.

Denmark established systems whereby all local authorities must have advisory boards of senior citizens. In Sweden, 50 per cent of older people belong to at least one of five national pensioner organisations. There are pensioner bodies at national, county council and municipal level, acting as policy and service advisory bodies, the pensioner organisations being represented on them (Batljan, 2005). The Netherlands has a policy of co-determination for older people, which means that services for older people are run by boards part-elected by older people themselves, and older people are represented on bodies responsible for the implementation of laws affecting older people. In 1982, French law required all regional authorities and departments to set up consultative committees to involve the participation of older people in health and social services planning. Local councils of senior citizens were formed in Germany from the 1970s, and in the 1980s in Denmark. Consultative committees of older people were formed at regional and commune level in Italy. Local advisory boards have been formed in the Netherlands and Austrian regions; at local authority level in Flanders and at local, regional and national level in Spain. They have not been an important feature of the landscape of older people in the UK including Northern Ireland and have been almost absent in Ireland. Indeed, some argue that they would not sit well with the type of clientelist, personalised political system evident in Ireland.

The central problematic in social action for older people is the degree to which older people have common interests transcending their other social, economic and political interests. Most researchers stress the fact that older people are not a homogeneous group and their political interests are more likely to be strongly affected by their socioeconomic status, gender, race, culture, religion and locality.

Statistical coordination within the European Union has the added advantage of enabling us to compare the situation of older people between member states, while the open method of coordination enables us to make useful comparisons in the policy field as well. Despite that, and despite the common European background for policy for older people, European example had tended to bypass both the UK and Ireland. Both states have been slow to use European example to inform their social policy, preferring to use social policy examples from quite different and often very distant countries and hemispheres. Ireland in particular has shown a strong preference for the Atlantic, rather than the European, social model (Lee, 1985). This is more than an abstract issue, for when the assistant secretary general of the Department of Health and Children spoke of how his department planned to develop services for older people in Ireland, he stated that they would be informed by the model of the United States (Smyth, 2005).

Conclusions

The voluntary and community sector working with older people in both parts of the island of Ireland does so in the context of:

- Demographic ageing, in which the proportion of older people in the population will grow considerably in the first half of this century both in continental Europe and on the island of Ireland
- A growing competence and interest by the European Union in shaping policies for older people according to a common set of principles and values
- A history of the development, in several waves, of organisations for older people in the continental European countries, with the adoption, by government, of systems of consultation with older people.

Perhaps the most striking feature of voluntary action for older people in Europe is the high level of mobilisation of older people into non-governmental and social movements, Germany being the most striking case. This has prompted a significant government response in the form of recognition and participation in the decision-making and political process. It is arguable that earlier mobilisations of older people have helped shape a European policy response that has increasingly acknowledged group rights, both in European and national laws. Insofar as this is the case, we would suggest that the liberal, indeed *laissez-faire*, approach to welfare in Ireland in particular, and Northern Ireland rather less so, has facilitated the emergence of forms of voluntary action that are reactive and focused on private needs. Paradoxically, it may be the case that welfare state restructuring around the concept of group rights now evident in both jurisdictions is challenging these organisations to be more effectively engaged in the policy process. It will be intriguing to see whether these developments have been matched or even echoed in Northern Ireland and Ireland.

2

Older People and Public Policy: Northern Ireland

Introduction

The extent and nature of social needs together with the ways in which these are interpreted both by older people themselves and in policy are an important aspect of the context in which voluntary action in the field has developed. This chapter aims to describe and analyse the socioeconomic circumstances of older people in Northern Ireland and the development of public policy addressing their needs. There is a wealth of socioeconomic data on which to draw in profiling the circumstances of older people. However, Northern Ireland's status as a region of the larger United Kingdom gives policy analysts the problem of distinguishing between policy that originates in central UK government and is applied equivalently across the country, policy that originates centrally and is adapted to local conditions, and policy that originates within Northern Ireland itself. Of necessity, this chapter will address all three dimensions of the context.

This chapter begins with a description of the main features of the socioeconomic profile of older people in Northern Ireland. Because of the extent to which social policy is determined centrally, it will then discuss the national UK context before dealing with the extent to which policy varies in Northern Ireland itself. Whilst there are substantial differences in administrative arrangements between the constituent parts of the UK, the country is not a federalist state, notwithstanding the devolution settlement of 1998. Taxation and broad spending policies are decided centrally, with the consequence that there are more similarities than differences in social policy between the constituent nations of the UK. So far as Northern Ireland is concerned, it can be argued that there has been less divergence in policy since 1998 than in either Scotland or Wales, although as will be seen, there have always been substantive differences in both legislation and administration that set Northern Ireland apart from other regions of the UK.

16

Demographic trends

Demographic trends in Northern Ireland are summarised in a report provided by the Northern Ireland Statistics and Research Agency (NISRA) published in 2003. As in other regions in Europe, the population of Northern Ireland is ageing. At the time of the last census, in 2001, the total population was about 1,685,000, of whom 16 per cent were of pensionable age (sixty for women and sixty-five for men). This was a somewhat lower proportion than in the UK as a whole where the figure was 18 per cent, but higher than in the Republic of Ireland where the figure was about 13 per cent (NISRA, 2003).

Over the past fifty years, the population has aged considerably. 'Over the fifty years between 1951 and 2001 the proportion of children aged under 16 in the NI population has fallen from 29 per cent to 24 per cent, whilst simultaneously the proportion of those of pensionable age has increased from 12 per cent in 1951 to 16 per cent in 2001' (NISRA, 2003, p. 6).

The NISRA report provides a projection of demographic change into the future, suggesting that the proportion of people over pension age is likely to increase from 16 per cent in 2001 to 20 per cent by 2026 and 25 per cent by 2041, while the proportion of people under the age of fifty is projected to fall by 20 per cent in the same period (NISRA, 2003). The impact of the change is emphasised by a projected rise of 170 per cent in the numbers of people over the age of 85 in the same period.

These trends show that the population of Northern Ireland shares the more general situation of an ageing population that has been identified across Europe, albeit at a lower level in that the population is proportionally younger than in the UK as a whole and in most other European states. The most notable exception here is the Republic of Ireland which, as will be noted in Chapter 3, has one of the youngest populations in the European Union and the lowest proportion of elderly people, although the trend there is upwards also, and at a steeper rate. It is estimated that, by the middle of this century, the proportion of people over pension age in both jurisdictions in Ireland will be in the range of 25 per cent.

However, there are significant differences within Northern Ireland itself. In particular, it should be noted that, at 19 per cent, the proportion of people over pension age in the Protestant community is closer to the UK average and higher than the average. The 12 per cent of the Catholic community over pension age in 2001 more than compensates for this and accounts entirely for the relatively lower demographic profile of Northern Ireland as a whole, in comparison with the UK as a whole. These differences have consequences for the spatial distribution of ageing within Northern Ireland, with pensioners forming a higher proportion of the population in the

Protestant east rather than the Catholic west of Northern Ireland. As will be shown later in discussing its development, these demographic factors have influenced voluntary action around the issue of ageing.

There are also notable differences in the numbers of male and female pensioners. The most recent published estimates indicate that there were 95,407 males and 175,185 females over pension age in Northern Ireland in 2003 (Evason et al., 2004a). Females outnumbered males at all ages over pensionable age, but the difference widens significantly the older the age cohort. Just less than one-third of the 56,739 people over the age of eighty were male.

These differences become important in understanding the distribution of incomes among pensioners and the extent of pensioner poverty.

Social situation of older people

Recent policy initiatives and the launch of a major intervention in ageing and public policy by a large philanthropic foundation have produced a wealth of new data on the circumstances of older people in Northern Ireland. The increased salience of ageing as a public policy concern has taken place against a rather unhelpful background of popular debate about the 'burden' of an ageing population which tends to ignore both the taxes and national insurance contributions already made by older people in their working lives and their continuing contribution to informal welfare.

Incomes

Overall income poverty rates in Northern Ireland are equivalent to those in other regions of the UK, notwithstanding the high numbers of people receiving out-of-work benefits, the high numbers without paid work, the high rates of disability and the extent of low pay among those in employment (Kenway et al., 2006). An important reason for this is relatively low housing costs compared to all other regions of the UK, leaving more money available for expenditure on other essentials. High levels of disability-related social security benefits (the highest in the UK) are not necessarily indicators of income poverty since these are not means-tested, and households in receipt of these may have other sources of income.

About 20 per cent of pensioners in Northern Ireland experience income poverty (ibid., 2006). The risk of being in poverty for elderly people, relative to the rest of the population, is similar in Northern Ireland to that in the UK as a whole, but remains lower than in the Republic of Ireland (Hillyard et al., 2003). Using the 60 per cent of median income poverty threshold in the country concerned, 40 per cent of pensioners in Ireland are at risk of poverty, second only to Cyprus among EU member states, and

24 per cent of pensioners in the UK as a whole. Hillyard et al. (2003) break the figures down into smaller age cohorts in their study in Northern Ireland, and show a rate of 30 per cent for those aged fifty-five to sixty-four, 25 per cent for those aged sixty-five to seventy-four, and 22 per cent for those aged over seventy-five. A recent report from Help the Aged UK makes the point that a great many pensioner households live at just above the 60 per cent of median income poverty threshold and that these are at high risk of falling into poverty because of increases in fuel prices. The report suggests that in the UK, the rate of inflation experienced by people over pension age may be over 8 per cent a year, considerably higher than for the population as a whole.[1] Whilst the risk of income poverty is considerably lower than in the Republic of Ireland, it should be noted that the risk in the UK is the sixth highest among the twenty-five member states of the EU.

Those most at risk of poverty are females over the age of eighty. A combination of widowhood and dependence on their former husbands' national insurance old-age pension and occupational pensions, coupled with historic inactivity in the labour market, are mainly responsible (Evason et al., 2004a). Many women will have adopted caring roles during their adult lives and depended on their husbands' earnings and pension savings and will thus not have savings of their own. Occupational pensions often pay out only half to surviving widows. The relatively high numbers of women over the age of eighty mean that these processes have a relatively high impact, reflected in the heavier reliance among single female pensioners on means-tested income support (Evason et al., 2004b).

The relatively high risk of pensioner income poverty in Northern Ireland, whilst similar to the UK average, has to be set against a relatively high cost of living, reflected in both the price of food and fuel, where the proportion of household budgets spent on these items is higher than in the rest of the UK. Furthermore, income inequality is greater in Northern Ireland than in either Great Britain or the Republic of Ireland, although in the latter case only marginally so (Hillyard et al., 2003). High levels of income inequality are themselves contributory factors in rates of morbidity and other social ills (Hillyard et al., 2003).

Housing and fuel poverty

The definition of a 'decent home' was published by the Office of Deputy Prime Minister in 2002 and applies in England and Wales as well as Northern Ireland. It covers criteria that include meeting the current minimum standard for housing, state of repair, having modern facilities

---

1 Help the Aged Spotlight Report, 2007: *Spotlight on Older People in the UK.* Downloaded from http://press.helptheaged.org.uk/NR, 14 June 2007

and services and providing a reasonable degree of thermal comfort (NIHE, 2006). Older people living on their own are the most likely group of people to live in a house that fails at least one of the tests for a 'decent home' (NIHE, 2006). Thus 29 per cent of lone older households were in a non-decent home. The figure for older couples was lower at 21 per cent. Whilst other people living on their own and lone parents were also at risk of living in a non-decent home, nevertheless the link between age and risk of living in a substandard house remains evident.

A fuel-poor household is defined as one where more than 10 per cent of household income is needed to achieve a satisfactory standard of warmth (21 degrees centigrade in living rooms and 18 degrees in other rooms). People over pension age are much more likely to experience fuel poverty than younger people (NIHE, 2006). The figures suggest that it remains a significant problem in Northern Ireland that older people are at a particular risk of experiencing. They show that fuel poverty is experienced by 39 per cent of households where the household reference person was between the age of sixty and seventy-four, and 42 per cent of households where this person was seventy-five and over. In contrast, just 11 per cent of those where the person was aged between twenty-five and thirty-nine experience fuel poverty. Based on the house condition survey of 2004, these figures show a considerable improvement over those obtained in the 2001 survey. The proportion of fuel-poor homes fell from 33 per cent in 2001 to 24 per cent in 2004 (NIHE, 2006). However, it should be noted that the proportion in England in 2001 was 9 per cent. There was a similar drop in the proportion of homes failing the decent homes standard over the same period. In the view of the Northern Ireland Housing Executive, the reason for this improvement in both cases lies in rapid upgrading of heating systems from solid fuel to oil or gas.

Health and social care
The majority of older people in Northern Ireland report their health to be 'good' or 'fairly good' (Evason et al., 2005a). Almost two-thirds (64.6 per cent) report a long-standing illness or disability; however, this proportion drops to just over a half (50.1 per cent) for people who report a long-standing illness or disability that limits their activities. Whereas activity limitation is most common in those aged over seventy-five, nevertheless the majority in that age group are able to manage daily living without assistance; it is important to bear in mind that impairments that can result in some limitation in activities affect a much broader group of people than those requiring active help in daily living and personal care.

The extent of limiting long-term illness is accompanied by high levels of uptake of social security benefits paid to meet the additional costs of disability. Disability Living Allowance is payable to people under pension age on the basis of an assessment of their functional ability to undertake a range of everyday tasks and has a care and a mobility component. Once in receipt of this benefit, a person carries their entitlement into retirement. People over pension age can claim attendance allowance on the same basis. These benefits are not means-tested and are clearly particularly important in households that are otherwise dependent on means-tested benefits. Taken together, 48 per cent of pensioner couple households, 35 per cent of sole male households and 48 per cent of sole female households are in receipt of at least one of these benefits (Evason et al., 2004b).

In the context of the risks of pensioner poverty, these figures are an indication of a social policy success story in that they suggest that there may be almost a 100 per cent take-up of these benefits among those who are entitled to them. Furthermore, their contribution to pensioner household budgets suggests that they lift many out of poverty.

In their careful analysis of relevant data, Evason and her team undermine the popular assumption that old people are necessarily a burden on the health service. Most elderly people are seldom in contact with health service professionals. General Practitioner consultation rates among those over sixty-five are similar to those for women aged from forty-five to sixty-four. Rate of use does increase over the age of seventy-five, where the majority had visited their GP at least three times in the past year (Evason et al., 2005a). However, less than one-fifth (18.9 per cent) of this age group had been a hospital inpatient in the year before interview. Of the other health and social care services, only chiropody had been used by more than half.

Some care should be exercised in interpreting these data. As will be discussed below, there is considerable public dissatisfaction about the quality and availability of current services and this dissatisfaction is an important driver of current trends in policy that are looking for an increased role for voluntary organisations. It is possible that relatively low rates of usage of some of these services are related to their unavailability, unattractiveness or inappropriateness, rather than a lack of need.

One thing does seem clear, however, and that is the contribution of older people as caregivers. Evason et al. (2005a) note that around 12 per cent of older people have caring responsibilities, mostly within families to spouses (the most common) or to other family members. Almost one-third of these are providing help for more than twenty hours a week. Data from the 2006 Life and Times survey of public attitudes in Northern Ireland indicates that 23 per cent of adults are carers, almost a third (31 per cent) of whom are over the age of fifty-five (Evason, 2007). Since 1994, this

proportion of carers who are over the age of fifty-five has climbed sharply from 24 per cent. The pattern in Northern Ireland follows that of the UK in general where the economic value of the care provided by families and friends has been calculated at about £800 billion, many times greater than the value of care provided through state funding (Land, 2006). Of this, one-fifth (£160 billion) is provided by people aged sixty-five and over. The total UK budget for social care is in the region of £10 billion.

The evidence to support popular assumptions that old age is inevitably accompanied by loneliness, family neglect and social isolation is mixed. Drawing on data from the Northern Ireland Household Panel and the Health and Wellbeing surveys of 2001, Evason et al. (2005d) note that just 7.7 per cent of respondents felt left out of things, and well over 80 per cent reported being made to feel important, loved and encouraged by friends and family. A similar proportion felt that they had people around them on whom they could count for help if needed.

Whilst a small minority appear to be socially isolated, a large majority talk to their neighbours, meet people and have contact with their friends and relatives on a regular basis. More than 60 per cent attend religious services at least once a week and almost half are a member of an organisation. However, evidence quoted for the UK as a whole indicates that many elderly people's lives are restricted by a lack of money, poor public transport and fears for their safety.[2] As many as 13 per cent of survey respondents said that they were often or always lonely. Parti-cipation in voluntary activity is explored in greater detail in Chapter 4; these data, however, give an indication of the extent to which the everyday lives of many elderly people are enriched through organisational contact.

Public policies for older people

The welfare state in Northern Ireland has historically closely followed developments in the UK as a whole. Northern Ireland, as part of the UK, in general shares in the welfare regime to be found in the country as a whole (Esping-Andersen, 1990). Whilst, in a European context, the UK and Ireland are generally placed in the same 'liberal' category of welfare regime types (Esping-Andersen, 1990), nevertheless there are substantial differences in both the scope and nature of the welfare state in each, and this is fully reflected in Northern Ireland. Thus, the UK welfare state has been adapted to fit local political circumstances in Northern Ireland, but it remains based on similar principles, especially those concerned with taxation, extent of entitlement and the level of emphasis on redistribution. In the terminology adopted by Esping-Andersen (1990), it decommodifies

---

2 *Spotlight on Older People in the UK*, Help the Aged, 2007

welfare goods to the same extent as in Britain and, on that basis, belongs to the same welfare regime.

The deviations from a British norm are both legislative and administrative, and, whilst not fundamental, they reflect a different set of political circumstances and a different political culture. These have shaped the particular institutions of the welfare state which, in some respects, look very different from those to be found in England, Scotland and Wales, but the overall policy frameworks within which old age is addressed as a social problem remain the same. This section of the chapter will thus discuss the development of policy in a UK context before going on to outline the major administration and legislative differences that set Northern Ireland apart from the rest of the UK, albeit within a shared overall policy context.

As already discussed, the UK shares in a general European trend of an ageing population relative to the numbers of people of working age, as the so-called 'baby-boomers' (the generation born in the decade after the end of the Second World War) reach retirement age (Ellison and Pierson, 2003). This has sometimes been portrayed as a crisis threatening the intergenerational contract that has underpinned welfare states in the fifty years after 1945, whereby the costs of welfare enjoyed by people over pension age are borne by those currently in work, in the expectation that the latter group will, in turn, be supported by the next generation as they themselves grow older. Hence there has been an associated concern with the dependency index, the ratio of older to younger people in the population.

Whilst these trends are likely to impact greatly in the future on the financing of pension provision and health services in particular, it is arguable that a much more important recent change in the UK has been the trend towards private provision both in pensions and in the way services are delivered, evident since the 1980s. A consensus account of the development of the UK welfare state suggests that the postwar welfare settlement introduced by the Labour government between 1946 and 1949 survived without much question until the oil shocks and the collapse of the Bretton Woods international financial settlement in the 1970s (Lowe, 2005; Ellison and Pierson, 2003). The reforms of the Thatcher governments between 1979 and 1993 and under New Labour since 1997 have been described as 'a rare case of extensive welfare state adjustment — more extensive than the majority of the advanced democracies, with the possible exception of New Zealand' (Ellison and Pierson, 2003, p. 6).

The areas of reform of the 1980s and early 1990s that arguably had the largest impact on the lives of older people were in the fields of pension reform and personal social service provision. In the case of pensions, there was an effective abandonment of the state as the main guarantor of adequate pensions, with the decoupling of the link between the old-age pension and wages, on the one hand, and the reduction in the value of the State Earnings Related Pension (SERPS), on the other, to the extent that for all but workers approaching retirement age, private pensions were sold as more generous. These reforms were accompanied by deregulation of the private pension industry. Together, these reforms left a greater proportion of people over pension age dependent on means-tested income support. Changes in the labour market leading to greater job insecurity, coupled with insufficient savings by those in work, have both increased the risk of income poverty in old age. The government has responded by increasing the availability and attractiveness of pension schemes for those without access to company pensions and has more recently proposed increasing the retirement age to help cover the costs of state-guaranteed pension provision. The introduction of the pension tax credit was designed to address levels of income poverty, but this initiative has not been as effective as it could have been because of low levels of take-up. Recent estimates of the value of unclaimed tax credits have put it as high as £4 billion a year,[3] a situation compounded by a poor level of take-up of relief on local taxes.

Social care

Personal social service provision by the state in the UK has always been discretionary and means-tested. The 1948 National Assistance Act fundamentally reformed the administration of relief and support from the earlier poor law system. However, by retaining discretion over both eligibility for and the extent of state-funded support in its approach to social care in particular, it was based upon similar principles. The separation of cash support from care support that this legislation introduced remained the hallmark of the UK welfare state system until the 1990s, when reforms to the social security system and the introduction of direct payment legislation began to blur the distinction once again (Kemp and Glendinning, 2006).

However, the distinction remains analytically important. The reforms of the 1940s led to nationally guaranteed minimum income through either national insurance or means-tested benefits, or a combination. Social care, in contrast, remained a discretionary power of local authorities, the provision of which they have always been required to balance against other demands on their resources and their ability to raise local taxes. As a consequence, the availability of social care has been rationed by both a means test and the setting of tight eligibility criteria. The continuing gap between need and resources has been plugged by private provision,

---

3 Department for Work and Pensions, 2004

informal care by relatives, and charity. Of these, informal care dwarfs all forms of formal care put together. No overall assessment has been made in Northern Ireland of the extent and value of this gap. However, two recent reports on the current situation in England have suggested that there the gap is saving the state about £30 billion a year (Wanless, 2006) and that the people most at risk in this situation are those whose conditions are serious but not critical *and* who cannot afford to meet the full cost of private provision (CSCI, 2006).

In an assessment of the situation in England, the Commission for Social Care Inspection noted that currently fewer and fewer people are eligible and their needs must be greater even if eligible. The options for those who are deemed ineligible are limited (CSCI, 2006). It is estimated that between a quarter and a third of all older people in residential and nursing homes have no financial support from the state (Land, 2006). Few of these people receive any information or advice from local authorities. The Commission endorses the conclusion of the earlier Wanless report into social care that the current situation is untenable given the rapid increase predicted in the numbers of people over the age of eighty.

It cannot be doubted that the social care system in the UK as a whole shares these characteristics. Driven by a growing concern about 'bed blocking' in NHS hospitals whereby scarce hospital beds were occupied by people who were no longer ill, but who had no other appropriate accommodation, a Royal Commission on Long Term Care was established in 1997 and reported in 1999. It recommended an extension of the right to a free service at point of need from those covered by the NHS to include intimate personal care outside hospital settings. This was accepted and implemented by the Scottish Executive, accepted in principle but not implemented in Northern Ireland and Wales, but explicitly rejected in England (Land, 2006). As a consequence, outside Scotland much of the cost of nursing-home care is subject to a stringent means test, requiring those with a place to realise and use up almost all their assets, including their home if there is no surviving partner still living there, before being eligible for more than a basic contribution from the state — in Northern Ireland £100 a week in 2007/08.

A further defining characteristic of the system of social care in the UK is its fragmentation. It has been argued that one result of the extent of discretion was always a variable mixture of charitable and semiformal sources of care support; continuity, in the basis on which the state offered support, with the system that developed in the late nineteenth and early twentieth centuries resulted in a degree in continuity in the range of ways that the support was offered. But the reforms to community care in the early 1990s that sought to introduce market principles into the management and funding of social care fundamentally changed the range and types of organisations involved. Responsibility for funding residential care was moved from the social security budget to local authorities which were to use the money to develop a range of alternatives from independent providers in both the voluntary and the private sectors. In England, local authorities were obliged to spend at least 85 per cent of this 'new' money on independent providers and, whilst this stipulation never applied in Northern Ireland, nevertheless the impact of the changes has been as profound as it was in England.

Thus, use of markets in allocating social care and in deciding between providers has become a core feature of social care in the UK. It is based upon a consumerist approach that seeks to copy the kinds of choice exercised in the market place for consumer goods, on the premise that this will increase the autonomy of the service user and drive up standards in service provision. Critics have pointed out that the model of empowered individual consumers making choices between different suppliers sits uneasily with the disparities in power in the relationship, and that the availability of publicly funded care is mediated by care managers and other functionaries who retain a rationing role (Barnes, 1997; Land, 2006). Furthermore, the stress on individualist solutions that is implied by consumerist assumptions undermines the exercise of citizenship among those who require care support. The emphasis on the market discounts the value of civic engagement in collective decisions about resource allocation and priorities.

The particular impact on the voluntary sector will be discussed below; here, however, a number of general points should be noted. Firstly there was a rapid decline in the extent of services directly provided by the state, and in the UK as a whole the state now employs less than a third of all care staff (Land, 2006). Secondly, the market in residential and nursing-home care matured much more quickly than that in domiciliary care, with the consequence that it is dominated by private-sector providers, increasingly grouped into a small numbers of conglomerates, some owned by banks and hedge funds, that can apply the necessary economies of scale to address the regulatory regime, particularly regarding space standards, whilst achieving adequate returns. There is a relatively small voluntary-sector presence in this market, and, where it is to be found, it is mostly in small specialised subsectors such as accommodation for younger disabled people with high-dependency needs. With some notable exceptions it is relatively absent from the much bigger elderly residential and nursing-home markets. Nevertheless, in Northern Ireland, there are about 1,500 places in voluntary-sector managed homes, the same as in the statutory sector. In contrast, the domiciliary care market is less mature, with a greater range of providers and a considerable degree of 'churn', that is to say rapid entry and exit from the market by a number of relatively small players. Overall the voluntary sector is much more active in this market than the residential and nursing-home market.

The third general issue is the extent to which contracts and service agreements are underfunded across the board. Private-sector residential and nursing-home providers in England have together estimated that they need an additional £1 billion a year from the state to give them what they consider to be a reasonable return (about 70 per cent of residents are funded by the state at fixed prices (Land, 2006)). It has remained a constant source of complaint from voluntary-sector providers, along with problems created by the short length of many contracts. According to the Association of Chief Executives of Voluntary Organisations (ACEVO), current practice creates unnecessary barriers, causes services to fail and results in poor outcomes for service users (ACEVO, 2006, accessed 16 January 2007). Notwithstanding government policy in favour of full-cost recovery on contracts, there is little evidence that matters are improving (New Philanthropy Capital, personal communication, 16 January 2007).

The government has been particularly keen to promote the use of individualised budgets for people eligible for care support from the state. Introduced by the former Conservative government in 1996, direct payments in lieu of services were initially designed to be used by younger disabled people, but their availability has been extended to all age groups and to carers, in addition to those people requiring care support. The government's aspiration is that these payments will become the norm in social care; those receiving payments will be able to buy the services and support that they need, as they require them. The system in the UK is, however, more limited than in some other European countries, for example Belgium (Breda et al., 2006). In the UK, payments to close relatives who are providing care can be made only in exceptional circumstances, retaining a clearer distinction between social security cash benefits available to carers, and cash provided in lieu of services, although the availability of social security benefits such as Disability Living Allowance and Attendance Allowance to households asking for support are taken into account in local authority means testing. However, the replacement of care support in kind with cash payments does not address the evident problems of there being insufficient resources to meet expressed need, let alone the latent need there may be that has not been identified.

A strategy to address an ageing society
An important characteristic of the Labour administration that assumed power in 1997 was the establishment of a set of interdepartmental policy-drivers, to give an overarching and strategic direction in policy areas that

cut across normal departmental boundaries. Thus, in 1998, the government established an interministerial coordinating group on older people, replaced in 2001 by a cabinet subcommittee on older people. Both these initiatives were supported by partnerships with representatives from older people's organisations, most notably the Better Government for Older People network.

In the context of the perceived challenge of an ageing society, these policy fora began to look at the issue beyond current public service responsibilities. This process led to the development of a strategy on ageing, *Opportunity Age: Meeting the Challenges of Ageing in the 21st Century* (DWP, 2005). The strategy aimed to be a 'document for the UK as a whole' (ibid., p. ix) and sets out 'a coherent framework for developing policies, and the principles that government believes must underpin progress' (ibid., p. xiii). It focuses on three areas of policy: achieving higher employment rates among people of working age over the age of fifty; enabling older people to play a fuller and more active role in society with an adequate income and decent housing; and sustaining the level of independence and control over their lives.

The strategy brings together service improvement targets across a wide range of government functions, alongside measures to address ageism. It points out that in addition to the need for legislation against age discrimination in employment, 'there is a wider task in transforming cultural stereotypes about ageing, including those among older people themselves' (ibid., p. xiv).

Since the publication of the strategy, the government has legislated against age discrimination in employment and overhauled the enforcement regime in antidiscrimination and equality legislation as a whole. In October 2007, a single Equality and Human Rights Commission was established to replace the Equal Opportunities Commission, the Commission on Racial Equality and the Disability Rights Commission, bringing the organisation of equality enforcement more closely in line with the position in Northern Ireland with the single Equality Commission and the Republic of Ireland's Equality Authority.

An important part of the background to these developments in policy has been the work of the Social Exclusion Unit, an innovation that also dates from the period immediately after the election of the government in 1997. The Social Exclusion Unit has now been incorporated into the Cabinet Office as a social exclusion task force, but its earlier work on the impact of social exclusion on older people was clearly influential both in the decision to establish a strategy and in the strategy's actual contents. A review of the impact of government policy on the social exclusion of older people identified four drivers of social exclusion: age-related characteristics; cumulative disadvantage; community characteristics; age-based discrimination (Phillipson and Scharf, 2004). It concluded that policy had been more effective in addressing the first and the fourth of these than the second and third. Older people were now less likely than in the past to experience income poverty because they were old, and measures designed to address age discrimination were beginning to produce a cultural shift in perceptions of older people. However, people who had experienced poverty throughout their lives remained likely to continue doing so in old age. The authors concluded that there was a 'hard core' of older people who had experienced poverty in earlier stages in their lives and continued to do so. These people were the least likely to use public services. Poor neighbourhoods also remained a significant source of social exclusion for those older people who lived there. Neighbourhood renewal strategies were not effectively addressing the needs of this group.

Differences between Northern Ireland and the rest of the UK

This chapter has focused on the general development of policy towards older people in the UK as a whole. Lack of devolution of substantial taxation powers has meant that policy remains driven largely from the centre and it is notable that the only substantial variation in policy on ageing across the country as a whole is the availability in Scotland of funding for personal care outside hospitals. Northern Ireland follows the pattern. Once the principle was accepted that the difference between income from taxation raised within Northern Ireland and public expenditure in Northern Ireland should be met from central government funds, the social contract between the state and citizens has followed the national pattern since the early days of the welfare state in the 1940s. Levels of public expenditure available to Scotland, Wales and Northern Ireland are decided on the basis of the so-called 'Barnett formula', which allocates money from the centre. In Northern Ireland, local taxation in the form of the regional rate contributes to, but far from meets the costs of, major regional service responsibilities including health and personal social services. Recently there has been a substantial increase in the size of the regional rate, doubling the liability of some households to bring local taxation rates more closely into line with those in the rest of the UK.

Social security entitlements are identical across the UK, although in Northern Ireland they are administered by a separate agency accountable to a regional government department, currently the Department for Social Development. There are more substantial differences in the administration of social care where Northern Ireland has retained its combined health and social services structure, introduced in 1972 and to be found nowhere else in the UK, but more closely following the administrative model in the Republic of Ireland. Thus, one of the core themes of debate in Britain concerning relationships between the NHS and social services run by local authorities, particularly since the introduction of the reforms to community care in the early 1990s, has little parallel in Northern Ireland.

The origins of a recognisably modern system of social care in Northern Ireland go back to the 1949 Welfare Services Act, which brought Northern Ireland into line with the rest of the UK. The Act finally abolished the Poor Law system that had been first established in Ireland in 1838. Old-age pensions had been introduced in 1908, but up to 1949 both supplementary income and welfare for those in need were administered by the Poor Law Guardians who managed the 'Union' workhouses and outdoor relief. National Assistance, set centrally at UK national rates, replaced outdoor relief and, in the place of the workhouse, welfare committees were established in each of the eight county and city councils, with permissive powers to meet the welfare needs of people in need, including providing domiciliary support and old people's residential homes. Working from an initial task of closing the existing workhouses and finding alternative accommodation and support for those people who still lived there, the new committees made slow progress but by the mid-1950s the home-help service had been established and new old people's homes had opened that began to address the needs of elderly people who would not have qualified for any state help before these reforms.

The county welfare committees were abolished in 1972 as part of a fundamental reform of local government structures. The eight councils were themselves abolished, replaced by twenty-six district councils with residual functions and powers. Welfare services were amalgamated with health structures in four new health and social services boards, while housing became the responsibility of a new regional body, the Northern Ireland Housing Executive. The years that followed saw further substantial increases in the volume of support that was available, accompanied by the rapid expansion and professionalisation of the workforce. Some critics have suggested that the changes introduced a large bureaucracy that served to undermine professional social work values rather than enhance them (Caul and Herron, 1992). It was certainly the case that welfare spending remained dwarfed by spending on acute hospitals and community health services. Although arrangements were put in place for consultative mechanisms with voluntary organisations (see Chapter 4), the new structures provided for little direct input from service users.

The reforms of the early 1990s, with the separation of the commissioning and the provision of functions in the health service in Britain, were imported into Northern Ireland, producing a complex system of four Health and Social Services Boards responsible for commissioning services, and nineteen independent provider trusts, eleven of which provided social care services, some of which were responsible for hospitals only, some for both hospitals and social care and others for social care only. As in Britain, with local authority services, the trusts were encouraged to subcontract social care services to independent providers. As a consequence, in the 1990s, considerable sums of 'new' money flowed from the trusts to both voluntary and private-sector providers (Acheson et al., 2004).

Since devolution, there has been scope for emerging differences in policy detail among the constituent countries of the UK, particularly in the social care field so far as policy on ageing is concerned. In practice, divergence has been slow to emerge. While it is quite possible that with a functioning local Assembly, there might have been greater divergence in policy between Northern Ireland and elsewhere in the UK since 1998, in practice the pattern established in the earlier years of direct rule from 1972 has continued. As noted earlier, the differences have been administrative rather than substantive.

The recent Review of Public Administration in Northern Ireland, published in 2005, has rationalised this situation although not reformed it fundamentally. The reforms were introduced in April 2007. The combined structures remain, but they have been simplified with the numbers of Trusts reduced to seven in total (five of which deliver health and social care). The initial intention of the Review to replace the four Boards with one regional health authority that would have taken over some of the functions of the Department of Health, Social Services and Public Safety (DHSSPS) and its agencies has been revised by the Northern Ireland Executive that assumed office in May 2007. In a statement of 4 February 2008, the Minister announced that there would be one health and social care board for Northern Ireland, responsible for commissioning, financial management and performance improvement across the full range of health and social care functions. This will produce a structure that will remain quite different from that in England in particular. There the combined local authority social services departments, introduced in the late 1960s, have been abolished, with children's and adult services being split, with children's support being amalgamated with education, leaving social care a separate function remaining under local authority control.

The continuity in the legal framework for social care is emphasised by noting that the substantive legislation in this area remains the Health and Personal Social Services Order (1972), notwithstanding subsequent legislation that spelled out in greater detail the services that the state could provide, rights to an assessment of need, additional rights for carers, and the introduction of direct payments. All these followed initiatives taken in Britain and then 'read across' to Northern Ireland. The 1972 Order reproduced the powers available to the state that originated in the 1949 Welfare Services Act in Northern Ireland, itself replicating the National Assistance Act of 1948 in Britain.

Social care policy in Northern Ireland has not been updated since the early 1990s and the service has been subject to less scrutiny than elsewhere in the UK, since the publication of the policy paper, *People First*, which in 1990 introduced the changes to community care. Officials from within the DHSSPS acknowledge that this remains the guiding document. Nonetheless, a Review of Community Care was commissioned by the Minister for Health in the then NI Executive in 2001. Chaired by the chief executive of the largest provider of social housing in Northern Ireland, the review team reported in 2002 (DHSSPS, 2002a). The report made no attempt to cost the extent of unmet need, but in the absence of other reliable evidence reported on the numbers of people with assessed needs who were waiting for services. In July 2001, there were 2,271 people waiting for community services and 365 people whose discharge from hospital was being delayed because of the unavailability of community support (ibid., pp. 88–9).

Of equal note was the report's finding that whilst the availability of all services had increased substantially between 1995 and 2001, numbers receiving support for residential care had increased by 123 per cent, whilst numbers receiving support in their own homes had increased by only 42 per cent. Relative to the population of older people, Northern Ireland has substantially more nursing and residential home places than any other part of the UK or the Republic of Ireland, although the report is careful to note that this may reflect greater levels of need rather than a greater propensity to use residential services.

Notwithstanding this caution, however, in the light of the evidence outlined in this chapter, on the circumstances of older people in Northern Ireland, there may be grounds for concluding that social care in Northern Ireland is biased towards nursing and other forms of residential care when compared to that of other parts of the UK. Although the reasons for this are doubtless complex, it is unlikely that variation in levels of need is one of them. Indeed, the report notes the view of social care staff that there is an incentive towards residential options since the cost is shared with social security payments for housing and other costs, making it cheaper for trusts than intensive support in people's own homes. This perception may be another indicator of the severity of underresourcing.

The report noted that service users felt that the service was under severe pressure with a general lack of resources, dissatisfaction with the system of means-testing and a sense that the system was biased against families who wanted support in the home. Possibly reflecting the date of the review, it is notable for omitting any mention of the potential of direct payments to either older users or their carers as a means of addressing the concerns it identified. As we have noted, these have subsequently become the UK's aspiration for the delivery of most social care in the future. As yet there is no indication of how this policy may be implemented in Northern Ireland.

The reforms introduced in the early 1990s have emphasised market-driven, value-for-money approaches to service delivery, with the consequence that voluntary organisations have primarily been viewed as more or less efficient and effective deliverers of a narrowly defined service portfolio.

Investing for Health

However, whilst the largest sums of government money for voluntary sector involvement in older people's welfare continue to be committed within this policy frame, this is still only half the story. Indeed, it is arguable that other developments are having at least as profound an impact both on how the task of government on older people's health and welfare is conceived and on the role of voluntary organisations within this. Chief among these has been the 'Investing for Health' initiative.

Promulgated in 2002, 'Investing for Health' is a health promotion strategy adopted by the Northern Ireland Executive and prepared by the DHSSPS. The strategy 'seeks to shift that emphasis (on treatment of ill-health) by taking action to tackle the factors which adversely affect health and perpetuate health inequalities' (DHSSPS, 2002b, p. 7). Its background is the World Health Organisation policy framework, 'Health 21', adopted in Copenhagen in 1998 by all fifty-one member states of the WHO European region, and it thus follows developments elsewhere in Europe and in other parts of the UK. The consultation document produced in 2000 had proposed a focus on identified groups of people including elderly people, but this approach was in the end rejected in favour of an approach that focused on health inequalities across groups. Its targets are consequently wide-ranging and at a high level, for example seeking to improve life expectancy and halve the gap in life expectancy between the poorest and the wealthiest areas and to reduce the gap in ill-health between the poorest and the wealthiest areas.

Focusing on the causes of ill-health and of inequalities in health, the strategy crosses departmental boundaries and seeks to create a framework 'which is based on partnership working amongst departments, public bodies, local communities, voluntary bodies, District Councils and the social partners' (ibid., p. 7). A regional Investing for Health forum has been established with voluntary and community sector representation, and each of the four health and social services boards has established area Investing for Health partnerships, themselves linked to existing partnership initiatives such as the Belfast and Derry Health Cities and the health action zones where they have been established. These partnerships comprise 'key voluntary, community and statutory organisations in the area' (DHSSPS, 2002b, p. 145).

Built on different principles from those underpinning the delivery of social care, this framework is providing a separate set of opportunities for policy influence of older people's voluntary organisation and, as will be demonstrated in Chapter 4, is beginning to have a profound impact on the ways in which these organisations relate to state agencies at the local level, and is starting to influence the resources to which they can have access. It is also beginning to change the way in which social care is understood at the local level by the health and social care trusts, with more emphasis being given to community development as a method of intervention.

Equality and strategic policy on ageing

As in Britain, however, there have been substantial changes since 1998 in the degree of protection from discrimination that older people have enjoyed. The so-called 'equality duty' of the 1998 Northern Ireland Act, requiring public authorities to provide services on a basis that did not discriminate extended to the grounds of age, adding to the protection offered by the 1995 Disability Discrimination Act, which applied in Northern Ireland as well as Britain for those older people falling within its definition of disability. Laws against discrimination at work on the grounds of age have recently been extended to Northern Ireland.

Similarly, the government in Northern Ireland has attempted to establish an overview of the strategic policy challenge of an ageing society in a process that closely paralleled the publication of *Opportunity Ageing* in Britain. Within the terms of government's antipoverty strategy of the time, 'New Targeting Social Need', a programme-for-social-inclusion working group on older people was established in 2002 'to consider the factors that cause older people to be at risk of exclusion.'[4] The working group, serviced by the equality unit in the Office of First Minister and Deputy First Minister (OFMDFM) comprised people drawn from relevant government departments, other relevant public bodies and age-sector voluntary organisations.

The working group produced a draft consultative report in June 2004, which was followed by a period of five months' further consultation. Its

---

4 (http://www.ofmdfmni.gov.uk/age-ageing-in-an-inclusive-society.htm, accessed 22 January 2007)

conclusions on the drivers of social exclusion closely reflect the findings of Phillipson and Scharf (2004). It identifies lack of income, where an older person lives, discrimination, incidence of ill-health or disability and lack of transport (Walker, 2003). The final version of the strategy, *Ageing in an Inclusive Society: Promoting the Social Inclusion of Older People*, was published in March 2005 and sets out a strategic vision:

> To ensure that age-related policies and practices create an enabling environment, which offers everyone the opportunity to make informed choices so that they pursue healthy, active and positive ageing.

Six strategic objectives are proposed, ranging from accessing sufficient financial resources, living in a safe and decent environment, accessing integrated services that meet older people's needs and priorities, promoting equality of opportunity and combating ageism, to improving coordination in government.

The strategy is monitored by means of biennial action plans and annual reviews on progress. An action plan for 2005/06 was published at the same time as the strategy and was subsequently updated in autumn 2005, with the first annual report published in March 2006. The action plans are organised around the strategic themes, each with a set of areas of action. Departmental-led responsibility is set against the areas of action. In the first half of 2008, the devolved administration had yet to adopt the strategy formally as policy, and consequently the process of action planning and annual reviews had been frozen. There was no annual report in early 2008 as there had been a year earlier.

Since the strategy was published, the government has updated its overarching antipoverty strategy to replace 'New Targeting Social Need'. The government's antipoverty and social inclusion strategy for Northern Ireland, *Lifetime Opportunities*, was published in 2006. Forming part of the UK's National Action Plan on poverty, it acknowledges that 327,000 people in Northern Ireland are living in poverty, 54,000 of them pensioners, and sets a target of eliminating poverty by 2020. It sets an overall goal for older people to:

> Ensure older people are valued and respected, remain independent, participate as active citizens and enjoy a good quality of life in a safe and shared community.

Its targets include reducing the gap in life expectancy between the poorest and wealthiest areas, and securing an adequate income, decent housing and access to support services. The antipoverty strategy is designed as an overarching framework within which specific social inclusion strategies such as that on ageing are set.

The process of monitoring and review were to be coordinated by the Equality Rights and Social Inclusion Division of the Central Anti-poverty Unit at the Office of First Minister and Deputy First Minister, which chairs an interdepartmental equality and social-need steering group. The incoming devolved administration has, however, instituted a review of anti-poverty strategy and, whilst this is in progress, these arrangements are effectively in abeyance. The review process established was based upon a ministerial poverty forum, whose members include 'relevant stakeholder groups', described in the strategy as being local politicians; employers; trades unions; the statutory, voluntary and community sectors; the social economy; and individuals experiencing poverty and social exclusion (OFMDFM, 2006, p. 62, para 162). The forum's role was envisaged as overseeing the whole antipoverty and social inclusion strategy and promoting a participative approach through modelling joint work between government departments and other agencies, as well as monitoring departmental actions and targets.

The context of the National Action Plans on poverty, shared across the EU, links the Northern Ireland process clearly to other EU jurisdictions, particular the Republic of Ireland. The strategy envisaged a process of North–South consultation, co-operation and common action that would report on common and current areas of co-operation and identify ways in which these could be promoted in the future (OFMDFM, 2006, p. 64, para 171). The future of these initiatives is rather unclear since the Northern Ireland Executive's Programme for Government published in early 2008 makes no mention of them.

Conclusions

This chapter has sought to describe and analyse the socioeconomic circumstances of older people in Northern Ireland and to analyse the policy response across a range of areas. Older people form a smaller proportion of the population in Northern Ireland than in the UK as a whole, while remaining a larger proportion than in the Republic of Ireland. However, this masks differences between the Catholic and Protestant populations in that the former closely follows the demographic pattern in the rest of Ireland while the latter is closer to the rest of the UK.

The risk of an older person being in poverty (60 per cent of median income) is similar in Northern Ireland to the rest of the UK and lower than in the rest of Ireland. Women over the age of eighty are at the highest risk. Whilst there is evidence that many older people experience isolation, loneliness and poor health, the overall picture is that the majority enjoy reasonable health and have access to social contacts, although they remain among the groups most at risk of living in substandard housing. A substantial proportion of those aged over fifty-five are carers.

Public policy on ageing closely follows policy in the rest of the UK and indeed may be closer to policy in England than to that in either Scotland or Wales. Differences are mainly administrative, the most substantial of which is the combined health and social care system which is closer to the arrangements in the rest of the island of Ireland than to those anywhere else in the UK. There the split between NHS services, on the one hand, and local-authority-run and social care and children's services, on the other, remains a core feature of public administration, whereas in Northern Ireland all three functions remain rolled into a single set of combined agencies.

3

Older People and Public Policy: Ireland

This chapter outlines the situation of older people in Ireland, beginning with demography and demographic trends, before examining the social situation of older people. Next we look at policies for older people under a number of subheadings, including health, welfare and income support, poverty and social inclusion, housing and equality. Critiques of these policies are then reviewed before conclusions are drawn.

Demographic trends

A brief outline of the situation of older people in Ireland is first provided, focusing on those aspects likely to be most relevant to voluntary and community action.

In the last available census, 2006, there were 467,926 older people (sixty-five and over) in Ireland (Central Statistics Office, 2007), 11 per cent of the population, the smallest proportion of the European Union (EU25). Over a third live alone. The elderly population is quite unevenly distributed, being higher in the west and lowest in the rapidly expanding commuter counties around Dublin: the average age in Roscommon is 38.3 years, with Fingal having the youngest average, 32.2 years (Central Statistics Office, 2007).

Chapter 1 set the European backdrop to ageing and here we deal with some specific aspects of this process in Ireland. Looking at ageing first, in the European Union, life expectancy at birth rose from sixty-seven in 1960 to seventy-four in 2002, for men, and from seventy-three to eighty for women in the same period (EU25) (European Commission, 2005a). Life expectancy in Ireland in the same period rose from sixty-nine to seventy-five for men, and from seventy-two to eighty years for women. Life expectancy is expected to rise to eighty for men and to eighty-five for women by 2050 (Eurostat, 2007).

Turning to the proportion of older people, Table 3.1 illustrates the most recent estimates for projected growth in the population aged sixty-five and over.

Table 3.1: Projected growth in population aged sixty-five and over in Ireland

	2006	2011	2016	2021
65s and over (000)	467	531	631	741
State total (000)	4.239	4.488	4.811	5.07
Proportion 65s and over (per cent)	11.0	11.2	13.1	14.6

Source: Central Statistics Office, 2005: *Regional Population Projections, 2006–2021*, Cork: Central Statistics Office and Central Statistics Office, 2007. See also Connell and Pringle (2004).

Projecting even further ahead, the National Economic and Social Forum (2005) estimates that the proportion of older people will rise to 25.9 per cent by 2050.

Table 3.1 emphasises the point that the older population in Ireland will grow in relative terms — but not yet. Garret FitzGerald (2005) rightly reminds us that this is still a young state. In his interpretation of current population trends, he also draws attention to a continued flow of young people into the labour force, which will sustain this older population, a benefit not available in most other European Union countries.

Ireland's population profile has been unusual in a European context. High rates of emigration meant that until the 1990s substantial numbers of young people left the country, not to return. As a result, the ageing of the population will be delayed and on a smaller scale than other European countries (FitzGerald, 2000). High immigration by young workers will keep the dependency ratio down. A similar scenario was envisaged by NCB (2006). This predicted that the over sixty-five population would grow to 29 per cent by 2050 (still just under the European average of 31 per cent), but it also predicted a further fifteen years of economic growth and that the immigrant population would double to 1 million, keeping the dependency rate down until the 2040s.

Looking at CSO predictions in more detail, it can be seen that growth in the older population is not evenly spread either geographically or within the age cohorts, being concentrated in the mid-east (+133 per cent) and Dublin (+75 per cent) with a two-thirds increase in the over eighties, again concentrated on Dublin and the mid-east. The National Council on Ageing and Older People (2005a) estimates that the numbers of over eighties will rise from 100,000 in 2002 to 137,300 in 2021. At present, 34 per cent of over sixty-fives live alone, a proportion expected to rise. Other features of these predictions to note are:

- Western counties will continue to have the highest *proportions* of older people.
- Midland and eastern counties will have the highest *numbers* of older people.
- The numbers of single, never-married older men and women will decline and there will be an increase in formerly married older people, widows and widowers.

The implications of such a population rise are more difficult to determine and are controversial. Conventional wisdom is that such a population growth will cause a growing and unbearable demand on state pension systems, health and care services, including those likely to be provided by voluntary and community organisations. This approach, especially evident in European Commission commentaries on ageing throughout the Union, has recently been criticised for its apocalyptical nature. Fahey (1995) challenges the importance of demographic change in determining these social pressures: people's expectations are more important and, if these are low, the pressures will not rise as much as might be expected. His colleague Layte (2005) points to the manner in which Irish older people are experiencing *good* health in old age, have responded to the promotion of healthier lifestyles by adapting their behaviour, are receiving more appropriate and less costly health services and are more able to pay for them. The *Irish Times* 50+ poll, conducted in autumn 2006, painted a picture not of a declining, dependent elderly population, but instead of one that was reasonably confident, in good health, computer-literate, active, socialising and taking holidays (O'Brien, 2006c).

Social situation of older people

Numerous reports and extensive research has been carried out into the situation of older people in Ireland and, in this contextual section, we pick out those features most relevant to the current circumstances of older people, which may shape voluntary action.

Ireland is the second richest member state of the European Union (EU25), its income per head being 144 per cent of the European average (European Commission, 2007c). Growth rates have been phenomenal since the mid-1990s, averaging 9 per cent a year from 1995 to 2002 (Dimas and Almunia, 2004). The benefits of economic growth have not been well shared, for Ireland long had the highest relative poverty rate in the European Union, with 21 per cent of the population living below the standard 60 per cent reference line, 23 per cent in the case of women (Eurostat, 2005). Social spending in Ireland fell to an all-time low of 14.7 per cent of gross domestic product in 1999, recovering to 16 per cent in 2002 (Eurostat, 2005). This rate was not only the lowest in the EU15, but it was by far the lowest, comparing poorly to a European Union average of almost 28 per cent and rates over 30 per cent in the Scandinavian countries (39 per cent). Looking specifically at pensions, the proportion spent on pensions was 3.6 per cent of gross domestic product, a quarter of the European average of 12.5 per cent (EU25). This partly reflects both the small proportion of older people in the population and the greater role for private pensions in Ireland (European Commission, 2005b). Taking all social spending on older people together, Ireland's level of spending is dramatically low. In the European Union as a whole (EU15), social spending on over sixty-fives is as high as 19,516 PPS (Purchasing Power Standard) in Denmark and 16,495 in the UK. Ireland is by far the lowest, at only 6,439 PPS, trailing the next lowest, Spain, by a large margin (9,771) (National Economic and Social Forum, 2005). Health spending is the lowest in western Europe (Cullen, 2007).

Health and social services are probably the most important part of public services for older people. The proportion of spending on health services in Ireland has been falling since the 1970s and is the second lowest in the European Union (EU15), with low rates of health service employment, doctors, dentists, preventative medical services and hospital beds (Eurostat, 2001).

In the late 1960s, both Irish and European figures showed that older people were a group at high risk of poverty (European Commission, 1981). The ground-breaking study by Power (1978), an all-Ireland study, provided disturbing detail on the housing circumstances in which a substantial minority of older people found themselves, such as the poor physical fabric of their homes, with many lacking water, electricity, toilets, heating or telephones. By 1985, thanks to a significant investment in pensions and related benefits, the situation of older people in Europe had significantly improved, dramatically so in the Irish case, where the numbers of older people below the 50 per cent poverty line had fallen 55 per cent (European Commission, 1991). Indeed, Cousins (2000) later viewed the late 1970s as the high point of the expansion of the Irish social welfare system. Older people benefited from relatively generous rates in the early 1980s, but fared worst of all the welfare groups in the decade after 1987 (Callan and Nolan, 2000). Ó Riain and O'Connell (2000) characterised the evolution of the Irish welfare state as one of delayed and interrupted development, lagging behind the European pattern, making rapid progress during the economic difficulties of the mid-1970s and mid-1980s, but coming to a halt in 1987. Garret FitzGerald (2005) confirms this, illustrating how the value of the pension increased by almost 80 per cent from 1972 to 1982.

The risk of poverty for older people rose dramatically in the 1990s (Layte, Nolan and Whelan, 2000) to reach a peak early in the new century. Whereas in 1994, the risk of poverty for older people had fallen as low as 6 per cent, by 2001 this had risen to 44 per cent, being most acute for those living alone and dependent on the state old-age pension (Whelan, Nolan and Maitre, 2005). This compared unflatteringly to a European average risk for this age group of only 17 per cent (EU25) (Dimas and Almunia, 2004). Older people began to appear as one of the groups most prominently at risk of poverty. Layte, Fahey and Whelan (1999) in their detailed analysis of poverty among older people point out that the picture of old-age poverty is a complex one. Some groups of older people are more vulnerable to poverty than others, especially women and those in poor housing. Although cash incomes of older people are low, these are offset by accumulated resources through housing, free schemes (worth an estimated bonus of 13 per cent on incomes) and free access to medical services. At the same time, the level of public services may be more limited than in other parts of the Union and the authors drew attention to the 'profound deprivation' likely to arise when health or social services are unavailable, too costly or of poor quality. Ireland reached the highest rate of poverty among older people in the European Union after Cyprus, with the poverty rate for older women over seventy-five years reaching an astonishing 63 per cent (Zaidi, 2006b).

Much the most recent figures on poverty among older people come from Prunty (2007) and from the Central Statistics Office (2007). Prunty gave an Irish income poverty rate for older people of 27.1 per cent, compared to 21 per cent for children and 17 per cent for people of working age. The proportion of older people in consistent poverty was low, as was the proportion of older people without basic household items under long-standing deprivation indicators. Where poverty levels for older people shot up was when she looked at housing-related factors. When it came to lack of bath/shower, lack of central heating, lack of hot water, presence of damp, excessive darkness and lack of toilet, older people scored consistently higher than children or people of working age. Up to 15 per cent of older people lived in damp conditions and 17.7 per cent had no central heating. Prunty observed, over time, the fall in the value of the pension from 38 per cent of average wage in 1987 to 31 per cent in 2004.

The data published by the Central Statistics Office (CSO, 2007) is more recent, showing an encouraging trend which indicates that the risk of poverty for older people may have peaked and is now falling. The overall risk for older people had fallen back to 13.6 per cent in 2006, halving the levels of only two years earlier.

Subgroups of older people are affected differently. Few Travellers, for example, live to old age at all. Older people comprise a significant component of the homeless population, typical figures showing 36 per cent of those assisted by homeless services being over fifty years old (McCrumm, 2002). Figures published by the Homeless Agency (2006) found even higher proportions of older people in the Dublin homeless population. The Economic and Social Research Institute found that older people were twice as likely as the rest of the population to have a problem with their dwelling in dampness, sanitary facilities or ventilation (Watson and Williams, 2003). Ó Riain and O'Connell (2000) observed how the difference between the contributory pension and non-contributory pension, hitherto small, was now 12 per cent. A significant group of retired middle-class and upper-income people, male, working for large organisations, managed to supplement contributory pensions with occupational and private pensions, giving them a good income in old age. By implication, those below such a threshold were not able to benefit from the reconfigured tax, benefit and pension system, reinforcing market-based inequalities.

Despite an image projected by government that the state looks after older people well, Murray (2004) characterises their situation as a difficult one, citing poor housing, high rates of poverty, widespread discrimination, insufficient social support for carers, unaffordability of nursing care and insufficient incomes in old age. The government's own National Council on Ageing and Older People has drawn repeated attention to the insufficient level of services and inequities in meeting the needs of older people (National Council on Ageing and Older People, 2000). Despite improvements in the conditions of older people over the years, social services lack comprehensiveness and some older people slip through the net to live in very difficult, sometimes squalid, circumstances, without appropriate support (Hurley, Scallan, Johnson and De La Harpe, 1997).

Most older people in Ireland live in their own homes. The proportion of older people owning their own homes is in line with the national average (81 per cent), followed by private rented (10 per cent) and local authority homes (6 per cent) (National Council on Ageing and Older People, 2005a). Some studies have given a higher figure for older people, 86 per cent (Irish Council for Social Housing, 2005). Some older people find themselves in very poor housing and traditionally this was most acute in owner-occupied rural and western housing. Photo essays by Bermingham and Ó Cunaigh (1978, 1982, 1989) shocked the nation about the extreme urban housing circumstances in which some older people found themselves. In their study of deprivation among older people, Layte, Fahey and Whelan (1999) found significant problems of lack of heating (7.8 per cent), damp (11.4 per cent), rot (8.3 per cent) and leaks (4.4 per cent), these problems being most severe among private rented tenants, local authority tenants and home owners, in that order. The National Council on Ageing and Older People (2005a) reported that 8 per cent of older people still do not have hot water, while 40 per cent still do not have central heating. A study of the work of City and County Development Boards found that housing for older people was one of the most recurrent priorities in the work of these boards (Delaney et al., 2005). Irish older people living alone have the highest rate of fuel poverty in northern Europe (National Council on Ageing and Older People, 2005c).

Although the image of old age is one of retirement, Ireland is exceptional, in a European context, for the late age at which people leave the workforce. The average age of retirement is sixty-four, the highest in the European Union, where the average age in a number of countries is in the fifties age group. Although the Lisbon strategy set a target of 50 per cent of older workers being in the workforce, this was a somewhat redundant exercise for Ireland, which is already well over the 50 per cent mark (O'Brien, 2007).

Surveys show that older people regard themselves as in comparatively good health, with a low rate of self-reporting of poor health. Between two-thirds and three-quarters regard themselves as in good health and self-sufficient in terms of daily living (Browne, O'Mahony and Murray, 2002). A proportion, though, is not. The National Council on Ageing and Older People has estimated that 30,000 people suffer from dementia, with a greater proportion in counties with a high age profile (for example, rural, western areas) and a lesser proportion in eastern areas of new population growth. In less affluent communities, the level of self-reporting of good health falls significantly (Rourke, 2005).

Social inclusion was a concept introduced to Ireland through the European programmes against poverty, and encouraged policy-makers and practitioners to think beyond the static connotations of 'poverty' to the dynamic processes that included or excluded people from participation in the life, goods and processes of the community. Here such issues as access to transport are important. The National Council on Ageing and Older People has identified, as a significant problem for older people, difficulty of access to transport in the rural areas where the older person does not have the use of a car in places where public transport services are limited. In its study of social contact among older people (National Council on Ageing and Older People, 2005c), the Council found that most, 73 per cent, had a good level of social contact and supportive networks. A minority of 50,000 people, 11 per cent of the total, had limited social contact and could be considered isolated, and these tended to be older elderly, rural, widowed, women, people in poor health, and those without their own transport and of low educational standards.

Policies for older people

Policies for older people may be traced to the Irish Parliament, which in the early eighteenth century passed the House of Industry Act, 1703, which ordered the construction of what became a network of 130 workhouses in Ireland. The workhouses were specifically intended for the old, the infirm, the poor and the destitute. Accounts suggest that destitute older people constituted one of the largest constituencies of the workhouse system. They were still standing two hundred years later and the Irish Free State inherited 127 such workhouses, which were the starting point of the present Republic's policies for older people.

Over time, policies were developed in the areas of health; welfare and income support; poverty and social inclusion; housing; and equality. These are reviewed here, in each case with an eye to how they might impact on voluntary and community action.

Policies for older people: health

Until the Department of Health was set up in 1947, policies for older people were determined by the Minister for Local Government. Early on, the Irish Free State rationalised the workhouse system, leaving thirty-three, essentially one for each county or borough area, and renamed them county homes. These county homes remained the cornerstone of the state's obligation to older people, even though many of these homes were in quite poor condition (Coakley, 1997).

The new state's first policy for older people was the interdepartmental committee chaired by J. J. Darby, called the *Care of the Aged* report (Department of Health, 1968). This policy was important for two reasons. First, it introduced the policy theme, followed to the present day, of the promotion of the independence of older people, the maximising of their lives in their own homes and communities, and the avoidance of institutionalisation and dependence. Second, it set down the principle that services for older people should be gradually extended beyond the then limited category of the destitute. *Care of the Aged* put forward a range of enlightened proposals for community-based services (for example, occupational therapy, physiotherapy, social services) and, for those for whom institutional care was appropriate, geriatric assessment units within the hospital system and day hospitals. Third, it moved services for older people from the local authorities, through which health services were provided (and financed through domestic rates), to a national system of eight health boards under the Department of Health.

The role of voluntary and community organisations was mentioned. *Care of the Aged*, in advocating the principle of community care, suggested that this should be done by the community and its organisations. There was a role for the state to provide some modest assistance to voluntary organisations and to monitor their work, but no more. Indeed, a departmental circular, issued in 1972 to the new health boards, specifically instructed the boards not to employ home helps unless voluntary agencies could not be utilised (Lundström and McKeown, 1994). As a consequence, a number of voluntary agencies began to provide home-help services in the 1970s (Prendergast, 2006). Voluntary-sector involvement in the home-help service is thus much more extensive than in Northern Ireland where it has been largely retained as a core function of state welfare services, notwithstanding the use of voluntary agencies for other forms of social care support.

The broad thrust of the *Care of the Aged* report was implemented through the subsequent Health Act and through departmental circular. The Health Act, 1970, was a wide-ranging reform, giving the new health boards a broad mandate for community care, and empowering but not obliging them to provide home-help services. In the event, there was a significant expansion in domiciliary services for older people in the early 1970s, principally in the areas of public health nursing, meals-on-wheels and home-help services. This expansion did not last. Indeed, in the history of the development of community services for older people, the speedy and pro-active manner in which local authorities supported new projects with older people in the 1960s can be contrasted with the growing difficulty these organisations experienced in attracting health board support in the 1980s. Despite a bright start, Ireland's pace of development was not sustained. Haslett, Ruddle and Hennessy (1998) recorded that by the end of the twentieth century there were 12,000 home helps serving 20,000 recipients, but that only 3 per cent of older people received such a service, compared to 14 per cent in Northern Ireland and 19 per cent in Sweden.

A more subtle effect of the 1970 change is that in removing services for older people from the local authorities, it defined post-1970s services for older people within a medical, institutional paradigm (some say an unrestrained one), one in which considerations of planning, community and the physical environment diminished in importance, and services for older people became separated from important local authority roles such as housing, amenities and environmental services. Whilst health services found the separation from the local authorities liberating, it is less certain that services for older people did. As important as those that happened were those developments that did not occur. The new dispensation in health was slow to take on social work staff and, where it did, this was limited to medical social workers. A significant social work service for older people never developed and, to this day, it remains the least developed of all services for older people (Rourke, 2005). The legacy of the change is that older people are still more likely to be helped by public health nurses than by 'social'-type services.

Geriatric medicine and facilities grew rapidly over the decade following *Care of the Aged*. The thirty-three county homes were converted into geriatric hospitals, catering better and for smaller numbers, while thirty new welfare homes were built for those who required less intensive levels of care. The numbers of places in private and commercial nursing homes rose substantially and they were used by both fee-paying patients and low-income patients placed in them at the expense of the health boards (Curry, 1993). The proportion in nursing-home or long-term care has been almost unchanged over the past forty years — 5.2 per cent in 1968, 5.1 per cent in 2001 (Donnellan, 2005).

One of the most positive features of the Health Act was the introduction of the medical-card system for people on low incomes. This made provision for free medical cover for up to 40 per cent of the population (at present, it is in the order of 30 per cent). Most older people qualified for the medical card and this lifted a substantial financial burden from them.

Although the developments that took place after *Care of the Aged* were impressive at one level, the state was starting from a very low base in which provision had been virtually frozen for fifty years. It is still far from comprehensive: CareLocal (2001), in its comments for the National Anti Poverty Strategy, pointed out that for older people, the quality, reach, coverage and delivery of public services was as important as the level of income support. Tansey (2001) painted a picture of unevenness, lack of transparency and confusion as to entitlement to home-help service, which still had very low coverage. Similarly, Boyle (1997) described home-help services as discretionary and discontinuous. In the same way, community support services for urban local authority flats for older people ranged from the excellent to the ad hoc to the non-functioning or non-existent. Research by the National Council on Ageing and Older People (2005b) confirms the perception by older people that such community services are underresourced. Eithne FitzGerald (2000) points out that health services have never been under an obligation to plan for care of older people. Such an obligation has for many years been sought by the National Council on Ageing and Older People. By contrast, statutory planning requirements already existed on public bodies in respect of health and safety, Traveller accommodation, litter and waste management.

The general picture of patchiness is confirmed in microcosm if we look at palliative care services (Hospice Foundation, 2006). Even though Ireland was the second country in Europe to recognise the discipline of palliative care, such services developed in an extraordinarily uneven manner, with investment ranging from €1.50 a head in one former health board area to €31 in another, some counties having well-developed services, while others had almost none. What is most relevant here is the support for voluntary activity. Home-care services were typically 80 per cent funded on a voluntary basis, but in some parts of the country it was 100 per cent and in others 0 per cent. In the former south-western health board area, 5 per cent of funding for specialist palliative-care nurses came from voluntary sources, but it was 85 per cent in the western health-board area. Within Dublin, the proportions ranged from 0 per cent in the east-coast board area to 67 per cent in the northern board area. Individual subtypes of services were, for some reason, funded out of voluntary subscriptions, most prominently night nursing. Five major inpatient services used volunteers; four did not.

The principal dedicated exposition of policy for older people now is *The Years Ahead — A Policy for the Elderly* (Department of Health, 1988). This report, our second landmark, followed the broad themes laid down by the *Care of the Aged* report. *The Years Ahead* likewise outlined the importance of community-based services to enable older people to live in their own homes as long as possible. It recommended the refinement and development of institutional and community-based medical and para-medical services for older people. The report stressed the importance of community-care teams and improved liaison and coordination. It was critical of the uneven provision of services for older people, especially in domiciliary services. Moreover, *The Years Ahead* drew attention to the poor housing conditions of some older people, recommending the further development of housing repairs and the installation of basic facilities for older people in poor-quality housing that they owned.

Policies for older people featured in subsequent departmental frame-work strategies. The first framework policy was *Shaping a Healthier Future* (Department of Health, 1994) which had a section called 'Ill and dependent elderly'. This endorsed *The Years Ahead — A policy for the Elderly* and gave a commitment to continue the improvement in services for this group, with a target that 90 per cent of older people over seventy-five should be sustained in their own homes. The *Plan for Women's Health 1997–9* (Department of Health, 1997) affirmed, in a single page devoted to older women, the ideal of maintaining healthy living into old age, with specific commitments to quality in residential care. A specific health promotion policy for older people actually predated the national strategy, *Adding Years to Life and Life to Years — A Health Promotion Strategy for Older People* (Department of Health and Children, 1998). This set the objectives of longer life expectancy, improved health and greater autonomy for older people, with a reorientation of health services around older people in the community. The *National Health Promotion Strategy*

2000–5 (Department of Health and Children, 2000) reinforced this approach with a strategic aim to 'enhance the quality of life and improve longevity for older people'. Irish people should live as long as their European counterparts and this could be achieved through supportive environments, lifestyle change and 'appropriate services'.

The current health policy for older people is to be found in the present national health strategy, *Quality and Fairness — A Health Strategy for You* (Department of Health and Children, 2001). Three pages of the 200-page document are devoted to services for older people. The strategy promised to rectify current gaps in the provision of community support, acute hospital and long-stay services. Under 'Actions for older people', the strategy pledged government action in the area of improved access to nursing homes and residential care, listing targets of 7,000 day-centre places, 1,370 rehabilitation beds, 600 day hospital beds and 800 additional community nursing places. Although the commitment to community care was by no means abandoned, the emphasis of the strategy was on delivering hospital and institutional solutions. Murray (2006) has been critical of the pattern of Irish spending on services for older people: it is too low (0.67 per cent of GDP, compared to an OECD average of 1 per cent) and its orientation too institutional (50 per cent goes on residential care, used by only 5 per cent of the older population).

The provision of community-based home-care services is now a frontier area in services for older people. The European Commission (2007a) estimates that demand for home-help care will rise in Europe by 150 per cent by 2050. In Ireland, the Department of Health and Children adopted the approach of 'care packages', namely that older people living in the community were entitled to a package of care services, objectively assessed and delivered in a systematic way. Care packages could be delivered through voluntary services, which makes them especially relevant for this study. In 2005, the Tánaiste and Minister for Health and Children, Mary Harney, announced a €150-million package of services for older people over 2006/07, which she described as the largest ever increase in funding for this group. Three quarters, €109 million, was for community supports and most was for home-care support packages (to rise from 1,100 to 3,100), home helps, funding for day and respite-care centres and palliative care. In the event, commercial organisations were quick to respond to these opportunities and, in 2006, the Minister for Health and Children launched the Irish operations of the American franchise, Comfort Keepers, which aimed to attract funding to provide 1,000 part-time home-care jobs.

The introduction of care packages may have a significant impact on the voluntary and community sector. Both the Department of Health and

Children and the Health Service Executive are open to such services being delivered by voluntary and community organisations — indeed, they may favour them over private, commercial suppliers. Equally, they pose a challenge for voluntary and community organisations, for the health service will expect such services to be delivered according to high professional standards, with calculated unit costs, performance indicators, transparent payment systems, garda clearances, complaint systems, staff training, ability to demonstrate value-for-money and fully audited accounts.

The historic underinvestment in the service became evident when home-help militants began to demonstrate against zero-hour contracts and for a significant improvement in their work and conditions (Gartland, 2006), and the matter was also raised in a special debate in the senate.[1]

An important trend within health policy for older people is the emphasis on *active* ageing and is connected to broader policies for active citizenship, exercise and fitness, preventative health strategies and continuing education into old age (Boldt, 1998; Dempsey, 2002). The term originated in the World Health Organisation and was subsequently endorsed by the European Union. This has implications for voluntary action, for through the programmes of Age & Opportunity and through local active-retirement organisations the government has sought to fund and reinforce community activity in support of these objectives (Carey, 2004). The Equality Authority (2002) has stressed the importance of the term being used to connote citizenship and participation — much more than physical wellbeing.

Age & Opportunity was set up by the National Council for the Aged in order to promote positive approaches to ageing, challenge negative attitudes and promote the greater participation of older people in society. The Council organised the first national day on ageing (1988), followed by a national age week, in the course of which the idea of a more permanent inspirational focus took root. Age & Opportunity was formed and floated off to become an independent organisation with its own board, now funded through the Health Service Executive. It provides a strong practical underpinning to the sentiments and policies around healthier lifestyles, active ageing and the active community, with programmes for active living and sports, arts, training to promote arts in care, equality workshops ('Agewise') and courses for positive ageing. Two of Age & Opportunity's main programmes are 'Go for Life' and 'Bealtaine'. 'Go for Life' provides small grants, over 500 in 2005 in the range €500 to €2,000, for voluntary and community organisations working with older people in physical activity and sport. 'Bealtaine' is a month-long festival of arts events involving over a thousand events and about 40,000 older people. A world

---

1 Seanad Éireann, *Debates*, 19 October 2005, 694–728

first, it is now arguably Ireland's biggest arts festival and runs an extensive programme of media work, talks, lectures, workshops, resources (*Opportunities in Retirement* guide) and information-giving (for example, *Challenging Attitudes* newsletter).

In 2004, the health boards established in 1970 were replaced by the Health Service Executive (HSE), and here may be found the present articulation of policies for older people. Shortly after it was established, the Health Service Executive published a *National Service Plan 2005*, which included a six-page section, 'Services for older people', committing the HSE to providing a broad and improving range of home, community, hospital and continuing care services to older people. Specific targets were set for the level of influenza vaccinations (60 per cent) and the proportions receiving home help, day care and respite-care services (7 per cent, 6 per cent and 1 per cent respectively).

Policies for older people: welfare and income support

The Irish state inherited from the British administration the pension introduced by the then Liberal chancellor, Winston Churchill, in 1909. But in an inkling of what was to follow, Irish Home Rule MPs in Westminster, who were far from enamoured of the social reforms presented by the last Liberal government (1906–16), opposed many of them. The fall of the Nationalist Party in the 1918 general election was briefly thought to herald a more enlightened social policy. The *Democratic Programme of the First Dáil* (1919), a reference point for the new state, subsequently referred to only fleetingly, declared that older people should no longer be regarded as a burden but rather entitled to the nation's gratitude and consideration.

In the event, the social policy of the Irish state was unadventurous, conservative and minimalist. This was not an environment in which one could expect to find significant policy statements for the wellbeing of older people. Indeed, an early decision of the Free State government in 1924 was to reduce the value of the pension (McCashin, 2005). As Lee (1985) was later to note, the old and vulnerable soon felt the lash of their liberators.

The year 1949 marked a crucial point, for the government published, at the prompting of the Labour Party Tánaiste William Norton, a white paper expressing the ambition that Ireland match the construction of the welfare state then in progress in Great Britain and Northern Ireland (*Social Security*). The white paper proposed a single, unified, flat-rate national insurance scheme for employees, with, for old people, a retirement pension followed by old-age pension and, in the subsequent Social Welfare Bill, 1950, a significant increase in the pension level. The government fell on the second day of the second reading of the Bill that was intended to put the white paper into effect. The subsequent Social Welfare Act, 1952, of the succeeding Fianna Fáil government was a pale imitation of what might have been (Ó Cinnéide, 2000). Governments from that period on pursued a structurally incrementalist approach to social policy, one formally endorsed by the landmark Commission on Social Welfare report (1986).

Pensions policy is, by definition, a core policy issue for older people and central to the system of income support for them. Irish pensions policy is a vast field, but its key lines will be explored here because of their relevance to the living standards of older people, a determinant of poverty in this group, and consequent voluntary action in response.

The pension introduced during the Liberal government remained the core of the pension system for over fifty years. Indeed, the qualifying age of seventy years remained until the 1970s when it was progressively reduced to sixty-six years, where it remains to this day. A contributory pension, funded through the social insurance scheme, was introduced in 1961. Pensions thereafter followed two paths: a means-tested, non-contributory pension for those who had no, or insufficient, social insurance, and the new social insurance contributory pension set at a slightly higher level. There was also a retirement pension, introduced in 1970 to bridge the gap between sixty-five and pension age. The *Care of the Aged* report (Department of Health, 1968) influenced government thinking to prioritise older people. Between 1966 and 1985, the value of the old-age contributory pension doubled, while the value of the non-contributory pension rose 60 per cent in real terms (Coakley, 1997). Commentators appear agreed that this progress came to a halt in the late 1980s. Almost a hundred years after their introduction, the National Economic and Social Council (NESC) (2005) commented that pensions in Ireland still fulfilled only a limited, floor-providing, poverty-prevention objective, in contrast to other parts of the European Union where income-replacement objectives were ascendant.

Citizens with means could supplement such pensions with company or other private pensions. From the 1970s, government policy began to change, with three objectives:

- To reduce the numbers dependent on the state means-tested non-contributory pension
- To increase the proportion covered by state contributory pensions
- To increase the take-up of private or supplementary pensions (*A National Income-Related Pension Scheme*, 1976; *Social Insurance for the Self-Employed*, 1978).

ie proportion of those dependent on non-contributory pensions fell from per cent in 1990 to 24 per cent in 2001 and is projected to fall to

14.5 per cent in 2011, 6 per cent in 2026, and 3 per cent in 2056, while contributory pensions were extended across the workforce to include, for example, self-employed people. In 1998, the National Pensions Board set the objective that 70 per cent of the workforce should have supplementary pensions. The government introduced substantial tax advantages to encourage the take-up of such schemes. The shift in responsibility, flagged in the 1970s, accelerated rapidly in the 1990s. In a measure likely to reduce further the burden on the state, in 2005 the National Pensions Board recommended a series of proposals to encourage the delaying of retirement and pension age (Hennessy, 2005).

The respective balance of state, non-contributory, contributory, occu-pational, supplementary and private pensions is one familiar to policy-making throughout Europe. In the past generation, governments throughout Europe have taken steps to reform pension systems, these reforms taking the shape of substantial changes to the benefit rules (for example, retirement age, circumstances of entitlement), increasing the contributions expected or shifting the balance between public, private and occupational pensions, their main feature in common being a decline in the generosity of the public pension (Zaidi, 2006a).

Irish pensions policy stood out in the member states for its low level of state pension, the relatively small commitment of the state to funding pensions, the high and still-growing level of responsibility thrust on the individual, and dependence on private pensions (moreover, a weakly regu-lated industry). This clearly created a danger of low incomes for those older people who had not been part of the workforce, were already poor, women, or had not been responsible enough to protect their incomes privately. Stewart (2005) argues that the current trend of pension policy is sharply redistributive toward the better off and disproportionately enriches the private pension insurance industry. He warns that current trends will leave poorer people and those with atypical work records, women and the low paid, at significant risk and exposure to poverty in the future. Similar comments have been made by Stratton (2005) who has contrasted the way in which tax reliefs for pensions facilitate higher-income earners while, at the other end of the spectrum, the state pension provides less and less protection for those on low or modest incomes. The National Economic and Social Council (NESC, 2005) commented that a situation in which the state spends more on tax reliefs for private pensions than on public pensions is sharply regressive and exposes many more older people to poverty. The European Commission (2007b), in its review of pensions policy and developments, drew attention to Ireland's high poverty rate among older people, the low level of pension entitlements, the lack of income-related pension provision for most workers and the 'very low' spending on pensions.

From the 1960s, the government added a series of additional high-visibility social welfare entitlements for older people to supplement pensions. Most were available to all people either at the point of pensionable age or seventy years — for example, free travel on public transport (1967); free radio and television licences (1968); gas and electricity allowances (1967); and medical card (2000). These benefits, which were warmly welcomed by older people, created an image of a country that was progressive and enlightened in its treatment of older people. In reality, their actual financial value was quite small, but their political impact was high. They illustrate how policy for the elderly was incrementalist and never the result of an *ab initio* consideration of the objective needs of older people. In the words of Curry (1993), 'there was no particular pattern to the way in which the various schemes were introduced. There were particular circumstances to the way in which the various schemes were introduced . . . Development of the system was not planned in a coherent manner.'

Only in recent years have systematic attempts been made to identify the number of carers in the state, the first figures coming in at almost 149,000 (2002 census) but rising to 161,000 (2006 census). Typically, they are women in their forties and fifties (Healy, 2007). The time commitment varies, but of these 40,526, or 27.2 per cent, commit over forty-three hours a week to caring and may be described as full-time carers. Although precise figures are not available, older people constitute one of the main categories of people cared for, while 10 per cent of carers are themselves aged sixty-five or over (Cullen, Delaney and Duff, 2004). A substantial number of older people are looked after by carers; it is estimated that 97,500 households contain a carer who is looking after an elder (Browne, O'Mahony, Murray, 2002).

The work of carers is facilitated by the Prescribed Relative's Allowance (1968), subsequently the Carer's Allowance (1998), and Carer's Benefit (2000), but these schemes have been criticised for their restrictive criteria and ungenerous means tests. Of the 150,000 carers in the state, less than a quarter, 23,233, receive a carer's allowance. Put another way, 125,488 family carers receive no income support at all and the imputed savings to the state of their work is estimated at €1.5 billion (Carers Association, 2005).[2]

Policies for older people: poverty and social inclusion
'Poverty' is a term that re-entered the Irish and European discourse in 1975, with the commencement of the European programmes against poverty, an initiative by the government of Ireland. Older people were

---

2 Dáil Éireann, *Debates*, 19 April 2005, 1293–4

identified from an early stage as a group at risk of poverty, and a significant achievement of social policy by the governments of Europe was the subsequent marked reduction in the proportion of older people at risk of poverty.

The concept of setting an income floor was introduced in 1986, with the publication of the *Report of the Commission on Social Welfare*. This enunciated the principle that income adequacy be a key feature of the Irish welfare system, setting a band related to average industrial earnings. In doing so, the Commission probably had older people least in mind, for in the mid-1980s older people were already close to such a floor, the highest of all welfare groups and expressing the highest satisfaction with their position (Curry, 1993).

The government returned to this principle eleven years later in 1997 when it adopted a national framework strategy on poverty, the National Anti Poverty Strategy, *Sharing in Progress* (Government of Ireland, 1997). This identified older people as an 'at risk' group, noting how the situation of older people had improved in the 1970s and 1980s, taking a downward turn subsequently, and committed the government to improve income adequacy for all groups on social welfare. The policy was revised several years later as *Building an Inclusive Society* (Government of Ireland, 2002), setting a new target for the minimum social-welfare payment of €150 a week (in 2002 values) by 2007. *Building an Inclusive Society* also named older people as one of a number of vulnerable groups and gave commitments to reducing poverty among older people and for the provision of respite care, hip replacements and central heating systems in local authority homes.

Parallel with the National Anti Poverty Strategy, the government was required to submit to the European Commission, as part of the Open Method of Coordination approved by the Council of Ministers in 2000, National Action Plans for Social Inclusion (NAPSIncl). The first, covering 2001/03, identified older people dependent on the non-contributory old-age pension as vulnerable to poverty, especially older women, with the need for both income and non-income support in the area of medical and caring services and security. As a result, the government committed itself to raising pension levels and the provision of new services for older people, specifying 1,550 hospital beds, twenty-one day-care centres and twelve new social centres.

Increasing the value of the pension has been declared as at the heart of government strategy to prevent poverty among older people. Given the rapidly rising levels of income poverty among older people, this policy has yet to produce the hoped-for results. In their lengthy discussion of the most effective policies against the social exclusion of older people, Layte,

Fahey and Whelan (1999) outlined how the government had choices between pension levels, non-cash benefits and improved services (for example, housing, health, social services) or combinations of them. They noted the concerns expressed by the Department of Finance — remarkable in the light of the foregoing evidence to the contrary — that welfare pension levels for older people were already too high.

Policies for older people: housing

As in social welfare, older people were made, at a similar time, a defined priority within the housing system. From the early 1970s, local authorities, on the prompting of central government, set aside 10 per cent of new homes for older and disabled applicants, and a specific type of dwelling was introduced: the OPDs, or Old Persons' Dwellings (Curry, 1993). In some areas, the 10 per cent figure was exceeded, but not in others (precise figures for older people are not available, for they do not appear to have been kept) (Ruddle, Donoghue, Mulvihill, 1997). An unknown proportion includes some sheltered-housing projects, which provide communal facilities, alarms resident or visiting wardens and voluntary committees. Today, 14,839 households headed by an older person rent from the local authorities out of its stock of 105,000 units.

In the decades prior to 1987, local authority housing routinely ⸱ised 20–30 per cent of all national annual output, but this fell to less 10 per cent subsequently (Fahey, 1999). Older people in acute ⸱ing need soon found themselves competing for a rapidly diminishing ⸱urce. Tansey (2001) noted that the average number of OPDs built annually fell from an average of 736 a year over 1972–87 to an average of only 236 a year in the period 1988–95, down by more than two-thirds. The collapse of the local authority programme is evident if we contrast the total numbers of local authority homes built in the mid-1980s with the rate of construction following the introduction in 1987 of the *Programme for National Recovery*: 6,323 in 1985, down to 768 in 1989.

Although the building of significant local authority accommodation is out of favour with most present-day economists and policy-makers, its role for older people should not be underestimated. Even if historic OPD accommodation might fall short of today's standards and size, much was purpose-built, well maintained, affordable, heated efficiently, convenient to amenities and had a level of support services (Tansey, 2001). The uprooting of traditional housing policy in the late 1980s had swift, negative effects on low-income and vulnerable households such as older people (O'Connell, 1994).

Following the reports by ALONE, uncovering appalling living conditions for a number of older people (Bermingham and Ó Cunaigh,

1978, 1982, 1989), a special task force for housing assistance to the elderly was formed in 1982. This was organised under the aegis of the Department of the Environment but delivered by the health services, providing emergency and more substantial repairs to homes for older people that were in very poor condition. Although the work of the task force has been commended, no documentation on its work appears to be available, although this could tell us much about the nature of housing deprivation for older people (Ruddle, Mulvihill, Donoghue, 1997). We know that in 2004, 4,414 repair jobs were completed at a cost of €10.8 million, which gives us an indication of the scale of the undertaking, but is the sum total of information available.[3] There are several long-standing schemes for which older people are eligible, such as the essential repairs grant scheme and the disabled person's housing grant. Since these schemes are also little documented, their impact or value is impossible to assess.

Despite the focus on older people within local authority housing, Tansey (2001) makes the point that national social policy for older people has paid little attention to housing, and there has been no national policy for the housing of older people. Although local authorities have provided homes for older people, such housing need has been separated from welfare needs, with little resourcing or coordination of the two. At one stage, the local authorities had developed a much-valued warden service, but in the cutbacks of the 1980s this service was reduced to the inconsequential or abolished altogether. *The Years Ahead* was extremely critical in its comments on trends in housing policy and practice for older people, saying that little had been done to develop home designs suitable for older people or to incorporate assistive technology.

From the late 1980s, responsibility for the housing of older people was effectively transferred to the voluntary housing sector. Although the *Plan for Social Housing* (Department of the Environment, 1991) spoke of new thinking in responding to housing need and gave welcome scope to voluntary and social housing, the policy signalled the reality that meeting specialised housing need (for example, older people, homeless people, disability) would become essentially a voluntary-sector responsibility. This line of development was reinforced in a successor policy, *Social Housing — The Way Ahead* (Department of the Environment, 1995), although no assessment was made of the ability of the sector actually to meet such a need.

At first sight, the number of older people officially in housing need is small. The 2005 national assessment identified 43,684 people in housing need, of whom 1,727 were elderly (Cornerstone, 2006). The list, though, has a number of other categories, which may also include older people,

---

3 Dáil Éireann, *Debates*, 6 December 2005, 1419

and the assessment system has long been criticised for its inconsistencies and definitional deficiencies, which between them are likely to lead to underestimates. This is certainly the case if we compare the outcomes to Prunty (2007). Older people have not featured prominently in the discourse on housing policy, despite research by the National Council for the Aged, dating to the 1980s, indicating that although a higher proportion of older people may own their own homes, a disturbing number lived in accommodation of poor quality in both urban and rural areas.

Related to housing, the government introduced in the 1990s a scheme to improve the security of older people in their own homes. This is run as a grant scheme by the Department of Community, Rural and Gaeltacht Affairs, providing grants over €2 million annually since 2002, with the 2006 allocation rising to €3 million. It is important to note that although the funding is channelled through voluntary and community organisations, it is not a fund *for* voluntary and community organisations. The groups distribute individual grants to older people for specific jobs of work, examples ranging from €50 for smoke alarms to €150 for locks, chains and lighting.[4]

Policies for older people: equality
The equality discourse is an emerging one within Irish policy-making. Not until 1994 was a government department, the Department of Equality and Law Reform, charged with equality issues. From 1997, this department was integrated into the Department of Justice as the Department of Justice, Equality and Law Reform. An equality infrastructure of law and institutions was set in place. Under Irish and subsequent European equality legislation, discrimination against older people was made illegal in the field of employment, enforced by the Office for the Director of Equality Investigations (ODEI) and the Equality Authority, which had a broad remit to promote equality for older people. The Employment Equality Act, for example, permits positive action in favour of people over fifty in employment. Discrimination against older people in goods and services is prohibited under the Equal Status Act, 2000. Age-related cases comprised 9 per cent of the authority's subsequent caseload, typically covering access to insurance, transport, pubs and nightclubs (Equality Authority, 2002). This is an area of work likely to grow in the future, covering such formal issues as age limits on the provision of services and retirement ages, as well as subtler forms of discrimination through media portrayal and stereotyping (Crowley, 2005).

Murray (2005) has drawn attention to the many ways in which Irish society continues to practise and tolerate discrimination, sometimes by

---

4 Dáil Éireann, *Debates*, 21 February 2006, 384–5

state services (Breastcheck, not available after sixty-four), employment discrimination (the difficulty of getting salaried work for over fifties) and commercial services (car hire refused for older drivers). Whilst often falling short of direct discrimination, ageism can take many subtle forms, such as disrespect, being ignored, having decisions taken for them, or being denied medical treatment or services on the basis that they will not live long enough to experience their benefits (Rourke, 2005). There is a sixty-year-old limit on cervical screening, apparently based on the mistaken belief that women over these ages could not benefit (O'Brien, 2006b). Although Irish law and public administration does not have a tradition of social rights, the equality legislation and its enforcement agency, the Equality Authority, have introduced the notion of the right not to be discriminated against and this is likely, over time, to make a significant change for older people. Retirement was compulsory in the public service at sixty-five for all entrants coming in before April 2004, and it appears to be still the norm in private-sector employment.

The Equality Authority specifically addressed the situation of older people in *Implementing Equality for Older People* (2002), which made seventy-two recommendations in the areas of legal status, age limits, indefensible anomalies and exemptions, policy-making, work, income, education, health and community services. The authority was critical of the way in which older people were not properly consulted about issues that affected them, for example in such areas as the strategic policy committees of the local authorities, sports, culture and the arts. Here, the authority recommended that the state resource older people's organisations, develop their capacity, promote networking and coordination and strengthen their advocacy work. Specific recommendations were made to promote the involvement of older people's organisations in the planning and delivery of health and social services. The authority's report contributed to the reorientation of older people's issues around an equality, rights, anti-discrimination agenda.

The National Economic and Social Forum, in its *Care for Older People* report (2005), devoted a chapter to equality issues, illustrating their rising prominence within the broader discourse on older people. Called 'Rooting out ageism', the chapter brought together a bundle of concerns previously raised by the Equality Authority, the National Council on Ageing and Older People and voluntary and community organisations, ranging from the need for attitudinal change to discrimination practised by government itself and its agencies. It described ageism as a substantial barrier in progress for older people. A further chapter, 'Legal aspects of community care', explored the question of whether older people should have rights to services. This was, according to reports, a controversial issue within the forum and led to the weak recommendation that existing entitlements to community care services be 'clarified' (most commentators had already observed that there are no such rights to be clarified in the first place).

Critique of policies

This chapter has, so far, reviewed the situation of older people, policies for older people, and changes in the way in which older people have been seen within the policy framework. But what has been said about those policies and their effectiveness?

Most of the critiquing of policies for older people has been supplied by the National Council on Ageing and Older People, which has, since its foundation, provided a commentary on policies for older people. The Council has, from time to time, analysed the degree to which its recommendations have been accepted by government. In one, somewhat disheartening, exercise in the 1980s, it determined that of its 142 recommendations to date, only one had ever been adopted, one related to the carryover of unused free electricity units from one billing period to another. Analysts of policies for older people have identified the problem of implementation as a central issue (for example, Hodgins and Grieve, 2004a). Implementation is not a problem unique to policy-making in the area of the elderly, for it affects governments the world over. Nor have governments in Ireland been alone in struggling with problems of community care, for it is a familiar theme in the discourse in England and Wales (Brown, 1996).

The Council has not only sought incremental change to improve the welfare of older people across a broad range of fronts, but it has also dealt with the larger issues of how services for older people should be developed, and the models and values that should inform them. Two themes have stood out consistently:

- The importance of community-based responses to older people, especially those that value the autonomy and participation of older people themselves
- The need for those responses to be properly resourced, planned and coordinated, be they provided through state services or voluntary action (here, the Council would favour a mixture of the two).

A recurrent criticism by the Council is that community-based services for older people are underdeveloped, fragmented and poorly coordinated. In their analysis of the situation of older people in Ireland, Browne, O'Mahony and Murray (2002) argued that the shortfall of public services was the most serious and that the three most outstanding of these were housing, domestic care and affordable high-quality residential care. The level of service was low, uneven (some parts of the country getting none) and underfunded. The National Economic and Social Council (2005), in its analysis of Ireland's welfare state, agreed that while the country had developed a hybrid model that drew on the best points of systems from many other countries, there were serious deficits in many key areas, including elder care.

The problems with services reflected larger political and organisational issues. Browne, O'Mahony and Murray (2002) argued that essential for the future welfare of older people were rights-based services and a much-enhanced basis for participation in decision-making. They argued that older people must become 'better organised' as a group if they were to represent their interests successfully. There was a need for a strengthening of organisations of older people. Such umbrella organisations would enable them to develop common agenda and pursue them in the public arena.

The National Council on Ageing and Older People (2005a) took a critical view of the quality of policy-making for older people. The Council described many policies for older people as inadequate, inconsistent, limited and not properly planned, leaving older people with substantial health and social deficits. There was no agreed vision of the respective role of the state, individual or community. The principal determinants of policy-making were administrative expediency, affordability and dis-cretion, in preference to planning, standards, equity and consistency. Contrary to many policy advisory bodies which claim that they have made a profound impact on the policy process, the National Council on Ageing and Older People reached the opposite conclusion, often despairing of the limited impact that it has made.

Some analysts of health services, most recently FitzGerald (2000), explain this in terms of the unsuccessful competition by community-based services for health service budgets, against much stronger, institutional, hospital-based big-hitters. Murray (2004) attributes this to the quality of debate on the situation of older people, which he rated as low. Rarely do senior politicians initiate or even enter debates on matters affecting older people, he comments. Debates usually revolve around the levels of the old-age pension, or occasional crises that suddenly blow up, such as charges imposed on elderly patients in nursing homes. Murray has criticised what he calls the nod-and-wink attitude of politicians, the 'Didn't we raise your pension for you?' approach. Only one political party appears to have a specific policy for older people, the Green Party (*Citizenship, Equality, Respect — A Policy on Ageing and Older Persons*). Although Fianna Fáil circulated a policy document on the situation of older people (*A New Approach to Ageing and Ageism*), it appears to be the personal initiative of an individual senator, Mary White. Debates on older people can be dominated by relatively local issues, although the most recent parliamentary debate showed the resolve of a number of parliamentarians to raise the discussion to national and policy concerns.[5]

The most detailed analysis to be found of the problem of implementation of policies for older people is given by Ruddle, Donoghue and Mulvihill (1997). They examined the problems attendant on the implementation of *The Years Ahead* report nine years earlier. In its comments on their work, the National Council on Ageing and Older People attributed the problem of implementation to:

- The failure of government to put services for older people on a statutory basis
- The failure of government (it implied the Department of Health) to take responsibility for the policy report and lead implementation
- Governmental preference for a discretionary, 'goodwill' model of service delivery
- Subsequent policy development, which ignored, took little account of, or was at variance with *The Years Ahead*.

The authors themselves drew attention to 'ambivalence' toward the report at management level, at both health board and departmental level. This was a gentle description of the attitude (implementation theorists might use terms like 'high-level bureaucratic obstruction'). In their investigation of the implementation of individual recommendations, the authors looked, amongst many other things, at the recommendation for an advisory committee on the elderly in each health board area. They found that in six of the eight health boards, the programme manager had formed the view that they would be 'hard to manage' and had decided to do nothing. Similarly, in the area of housing homeless people, including homeless older people, formal arrangements for co-operation between health boards, local authorities and voluntary and community organisations had simply not been put in place (most of them were eventually established in the following century). In their conclusions, the authors explained at least some of these difficulties as the outcome of the lack of space made available for a consumer viewpoint and the voice of older people themselves in the planning and delivery of services for them.

Such problems continue to persist. When the National Advisory Committee on Palliative Care reported in 2001, it recommended that there be a national council for specialist palliative care. Even though this was not a costly reform, it still took four years to set up the council.

---

5 Dáil Éireann, *Debates*, 23 March 2006, 2072–2104, statements on care of the elderly

Mangan (2005), in her reflections on the Equality Authority's report, *Implementing Equality for Older People* (2002), echoed many of these comments about non-implementation. Nothing had been done about many key recommendations for protection against unfair dismissal past retirement age, age limits on social welfare and pension contributions, the right to core services, entitlements to care, and adjustment of the consultative process to allow for the participation of older people.

The National Economic and Social Forum (2003a) sought specifically to test the implementation of the recommendations of the Equality Authority (2002) in respect of older people, with the purpose of identifying the barriers and challenges to implementation. The forum confirmed, among other things, the inconsistency between official policy and its sluggish implementation, both in resource-sensitive areas and those where resource implications were minimal; the lack of commitment to consultation with older people in policy-making; the lack of cross-departmental working and insufficient political priority given to issues affecting older people. A number of proposals were made to government departments and state agencies which, the forum hoped, would ensure that issues affecting older people were more thoroughly structured, monitored, reported and acted upon. Although NGOs participated in the project team for the NESF report, issues concerning the role of voluntary organisations featured little in the report.

The National Economic and Social Council (2005) implicitly accepted the criticism that many services for older people were poorly coordinated, by proposing, in *The Developmental Welfare State*, that there be a national strategy for older people, modelled on the national disability strategy, forcing coherence across the many departments and agencies of government involved. Similarly, the National Economic and Social Forum (2005) recommended that there be a new national strategy on ageing, generated by the Department of the Taoiseach. In effect, this would move ageing policy from its traditional home in the Department of Health to a centralised position, one likely to produce a more joined-up result across government departments.

Conclusions

At the beginning of this chapter, we examined the demographic situation. We know that the European Union faces a rapid ageing of its population over the next decades, a rising dependency ratio and resultant financial strain. Although Ireland will definitely follow the ageing trend, it will do so later and to a much less marked extent. The ageing trend in Ireland will be geographically uneven, being at its greatest in the eastern counties.

Table 3.2: Landmarks in the development of policies for older people in the Republic of Ireland

Year	Policy
(1703	Houses of Industry Act)
1910	Old-age pension
1947	Department of Health
1949	White paper, *Social Security*
1953	Health Act, s.65 permitting funding for NGOs
1961	Contributory pension
1968	*Care of the Aged* report
1970	Health Act, 1970: introduction of health boards
1975	Pilot schemes against poverty
1981	National Council for the Aged established
1984	Defined scheme for voluntary housing
1988	*The Years Ahead — A Policy for the Elderly*
1986	Commission on Social Welfare
1994	Health strategy, *Shaping a Healthier Future* Social partnership extended to Non-Governmental Organisations
1997	National Anti Poverty Strategy, *Sharing in Progress*
2000	White paper, *Supporting Voluntary Activity*
2001	Health strategy, *Quality and Fairness — A Health System for You*
2005	Health boards replaced by Health Service Executive (HSE)
2006	NESF, *Care for Older People*

In the late 1960s, Ireland, like other European countries, identified older people as being at high risk of poverty. Substantial efforts were made to improve the economic situation of older people during the 1970s and 1980s, periods of considerable economic difficulty in Ireland, and these policies were successful in reducing that risk. From 1987, though, these gains were lost and the most recent studies of poverty indicate a dramatically rising risk of poverty for older people, especially older women. This risk is thrown into sharp focus if we consider the backdrop of Ireland having the highest rate of relative poverty and one of the lowest levels of social protection in the European Union. There is evidence of a small group of older people living in notably substandard housing. The issue of pensions is an important one for the future of voluntary and community activity. A pensions policy based on social insurance, social inclusion, intergenerational rights and responsibilities is more conducive to voluntary and community activity than a marketised, privatised, consumerised future with minimal state obligation, where voluntary and community organisations will play, unsupported, a residual role in trying to assist those unable to afford care.

The present policy architecture for older people is determined by the Department of Health and may be found in two key policy documents: *Care of the Aged* (1968) and *The Years Ahead* (1988). Several other national bodies also contribute to policies for older people, such as the National Economic and Social Forum and the Equality Authority. Policies for older people, especially for income support, may also be found in the more dynamic policy environment of programmes for government and the national social partnership agreements. The Department of Health is informed by the substantial research work undertaken by the National Council on Ageing and Older People.

Table 3.2 marks the main milestones in the evolution of policies for older people.

Policies for older people, articulated first in *Care of the Aged* and elaborated in *The Years Ahead,* marked the transition from a passive, dependent medical, institutional model of ageing to one that valued active, healthy old age, based on care in the community and services that enabled people to live well in their own homes. To what extent the state has been able to supply this community-based model has been at the heart of the subsequent policy debate. Neither the Free State nor the Republic prioritised the welfare needs of older people until the sustained expansion of income support in the two decades from the late 1960s to the late 1980s. Significant changes in pension policy in the 1990s appear to be redistributive toward the better off, and will leave women, those without sustained work records and other vulnerable categories at some risk in the future. An equally significant shift took place in the area of social housing, where supply was shifted from the local authority to the voluntary sector. A recent development in policy for older people has been that of equality, where affirmative action and protection from discrimination are now expected from the state, by both Irish and European law.

The place of voluntary and community action in this scheme of things will be examined in Chapter 5.

4

Community and Voluntary Action: Northern Ireland

Introduction

This chapter sets out the field of voluntary action concerned with older people in Northern Ireland. It is divided into a number of sections. The first discusses the context of the development of public policy towards the voluntary sector as a whole, indicating the ways in which this has helped to structure the development of those voluntary organisations addressing the needs of older people in particular. This is followed by a section drawing on survey data to describe the general features of the voluntary sector and ageing in Northern Ireland: its size, age, functions, activities, incomes, and numbers of people involved. The third section comprises a number of case studies of organisations operating at regional Northern Ireland level, and at subregional and local levels, that have a role in the development of voluntary action among older people and which may seek to influence directly the development of public policy. A number of specialist and general welfare and housing organisations that have developed services used by older people are described in Appendix A.1. The fourth section of this chapter discusses the development of an independent voice of older people in Northern Ireland. Finally some conclusions are offered.

The data are necessarily incomplete. First, it is impossible to obtain a reliable sampling frame of organisations, partly because no such thing exists, but also because the boundary of the category of older people's organisations is permeable and imprecise. For example, much voluntary activity carried out by older people is recreational and may not be labelled as being particularly aimed at older people. An example would be bowling clubs, or even book-reading groups. We have made no attempt to quantify this. There are also many general welfare service-delivery organisations whose work may be in part directed at older users, but they are not necessarily specialists. Equally important are church-based groups and institutions run by religious orders in the Roman Catholic Church, many of which may be very important in the lives of many older people, but they are not well documented and are often not well known to the 'secular' voluntary sector.

Second, it proved very difficult to access accurate and complete financial information, particularly from government sources. We have had to rely on a few indicative examples of the kinds of organisations funded and the amounts they receive. More research is needed in this area since our experience suggests that there is no accurate overview of the extent of government support for voluntary action in this important field at either regional or local level. The absence of an overview of the extent and nature of government support for voluntary organisations working with older people is a major gap in our knowledge, although it can, to an extent, be remedied with reference to example cases. The inability or reluctance of public bodies to respond to requests for information (also a problem, although to a lesser extent, in the Republic of Ireland) is unfortunate.

Public policy and voluntary action in Northern Ireland

The general development of voluntary action in Northern Ireland has been outlined by us elsewhere (Acheson et al., 2004). In considering the background to the development of voluntary action concerned with ageing, three aspects of that analysis should be noted. First, the early development of voluntary organisations was very closely related to the concerns of the clergy and, by the beginning of the twentieth century, a clear sectarian division of voluntary action was discernable which has persisted right into the start of the twenty-first century (Jordan, 1989: Acheson et al., 2007). The second and perhaps related factor was the remarkably conservative nature of voluntary action up until the social cataclysm that accompanied the outbreak of the 'troubles' in the early 1970s. Very few new organisations emerged between 1920 and 1970, and in that fifty-year period those that were around by and large continued doing what they had always done. There was very little contact between Protestant philanthropy and Catholic social action.

The third factor has been evident since the very earliest days of the extension of state-underpinned general welfare services from Britain in 1949, with the passage of the Welfare Services Act (Northern Ireland) (1949). This Act repealed the Poor Laws and established eight county welfare committees in Northern Ireland, with the powers to provide welfare services to those in need. The Act was followed by a government circular that stipulated that the new county welfare committees should 'give to voluntary bodies the recognition which they deserve, consult closely with them and generally assist them not only to continue in being, but to develop and expand' (Acheson et al., 2004, p. 32). The wording of the circular was perhaps chosen to reassure the voluntary sector that, unlike in the case of hospitals, which had effectively been nationalised, the state's new role in general welfare should not be understood as a threat.

The welfare reforms of the 1940s and the accompanying government circular on the future role of voluntary organisations led the Northern Ireland Council for Social Services to establish a number of standing committees, among them a committee on ageing and older people, an entity that was eventually to become Age Concern Northern Ireland.

It has thus been public policy since 1949 that the state should ensure a facilitative and enabling environment for voluntary organisations in the provision of welfare, and this has been an important factor in shaping the structures of voluntary action, particularly around key groups of welfare-users such as older people. Indeed, as Ditch (1988) has pointed out, a defining characteristic of the administration of welfare in Northern Ireland since the establishment of the welfare state has been the way in which elites from voluntary organisations have been recruited to quasi-governmental roles in a series of commissions and arms-length bodies.

The general tenor of welfare policy in Northern Ireland for the thirty years between 1950 and 1980 was conservative and incremental. The administrative reforms of 1972 that saw the abolition of the county welfare committees and the amalgamation of welfare and health services into four new Health and Social Services Boards was followed in 1974 by a further departmental circular on relations with voluntary organisations, which reiterated the themes of the 1949 circular and identified the value of partnerships both to harness the additional resources held by voluntary organisations and to make use of their ability to enable service users to identify their needs (Kearney, 1995). In retrospect, the circular appears more aspirational than realistic about what could be achieved. In the first comprehensive study of voluntary organisations in Northern Ireland, the authors concluded that these organisations showed little interest in social change, were readily accepting of existing categories of need and, most remarkably, were largely oblivious to the impact of the civil conflict (Griffiths et al., 1978). This evidence suggests that they were at that time an unlikely source of either civic participation or new ideas.

This study coincided with the publication of the report of the enquiry into voluntary action by the committee established by the Carnegie United Kingdom Trust, chaired by Lord Wolfenden. The committee had taken evidence in Northern Ireland. Its report, *The Future of Voluntary Organisations* (Wolfenden, 1978), is notable for being the first instance of the use of the term 'voluntary sector' in the UK. It promoted the value of intermediary bodies that would both foster local voluntary action and help to formalise and make more effective relations with government. The government's response to the Wolfenden report was to publish a consultative document, *The Government and the Voluntary Sector* (Home Office, 1979), which contained a separate chapter on Northern Ireland and which recognised the 'vital importance of the voluntary sector' and committed government to facilitating its ability to expand and innovate (Kearney, 1995).

In Northern Ireland, the Minister responsible for Health and Social Services launched a strategic review of government voluntary-sector relations, which recommended a strategic partnership between government and the voluntary sector, and this work carried on after the election of the first UK government under Margaret Thatcher in 1979. The review, conducted by the Coordinating Committee on Social Problems, set out the principles on which such a partnership should be based (CCSP, 1980; Kearney, 1995; Acheson, 2003). However, it rejected the need for a central point of coordination within government that would mirror the establishment of the Voluntary Services Unit in the Home Office in London.

An important outcome of these developments was the establishment, first of the Northern Ireland Voluntary Trust, in 1979, and second of the Northern Ireland Council for Voluntary Action, in 1985. The latter was the successor body to the Northern Ireland Council for Social Services (NICSS), which had been established in 1938, one of the only innovations in voluntary action that occurred in the period between the establishment of the Northern Ireland government in 1920 and the Second World War. From its inception, the NICSS had managed an older people's home in east Belfast and, from the 1940s, also housed the standing committee for old people, an entity that was to be floated off to become the Northern Ireland Council on Ageing, operating as Age Concern Northern Ireland on the establishment of NICVA.

These events illustrate an increasingly interventionist approach by government as it developed policy towards the voluntary sector which was accompanied by a growing formalisation of the mechanisms whereby the government and the sector were to relate. To a degree, these mirrored events in the rest of the UK, and certainly the growth in policy interest in the welfare contribution of the voluntary sector was one result of the crisis of confidence in state welfare that followed the oil shocks of 1974 and the consequent economic recession (Lowe, 2005; Ellison and Pierson, 2003).

As discussed in Chapter 2, there was one respect in particular in which policy in Northern Ireland closely mirrored developments in Britain. In both health and social care, the government moved to create a split between the purchase or commissioning of public services and the provision of those services. The role and nature of public administration were heavily influenced by the 'new public management', which emphasised rational, managerially led and evidence-based systems and the use of market mechanisms to drive innovation and efficiency. In Northern Ireland, the monolithic Health and Social Services Boards were broken up into a relatively small purchasing arm, in the form of the four Boards, and a complex assortment of more than twenty quasi-independent Trusts that between them were responsible for acute and community health care and for social services. Alongside their own services, the Trusts were, in turn, encouraged to develop relationships with a range of service-providers from both the private and the voluntary sectors.

The equivalent reforms in England and Wales required local authorities to use 85 per cent of the money that was transferred from the social security budget on independent service-providers. Whilst this did not apply in Northern Ireland, nevertheless the middle years of the 1990s witnessed a 400 per cent increase in the amount of money flowing to the voluntary sector from state health and social services agencies (Acheson et al., 2004). Acheson et al. note in that study that older people were the biggest single beneficiary group of this switch from public to voluntary-sector service-providers. However, as the evidence presented below will show, the trend has been to concentrate resources in a small minority of relatively large providers, one or two with over 500 staff, delivering services in England, the Isle of Man and the Republic of Ireland, as well as in Northern Ireland. Economies of scale and the ability to shoulder the costs of unsuccessful contract bids have tended to push the trend in this direction. Furthermore, there is evidence of the widespread practice of underfunding of contracts, leaving voluntary organisations subsidising costs out of charitable income.

In a review of the experience of these policy changes in England during the 1990s, Scott and Russell (2001, p. 60) concluded that 'the global picture appears to be more bureaucracy, greater financial dependence of voluntary agencies on the local state, improved administrative and legal skills and mission drift'. A study by the Northern Ireland Council for Voluntary Action revealed a very similar story in Northern Ireland. These issues have become more salient again in policy since the second term of the Labour administration. But their significance for the sector in Northern Ireland should be read in a context that shows how policy has also reflected local as well as UK national concerns. In a process that can be traced back to the mid-1980s, welfare policies and policies first to manage and then to transform the conflict have tended to converge and overlap, in circumstances that have at times led to considerable divergence between Northern Ireland and the rest of the UK.

In 1993, the Government published its groundbreaking *Strategy for Support for Voluntary Organisations and for Community Development*. It set out a vision of the respective roles of voluntary and community-based organisations in governance that has been the basis for the development of policy in Northern Ireland since then. It has also been argued that it played a seminal role in the development of policy throughout the rest of the UK, underpinning the thinking behind the Compacts of 1998 (Kearney and Williamson, 2001).

Thus, it is important to emphasise that the trajectory of policy towards the voluntary sector was rather different during the 1990s from how it was in Britain at that time, in that explicit support for community development as a source of social cohesion and civic participation dates from 1993 in the Northern Ireland administration's response to the Efficiency Scrutiny review (Home Office, 1993; DHSS, 1993; Kearney and Williamson, 2001; Acheson et al., 2004).

The civic participation and renewal theme became a stronger element in UK policy towards the voluntary sector after the 1997 general election and, in principle, the idea of a 'compact' between government and the sector, implemented in 1998 in each of the four 'countries' of the UK, incorporated a recognition that government support was necessary for the sector to fulfil this role adequately.

The Northern Ireland compact emerged in 1998, the same year as the 'Good Friday' agreement, subsequently endorsed by referendum in both Irish jurisdictions. The Northern Ireland Executive endorsed the compact as the basis of its relationship with the sector. The key role of the sector and the importance of involving it in policies and programmes aimed at strengthening 'community wellbeing' were clearly stated in the Executive's first Programme for Government for the three years from April 2001 and reiterated a year later in the second Programme for Government. But there is very little evidence that this made a great deal of difference in practice. The commitments expressed an idea about the necessary contribution of voluntary and community organisations to the reconstruction of Northern Ireland but left it up to individual government departments to specify what this might mean in practice. They have generally done this in a risk-averse and conservative manner.

The compact was followed up by a government strategy document, *Partners for Change: A Government Strategy for the Support of Voluntary and Community Organisations* (2003). This further embedded the principle that voluntary action was a complementary and necessary part of Northern Ireland governance that had its own validity, by setting out a number of core cross-cutting themes and principles that would inform all government voluntary-sector relationships. It brought into operation the commitments in the Compact for each of the eleven government departments. A joint government and voluntary-sector forum was set up to oversee its implementation. Knox suggests that the language used by government to describe the strategy is 'bold by any standard'. In his assessment,

> Even after stripping away the departmental rhetoric, the strategy suggests a significant role for the voluntary and community sector in the decision-making process of every government department. Its strict monitoring arrangements . . . implied departments cannot afford to pay lip-service to partnering the sector (Knox, 2003, p. 25).

The policy framework set out in *Partners for Change,* with its bold vision of the complementary and essential role of voluntary action for the good governance of Northern Ireland, was accompanied by concerns (expressed both by the voluntary sector itself and by elements within government) that the contribution of the voluntary sector was threatened by the unsustainable nature of its finances, much of which was based upon short-term government or EU-funded programmes. In early 2003, a 'Task Force on Resourcing the Voluntary and Community Sector' was established by the Department for Social Development to analyse the issues and suggest a way forward. Members of the Task Force were drawn from both government and the voluntary sector. It interpreted its brief widely and established working groups on government policy for support and funding, accountability and governance structures, infrastructure and sustainability, all of which took evidence and commissioned a series of detailed scoping papers.[1]

Despite the Task Force retaining a broad civic vision of the voluntary sector's role in addressing intractable structural social problems and cross-community divisions, policy in Northern Ireland towards the sector has swung back towards placing greater emphasis on the latter's role in modernising public services. The UK Treasury's *Cross-Cutting Review of the Voluntary Sector* in 2002 shifted the balance of government narratives on the value of voluntary organisations back to their perceived contribution to the delivery of public services and away from the focus on social cohesion that had been presaged by the Deakin review of 1996 (Osborne and McLaughlin, 2004). This change in policy focus was factored into government thinking during the period of direct rule between 2002 and 2007 and continues to be predominant in the current devolved administration.

Programmes supporting public service delivery are being moved to longer-term seven- to ten-year funding cycles, based on a social

---

1   The proceedings of the Task Force, including all the papers and submitted evidence can be found at http://www.taskforcevcsni.gov.uk/Documents/Working per cent20Groups .html.

investment framework and subject to performance against outcome indicators, reviewed on a three-year basis. As in the rest of the UK, albeit at a slower pace than in England in particular, there has been a continued rollout of public services into the voluntary sector and a trend to convert existing funding relationships into a set of contractual obligations on organisations that increasingly are required to compete for contracts to do work that had once been subsidised by grant aid.

Thus three strands in government policy have come to shape relations with voluntary and community organisations. First, there has been the recruitment of voluntary organisations to the modernisation of public services with, nationally, the government envisaging a greater degree of participation by voluntary organisations in public service delivery than has been the case in the past, extending to areas of policy such as the administration of social security and the management of the penal system that had not been considered before. The trend towards delivering increasing amounts of social care and possibly ancillary health services by voluntary organisations is likely to be consolidated so far as older people's services are concerned, impacting on existing specialist players such as Extra Care for the Elderly, but also drawing general welfare organisations into this field of public service delivery to an increasing extent.

Secondly, the 'Good Friday' agreement settlement of 1998 is based upon the recognition of group rights, the settling of long-standing group grievances, and the extension of such recognition to all groups that could potentially benefit. Since 1998, then, there has been an explicit recognition of older people's group rights in the legal and administrative arrangements for the governance of Northern Ireland, further reinforced in policy by the strategy on older people adopted in Northern Ireland as part of a wider UK initiative (see Chapter 2). This latter development has pushed the development of an older people's representative voice in these governance arrangements, giving them a degree of formal recognition in a legally structured set of obligations that is not closely replicated elsewhere, either in the UK or the Republic of Ireland.

This trend has been closely related to the third strand, the development of partnerships in addressing social problems, in many cases giving a primacy to voluntary and community organisations in these structures, a process that appears to touch almost all aspects of voluntary action in Northern Ireland. These structures have created new strategic challenges to voluntary organisations faced with deciding between insider and outsider strategies and understanding the extent of the power that they may wield (Taylor, 2003). Further, it is not always clear what the role expectations of voluntary-sector partners might be — as sources of good intelligence on 'what works' and what the problem is, or as the 'voice' of marginal groups in society, or as drivers of innovative policy intervention (Acheson and Williamson, 2007).

The first strand has generated a set of issues very familiar to students of voluntary action in welfare-state modernisation of the sort pursued by the UK government over the past ten years. The evidence available in Northern Ireland in no way replicates recent studies such as that carried out in 2007 by the Charities Commission for England and Wales,[2] which found that contracts and service agreements were predominantly held by larger organisations; that there was a continuing problem of recovering full costs of contracts, resulting in a charitable subsidy for public services; and that two-thirds of contracts were for periods of one year. Only a quarter of charities that delivered public services agreed that they were free to make decisions without pressure from their funders.

Much of the evidence in Northern Ireland is anecdotal. According to the chief executive of the Association of Chief Officers of Voluntary Organisations (since renamed Chief Officers Third Sector):

> There is a perception that charities and voluntary organisations are not service-providers or even partners. They are a junior partner that is supposed to contribute to whatever the Trusts or Boards feel is appropriate. There is no sense of the costs that independent providers have to bear.[3]

Whilst attending to group rights of sets of people who are judged to have been marginalised or subjected to discrimination has been an important change in welfare policy across the developed world to varying degrees (Banting and Kymlicka, 2006), in Northern Ireland this trend has been legally institutionalised by the provisions of the 1998 Northern Ireland Act, to a degree that is unusual. As will be shown, this has created a set of circumstances that has driven the emergence of a voice of older people. This voice has been incorporated in governance arrangements in a very particular way, potentially raising insider/outsider dilemmas for the smaller voluntary organisations that parallel those experienced by organisations that have ventured into public service delivery.

These issues will be returned to again at the end of this chapter. The discussion will first turn to an outline of what is known about the extent, shape and form of voluntary and community organisations concerned with older people in Northern Ireland.

---

2   Charities Commission for England and Wales (2007) Stand and deliver: the future for charities delivering public services http://www.charity-commission.gov.uk/Library /publications/pdfs/RS15text.pdf accessed 17 May 2007
3   Majella McCluskey, interview 26 February 2007

Voluntary and community action: a profile[4]

Evidence of the range, scope and size of the part of the voluntary sector whose primary beneficiaries are older people is drawn from two sources. As part of this study, a postal questionnaire was administered in autumn 2006 to 202 organisations, identified from the central database of voluntary and community organisations held by the Northern Ireland Council for Voluntary Action as having older people as their primary beneficiaries. There were fifty-five responses, a 27 per cent response rate. This questionnaire replicates that which was administered in Ireland, providing a basis for direct comparison across a number of key variables.

In addition, the authors have been given access to the dataset from a separate survey conducted by a research team at the Institute of Governance at Queen's University Belfast, on behalf of Age Concern and Help the Aged in Northern Ireland. The data have been reanalysed for this publication. This survey was administered in autumn 2006 by post to 1,306 voluntary and community organisations on a database compiled from lists held by Age Concern NI and Help the Aged. There were 375 respondents, a 28.85 per cent response rate.

The results from the survey by the team from Queen's University give an indication of the range and type of organisations, the numbers of people they reach and the extent of their voluntary contribution, as well as their funding.

Age structure and functions of the organisations
The age profile of this part of the voluntary sector mirrors closely the age profile of the sector as a whole in Northern Ireland (NICVA, 2005). Figure 4.1 shows that the rate of start-ups has increased cumulatively, particularly in the past twenty years. Figure 4.2 shows that of the organisations surveyed and in existence in autumn 2006, 61.4 per cent were founded since 1990, of which 35 per cent were founded during the 1990s. The pace of new arrivals has, if anything, speeded up since then, with a further 24.1 per cent appearing in the five-and-a-half years from 2001 to the survey date towards the end of 2006. In contrast, only just over 5 per cent date from 1970 or earlier. In summary, 38.6 per cent of organisations reported a foundation date before 1990 and 61.4 per cent after 1990.

---

4   This section has been written by the authors and by Nathan Emmerich of the Institute of Governance at Queen's University Belfast.

Figure 4.1: Cumulative percentage start-up of voluntary organisations in Northern Ireland concerned with older people by year of foundation

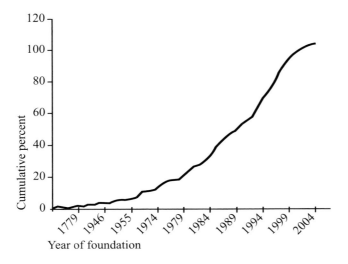

Figure 4.2: Percentage of new voluntary organisations in Northern Ireland concerned with older people before 1970 and by decade since 1970

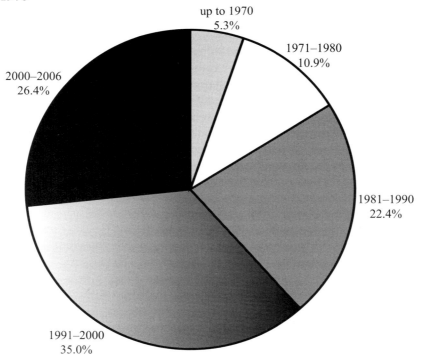

Whilst we do not have evidence on the numbers of organisations that once existed but have now folded, it would appear that the density of voluntary action in this field has increased markedly since the early 1990s. As might be expected, organisations that are consortia or fora are likely to be in the younger cohort, but there are few other differences. The most interesting finding is that younger organisations appear no more likely to be self-help organisations than older organisations. Table 4.1 shows that these are the commonest type of organisation and the evidence thus suggests that the increase in the numbers of older people's organisations has been driven by self-organisation among older people since the trend became apparent.

Table 4.1 shows that older people's voluntary organisations in Northern Ireland are most likely to be self-organised, that is, run and managed by their members, the majority of whom are themselves older people.

Table 4.1: Older people's voluntary organisations in NI by type

Type of organisation	Number	Valid percentage
Self-organised	156	51.8
Organised by people other than members	56	16.5
Forum or consortium	26	7.6

These organisations reach considerable numbers of older people, the majority of whom are women. Most respondents (71.8 per cent) said that their membership was entirely or mostly made up of women. Almost three-quarters (74.8 per cent) said that most of their members were over the age of sixty, although a further 17 per cent said that membership was divided evenly between those over and under the age of sixty. The median membership number of the respondents is forty, which would translate to approximately 52,000 people for the entire sample of 1,306 organisations. The research team that administered this survey is of the view that there are at least 500 additional organisations in Northern Ireland primarily concerned with older people. Factoring that estimate into this simple calculation would bring in an additional 20,000 people at least, suggesting that membership numbers of older people's organisations may be well in excess of 70,000, or about 25 per cent of the approximately 270,000 people over pension age in Northern Ireland.[5]

---

5   This may be a substantial underestimate in that the sample contained a minority of organisations with thousands of members each. The total number of members reported by the survey respondents alone was 41,068. The proportion of these people who are in any way active in their associations is unknown and is likely to be considerably lower.

These are rough-and-ready estimates as we do not have the evidence to show the actual proportion of members of these organisations who are over pension age. However, they give a guide to the pervasiveness and reach of older people's voluntary organisations into the lives of people over pension age and are an indication of their importance as a source of civic engagement and support.

Other than those that date from before 1970, where they are in a minority, the proportion of these organisations has remained fairly constant at around 50 per cent as the number of start-ups has grown. On the other hand, fora or consortia are more likely to be recent in that 72.8 per cent of the small numbers of these have been established since 1990, compared with 61.4 per cent of all organisations.

The field is dominated by many small and local organisations. Just 5 per cent of respondents indicated that their members travelled more than 32km (20 miles) to meetings and only 15 per cent had members who travelled more than 16km (10 miles). In contrast, 59 per cent of respondents indicated that their members lived within 8km (5 miles) or less of their organisation's address.

Incomes

The distribution of incomes emphasises this structure. Figure 4.3 gives a breakdown of income distribution for the year 2005/06. Just 17 per cent of the respondents reported incomes over £50,000 for the year whilst, in contrast, 38.2 per cent had incomes of less than £1,000 and just over half (50.2 per cent) had incomes of less than £2,000.

Table 4.2 shows the distribution of funding sources. Respondents reported a very wide range of funding sources, reflected here by the 56.2 per cent who referred to sources other than those that could be readily categorised.

Two features of these figures stand out. First is the relatively high percentage drawing in membership fees, which, at 53.1 per cent, was by some measure the biggest single category. Second, sources from public funds were dominated by the health and social services trusts, although local government was also important. At over 40 per cent, this was the largest source of funds other than membership fees. Relatively little money was accessed from European Union sources, including the Programme for Peace and Reconciliation, and an even smaller proportion from the main independent funder of local community development in Northern Ireland, the Community Foundation for Northern Ireland. It is notable also that in this scenario the role of the Big Lottery Fund becomes relatively important, being accessed by almost a quarter of respondents during the year in question.

Figure 4.3: Distribution of incomes among older people's voluntary organisations in Northern Ireland 2006/07

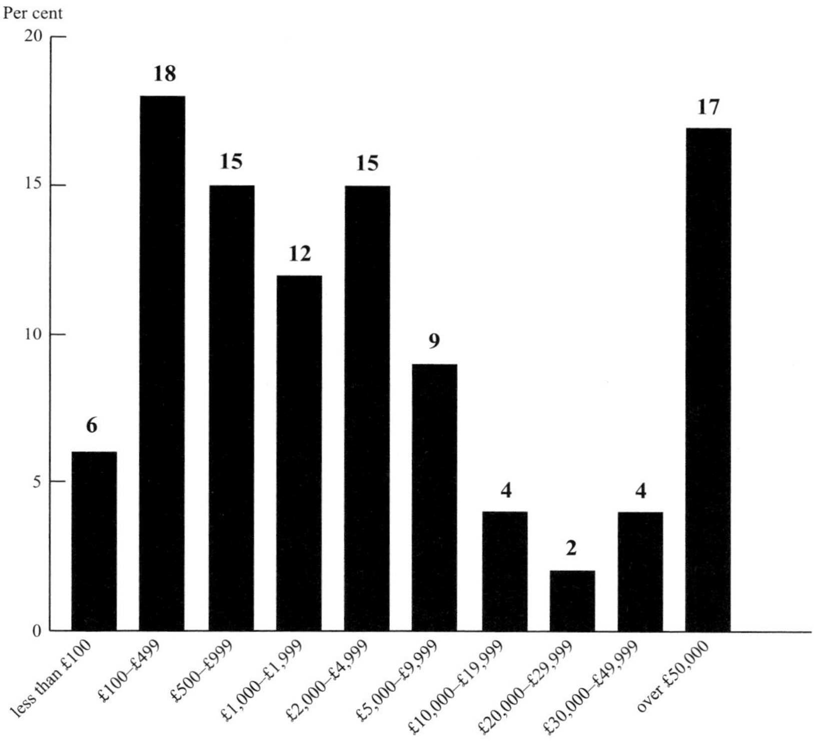

Per cent

Group Income Last Annum	Per cent
less than £100	6
£100–£499	18
£500–£999	15
£1,000–£1,999	12
£2,000–£4,999	15
£5,000–£9,999	9
£10,000–£19,999	4
£20,000–£29,999	2
£30,000–£49,999	4
over £50,000	17

The level of association between income and funding source is relatively low, with all income categories receiving funds from each of the main sources. A higher proportion of the smallest organisations have membership-fee income than is the case with the larger organisations. Thus 58.1 per cent of organisations with incomes of less than £1,000 and 68.4 per cent of organisations with incomes between £1,000 and £2,000 have membership-fee income, in contrast with 28.6 per cent of those with incomes over £50,000. However, the relationship is weak.[6]

Whilst it might be expected that funding from health and social services trusts would be concentrated among the bigger organisations, nevertheless the evidence does not support the view that this resource is accounted for wholly by the larger organisations. The relationship between size and the

---

6   Cramer's *V*: 0.307, p< .0001

likelihood of receiving money from health and social services is even weaker than it is for membership fees, although it is evident.[7] That is to say that the bigger organisations receive a somewhat higher proportion of the numbers of grants and fees available than the smaller, but not to the extent that the smaller are excluded. Instead, the evidence shows that many grants from health and social services are for very small amounts for the smaller organisations. Thus, 27.8 per cent of those with incomes less than £1,000 and 43 per cent of those with incomes between £1,000 and £2,000 report receiving health and social care grants. By definition, these must be for very small sums.

Table 4.2: Reported funding sources among voluntary organisations in NI addressing the needs of older people

Funding source	Numbers	Valid percentage
Membership fee	172	53.1
Economic activity	27	7.6
Big Lottery Fund	80	24.7
Community Foundation NI	26	8.0
Other charitable trusts	43	13.3
EU grants (including Peace Programme)	36	11.1
HPSS Trusts	132	40.7
Investing for Health	29	9.0
Local churches	17	5.2
Local government	69	21.3
Other government departments	37	11.4
Other	200	56.2

(N = 356; 32 missing)

Government funding is thus dominated by health and social care agencies in terms of the spread of grants. The Department of Health, Social Services and Public Safety (DHSSPS) provides core funding to a very select number of regional organisations to each of which it provides relatively generous support. Table 4.3 sets out recipients and amounts of core funding to each.

---

7   Cramer's V: 0.239, p<.005

Table 4.3: Core funding from DHSSPS elderly and community-care unit to regional voluntary organisations in Northern Ireland, 2007–08 (unless indicated)

Organisation	Amount (£)
Age Concern	170,298.00
Alzheimer's Society	38,581.00
Presbyterian Board of Social Witness	87,948.00 (2006–2007)
Carers Northern Ireland	37,994.00
Help the Aged in Northern Ireland	45,874.00 (2004–2005)
Relatives Association NI	18,486.00
Society of St Vincent de Paul	75,628.00 (2005–2006)

Source: DSD Voluntary Activity Unit, personal communication.

In addition, the DHSSPS awards non-recurring project grants. These have included £25,000 to Arthritis Care Northern Ireland in 2005–2006, and grants to each of Carers Northern Ireland and the Relatives Association, the latter two in addition to their core funding.

No comprehensive data on funding are available from trusts across Northern Ireland. Indicative data were obtained from what were at the time Down Lisburn Health and Social Services Trust and Sperrin Lakeland Health and Social Services Trust. Both trusts had responsibilities for acute hospital services as well as community-based social care services. The Down Lisburn data indicate the extent to which voluntary organisations have been drawn into mainstream service provision. It is striking that whilst the funding can be very important for the voluntary organisations involved, it still represents a tiny proportion of total expenditure on health and social care and appears to be dwarfed by expenditure on private-sector providers. According to the Trust's annual accounts for the year ending 31 March 2006, it spent £31,640,000 on buying care services from non-HSS bodies (the private and the voluntary sectors together), out of a total expenditure of £164,946,000 (just short of 20 per cent). According to figures supplied by the Trust for this research, total expenditure on the voluntary sector for the same year was £3,083,898 (less than 2 per cent), of which £860,380 was identifiable as being spent on services used primarily by older people. This sum was made up of twenty-four separate grants or service-level agreements, which ranged from the biggest of

£347,000 to the smallest of £100. Of the twenty-four awards, ten were for sums of less than £1,000.

The figures for Sperrin Lakeland Trust refer to grants given to local organisations rather than service-level agreements for the purchase of care services. They largely corroborate the survey data in that they show a large number of small grants. In the year ending 31 March 2006, the Trust granted a total of £51,380 to seventy-two local groups identifiable as primarily working with elderly people. The largest of these grants was for £1,160 and the smallest for £145.

Paid staff and volunteer resources

Table 4.4 indicates the estimated hours' work per annum provided by paid staff and by volunteers, both those external to the groups themselves and those by the members.

Table 4.4: Hours per annum of paid staff and volunteers in older people's voluntary organisations in Northern Ireland

Type of work	Hours	Percentage*
Paid hours per annum	335,262	43.11
External volunteers per annum	199,344	25.63
Member volunteer hours per annum	243,115	31.26
Total hours	777,721	100.00

* Rounded to two decimal places.

Almost three-quarters of the respondents (73.5 per cent) reported having no staff. Just under one-third (32.7 per cent) used external volunteers, while, in contrast, in 92.3 per cent, members contributed at least some hours. The contribution of members to their own organisations thus constitutes the biggest commitment in terms of the numbers of organisations, but paid staff together contributed more hours. However, these global figures hide an enormous variation in all three categories among organisations.[8]

These data provide a basis to calculate the value of the economic contribution of these organisations. The calculation is based on the national minimum wage as an equivalent value for volunteers. In 2006/07, this was £5.35 per hour. On this basis, the total value of the volunteer hours

---

8   Standard deviations: staff – 3314.391; external volunteers – 3757.502; member volunteers – 2893.256

worked comes out at £2,367,155.65 per annum. The significance of this volunteer commitment may be measured by comparing it to the value of all grants to the 83.4 per cent of organisations with incomes below £50,000 a year. The calculation is inexact and is based on estimates since respondents were asked to indicate their incomes within a range. It also excludes those organisations with incomes over £50,000. But based on the mid-point of each range, the total income for these organisations can be estimated as £1,273,950, or 53.81 per cent of the value of the volunteer hours. The importance of volunteers for these organisations is underscored by the 83.3 per cent who agreed or strongly agreed with the statement: 'Our group could not operate without volunteers.'

Activities

Respondents were asked to indicate whether they engaged in a range of activities. The results are summarised in Table 4.5. By far the most important reported were social activities for the members, cited by 87.7 per cent of respondents. Physical, educational and cultural activities were also important categories, emphasising the way that these organisations are to a great extent inwardly focused on the wellbeing of their members, albeit in a variety of different ways. Less than a quarter (24.9 per cent) reported engaging in advocacy, lobbying or representation.

Table 4.5: Activities cited by older people's voluntary organisations in Northern Ireland*

Type of activity	Number	Percentage
Social	293	87.7
Educational	149	44.6
Cultural	131	39.2
Physical	182	54.5
Religious	55	16.5
Advocacy and lobbying	83	24.9
Fundraising for group	201	60.2
Fundraising for others	60	18.0
Other activity	214	60.2

* The categories are not mutually exclusive. Therefore percentages add up to more than 100.

Perhaps it should not be surprising that almost all the respondents thought that their activities were a very important source of support for older people. Over 90 per cent either strongly agreed or agreed with the following statements: 'Our group makes a significant contribution to the wellbeing and health of our members'; 'We provide an important and basic social service'; 'Our group improves the quality of life for older people'; 'Older people's groups are an important social resource'. Very few (7.4 per cent) thought that 'Health and social services provide all the services required by older people', perhaps reflecting the realistic appreciation that it would be surprising if they did, as well as possible dissatisfaction with the services that they do provide.

Engagement in the policy process
The overall picture of these organisations is of many small and local groups, most of which are member-run and orientated and which generally engage in social and other activities of immediate benefit to the members themselves. Although only about a quarter of organisations surveyed reported lobbying and associated activities, the evidence suggests that it does not follow from this that they are not linked to wider networks. Reponses to the survey conducted by CVAS in 2006 to questions about networking and engagement in the policy process show that, while 40 per cent were not part of any network or federation, more than half the respondents (56.4 per cent) were, the most common being Age Concern (16.7 per cent). Numbers were very small in this survey, but the responses do indicate a range of other network bodies, apart from age-related ones, to which these organisations belong. These included the Rural Community Network, other local area-based community fora, Disability Action, housing bodies and advocacy organisations like the Northern Ireland Law Centre.

The interview data obtained suggest that the extent to which organisations are linked to wider networks varies from one part of Northern Ireland to another. These data will be discussed in greater detail below, in particular the view that the extent of networking activity is very highly resource-dependent, but the survey evidence does reveal that many organisations are embedded in wider networks, although there is no evidence on how actively they participate in these networks.

Debate about the extent of, and the best form of, networking support for older people's organisations has been a central concern over the past decade. The survey evidence suggests that the importance of this issue has been to an extent driven by an awareness of the reach of these organisations into the lives of many older people and that if only they could be organised as such, they could together constitute a powerful lobby on behalf of older people generally, despite the paradox that lobbying is a low priority for most of the organisations taken individually and is clearly not in general the main motivational factor behind individual older people becoming involved.

While politically minded activists within the sector may see the numbers of older people involved as a way of mobilising an older people's movement, it has also been the case that government departments and agencies have been looking for ways to engage with representative groups of older people. This policy imperative, together with the growing ubiquity of local older people's organisations, has tended to pull these into consultative and other governance mechanisms. The extent to which this is already the case can be seen in the responses on the matter to questions in the CVAS survey.

While care must be exercised in generalising from a sample of just fifty-five organisations, 27.3 per cent of these reported being formally represented on policy-making or advisory bodies, and 20 per cent reported being consulted informally regularly, with a further 27.5 per cent consulted occasionally. Well short of one-fifth of respondents (18.3 per cent) said that they were never consulted.

Respondents to this survey were further asked how much they felt that organisations like theirs influenced policy. The results are summarised in Table 4.6.

Table 4.6: The extent to which older people's voluntary organisations in Northern Ireland feel that they influence government

Extent of influence	Number	Valid percentage
'A great deal'	5	9.1
'To a limited extent'	22	40.0
'Rarely'	16	29.1
'Never'	8	14.5
Missing	4	7.3
Total	55	100

There may be a bias in the respondents in that these data may be drawn from a sample that is possibly more engaged in the policy process than that in the Queen's University Institute of Governance data. Nevertheless, the results are striking. While very few felt that they had a great deal of influence, almost 70 per cent felt that they might have at least some influence, with only 14.5 per cent suggesting that they never influence government policy.

These results tentatively suggest that many organisations have been drawn into a variety of governance mechanisms and that this has been a reasonably positive process among those organisations. It is, of course, quite another matter to suggest that participating in advisory and consultative processes actually constitutes an exercise of power, and indeed there is evidence to suggest that they can serve to screen out views that are awkward or inconvenient for government. Nevertheless, taken together, the data from both surveys indicate a thriving field of voluntary action that has, at least to an extent, been incorporated into the machinery of government in Northern Ireland.

Cross-border networks

There was a relatively low level of networking with organisations in Ireland, reflecting a more general feature of the voluntary sector in Northern Ireland. The question was asked in the CVAS survey, where 27.3 per cent of the fifty-five respondents said that they did have contact with organisations working with older people in the Republic of Ireland, well short of the proportion of organisations networked within Northern Ireland itself. For most of those with contact, this was irregular and occasional. Only three reported participating in a formal arrangement. This evidence suggests that from the perspective of organisations in Northern Ireland, cross-border links are a low priority and remain underdeveloped.

Voluntary and community organisations

The statistical information on its own provides little insight into how organisations relate to one another and to regional bodies and structures. Nor do the data provide much help in beginning to disentangle any reasons that might lie behind their rapid growth and development. We turn now to these issues. The data were collected through documentary research and through a series of interviews with individuals in relevant voluntary organisations at all levels and carried out in the latter half of 2006.

A paper[9] prepared in 2003 by Help the Aged in Northern Ireland, as part of consultation by the government task force on resourcing the voluntary and community sector, structured the field into regional, subregional and local layers. We follow this pattern in setting out accounts of the key elements in the field in Northern Ireland.

In the course of this research, a profile was compiled of some of the main voluntary and community organisations working with older people. Here,

---

9   Help the Aged (2003) 'The Age Sector Infrastructure'.

the main regional bodies were identified as Age Concern, Help the Aged, the Pensioners' Convention, the Age Sector Reference Group, the Older People's Policy Forum, ExtraCare, Belfast Central Mission, the Abbeyfield Societies, the Bryson Charitable Group, the Fold Association and Carers Northern Ireland. Many of these are well known and of long standing, the most recent being the Age Sector Reference Group, a regional body created to present the views of older people on equality and related policy issues. Because of their role in shaping the development of the older people's voluntary sector as a whole and expanding its capacity to act as a voice for older people, Age Concern NI, Help the Aged, the Pensioners' Convention, the Older People's Policy Forum, and the Age Sector Reference Group are discussed in the text of this chapter. The other regional organisations, more clearly focused on providing various forms of housing and social care services, are profiled in detail in Appendix A.1. Similar profiles will be provided for Ireland (Appendix A.2). Northern Ireland has a number of organisations at subregional level, generally taking the titles of 'forum' or 'consortium'. These are a particular form of organisational path, not matched in Ireland and are reviewed here in the main part of the text.

Regional bodies

Age Concern
At the regional, Northern Ireland, level there are two dominant organisations, Age Concern (NI) and Help the Aged. With a turnover in 2005/06 of just over £2.5 million, Age Concern (NI) is the bigger of the two. It is institutionally independent of other Age Concern organisations in the UK, but to a large extent it mirrors their structures and has close relations with them, benefiting in particular from joint fundraising initiatives (Age Concern NI, 2006). It emerged as an independent body in 1985, out of the wreckage of the old Northern Ireland Council for Social Services (NICSS) where there had been an older people's welfare committee (Acheson et al., 2004). It was one of three subcommittees of the NICSS floated off as independent entities at the time that body was wound up and replaced by the Northern Ireland Council for Voluntary Action (NICVA). An older people's home that had been run by NICSS since the 1930s was inherited by NICVA (quickly passed on to Bryson House Charitable Group), rather than by the new Age Concern, whose new brief was to focus on supporting a network of local Age Concern groups and on providing advice and support for older people, rather than as a provider of other direct services.

Formally incorporated as the Northern Ireland Council on Ageing, and operating under the trading name of Age Concern Northern Ireland, it is thus an independent stand-alone organisation, answerable to a group of local trustees. It combines a community development function and policy and research with a range of direct services. Its community development staff supports thirty local affiliated Age Concern groups, six of which are large enough to employ their own staff, together with a large number of older people and other community organisations participating in an 'Active Ageing' initiative designed to support local organisations providing physical activities for people over the age of fifty. The initiative run in partnership with the Northern Ireland Health Promotion Agency supports an 'Ageing Well Network', members of which can receive training, information and networking opportunities. In April 2007, it had 350 member organisations.[10]

In the early 1990s, in response to changes in community-care policy, whereby the Health and Social Services Trusts were encouraged to develop contracts with voluntary-sector and private providers, Age Concern established a separate trading company to develop and run a portfolio of direct services. These now include domiciliary and day-care settings in a number of locations across Northern Ireland, as well as an older people's home for people with dementia. These newer services, many of which have pioneered work with people with dementia, joined the longer-established telephone advice line run from the organisation's head office in Belfast. In the current policy context, in which voluntary organisations will be expected to undertake a greater amount of direct public-service provision, Age Concern anticipates that its service portfolio will grow further.

Help the Aged
The Northern Ireland office of Help the Aged is a regional outpost of the UK national and development charity working in the Indian subcontinent and Africa as well as the UK itself. The office in Belfast was first established in response to a query from a volunteer fundraiser for the charity in Northern Ireland who had wondered why it was raising money locally, but had no programmes. A local fundraising committee had been established in Northern Ireland to mark the charity's jubilee year in 1986 and it was as a result of representations by the person who chaired that committee that its 'careline' service was extended to Northern Ireland.

The focus of the charity is on poverty, isolation and neglect among disadvantaged older people. Its thirty-eight staff members in Northern Ireland support a policy, research and community-development function as well as community services consisting in the 'careline' service and home-support services. The organisation sees a 'tremendous advantage' in being

---

10   Age Concern Northern Ireland: http://www.ageconcernni.org/ageing_well.htm Accessed
     27 April 2007

part of a bigger national and international organisation. It is seen to be able to 'punch above its weight' because of these links. In particular, as a development charity, Help the Aged has maintained the ability to invest its own resources directly in local developments, including giving grant aid to local groups, additional funding that would not otherwise be available locally within Northern Ireland itself.[11] The importance of this work is reflected in that more than a fifth (20.2 per cent) of respondents in the Queen's University survey reported having received at least one of these grants in the year.

Development practice, pioneered elsewhere by the organisation, has been imported to Northern Ireland. In particular, the introduction of the 'senior forum' to Northern Ireland was to prove an important means for coordinating at regional level the concerns of local Age Concern groups and other local older people's organisations that were not a formal part of the Age Concern structures. At its height it claimed to bring together the interests of 800 local organisations. It was to provide the basis for the later establishment of the Age Sector Reference Group, for which Help the Aged continues to provide development support.

A crucial issue has been the relationship between Age Concern Northern Ireland and Help the Aged, which has not always been easy. Overlapping functions sometimes gave rise to conflict between them and never made coordination very straightforward. Interviewees from both felt that at times the two organisations tended to be played off against one another, and unresolved tensions had, in the past, tended to reduce the overall effectiveness of the older people's lobby. Changes in personnel had helped to resolve some of these tensions, it was felt, and at the time of the interviews (autumn 2006) interviewees in both organisations were optimistic about the strength and effectiveness of current joint working arrangements, in which roles and tasks have been more clearly negotiated and agreed and where there is a clearer sense of a shared agenda than there had been in the past. This had led to a joint campaigning and lobbying programme and activities.[12]

The Age Sector Reference Group
The Age Sector Reference Group is an affiliated group made up of the subregional networks (see below), issue or medical-condition-specific organisations and retired trades union sections. It represents an attempt to create a coherent single voice of older people's organisations in the policy process and was created to fill a specific niche in the emerging partnership requirements of the new systems of governance that emerged after the 'Good Friday' agreement in 1998.

11   Interview, Grace Henry, 15 November 2006
12   Interviews: Grace Henry (15 November 2006), Anne O'Reilly (24 November 2006)

It was established in 2000 after an approach to Help the Aged from the then new Equality Commission for Northern Ireland, which was looking for a partner in the 'age sector' to help with the consultations required under Section 75 of the 1998 Northern Ireland Act. This section established that public policy should be conducted in ways that treated a number of named minority groups in an equal manner; one of these minority groups was older people. Public bodies were required to establish equality schemes in respect of all the mentioned groups on which they were required to consult. The Equality Commission has had the statutory role of approving equality schemes against a number of criteria, including the robustness of the consultations undertaken. It thus had an interest in establishing a clear point of reference with older people's organisations.

Help the Aged, which already supported the 'senior network', a grouping of local older people's community organisations, met with Age Concern and the Pensioners' Convention, and it was agreed that there was a need for a better working relationship in light of the new legislation. The Age Sector Reference Group (ASRG) was established as a shared mechanism to enable a more effective response to the emerging policy environment. The ASRG had no formal independent status, but it enabled organisations that up to that point had had no formal links to work together on a shared agenda. It was further encouraged by other new arrangements for the governance of Northern Ireland, which also required the establishment of a Civic Forum (see Chapter 6), an advisory forum constituted of the main social partners on which there was a seat reserved for a representative older person. At that point, there was no single agreed mechanism for choosing who that person should be. The ASRG provided a mechanism for doing this, advertising for potential applicants and holding interviews.

As time progressed, other single-issue organisations joined along with trades unions retired members' sections, and the ASRG gradually found itself dealing with issues beyond those generated by the Section 75 equality schemes. Its role was further strengthened during the first period of devolved government in Northern Ireland, which sat on an on–off basis between 1999 and 2002. A cross-party group on ageing was established at the Assembly and the ASRG became a useful mechanism to feed policy concerns to sitting MLAs with an interest in the issues. Emphasising the reactive and rather ad hoc way the group acquired legitimacy and a role, an interviewee for this research commented: 'It seemed that the ASRG was the appropriate vehicle to work together.'[13]

The work of the ASRG has been facilitated by a staff member of Help the Aged, whose legitimacy as the group coordinator has been

---

13   Interview with Seamus Lynch, Help the Aged, 10 October 2006

democratically ratified by the group members. Up until the start of 2007, the ASRG had no separate constitution and there was no affiliation fee for members. Its running costs have been jointly and equally funded by Help the Aged and Age Concern. The group has had a chair and a deputy chair elected for a two-year term. It meets formally four times a year at the offices of the Rural Community Network in Cookstown. There are several working groups that are constituted as the need has arisen. These have been both policy focused — for example, the working group on the introduction of water charges in Northern Ireland — and focused on developing and sustaining the group itself.

A major strength of the group has been its legitimacy as a representative of local organisations with grass-roots members, some of whom have been suspicious of the motives and methods of Age Concern and Help the Aged, viewing it as 'their' organisation. These grass-roots members have been keenest to constitute the group as an independent organisation.

The process of constituting the group began in 2004 notwithstanding initial concerns about creating a fourth regional body that would be in competition with those that were already established. Matters moved rapidly forward in 2006, with Help the Aged and Age Concern jointly paying for a consultant who was appointed to develop a sustainability strategy and advise on appropriate structures for an independent organisation. The group was formally constituted in May 2007.

Although the ASRG has taken time to mature as an organisation, 'limping along at a pace it could afford',[14] it has, in its own judgment, been influential in policy development on key issues. One example given was the work it did in 2006 on the proposed introduction of water charges, where it organised a mass lobby and a postcard-writing campaign in which the government minister involved received between 7,000 and 8,000 postcards. The group sought and gained the support of all the political parties and secured a commitment that no older person would have to pay more than 3 per cent of their income on water and would have the right to have a water meter installed if they wished. The campaign was driven by the grass-roots members and this was seen as giving it legitimacy and strength. Given the subsequent political developments and the likelihood that the Assembly will review the policy, it may never be possible to measure the worth of this commitment. However, it is worth noting that the campaign stopped short of the demands of the Trade Union-led campaign to refuse to pay the charges if they were implemented, and the group resisted requests to sign up to that, because of reluctance among members to endorse non-payment of bills as a campaign strategy.

---

14   Seamus Lynch, interview, 10 October 2006

Older People's Policy Forum
Established and supported by the Northern Ireland Council for Voluntary Action (NICVA), it is one of four policy fora that were set up in 2004 and 2005 to address a perceived need to increase the capacity of voluntary organisations to address broad policy issues. The other three fora cover women's issues, the environment and the arts. The aim is to enable small organisations to impact on policy issues in a manner that they could not achieve on their own, and it is targeted at any organisation that mentioned older people as a beneficiary in NICVA's 'State of the Sector' census surveys. Meetings are chaired alternately by Age Concern and Help the Aged and the agenda for each meeting is agreed between the chair for that meeting and NICVA. Attendance at meetings is typically between thirty and forty people. Unlike the Age Sector Reference Group, the Forum has no representative function, but it has its own identity, responding to government consultations in its own name. However, it also acts as an informant for NICVA's own policy work on issues to do with the sector as a whole and clearly can add weight to the views of the specialist age-related organisations expressed through the ASRG.

The Pensioners' Convention
The Northern Ireland Pensioners' Convention was established in 1984 as part of the UK National Pensioners' Convention. An initiative from within the Trades Union Movement, its membership is made up of other organisations, mainly, although not exclusively, trades union retired members' associations. Each of the seventeen affiliated organisations sends two delegates to a quarterly delegate conference from which the executive committee is elected. The Convention sends two delegates to the biennial National Pensioners' Convention in Britain and every year sends one official representative to the Pensioners' Parliament in Blackpool, although as many as six other representatives from Northern Ireland are sent by their individual trade union.

It is an exclusively campaigning body, supporting national campaigns in whatever way they can. However, the Northern Ireland Convention can also act autonomously, running local campaigns on issues that it decides are important to members, such as concessionary travel. It has developed close working relations with both Help the Aged and Age Concern and was instrumental in establishing the Age Sector Reference Group.

Subregional network organisations

These organisations have no equivalent in Ireland. In its review of the age sector, Help the Aged (2003) noted that they were based on local expressions of need and local opportunities, with few resources and with a perceived low priority for other organisations, both in government and within the voluntary sector itself. The insecurity in funding and absence of strategic direction behind their development is reflected in their decline in numbers since 2003. At that time, there were twelve of these organisations in Northern Ireland, six of them large Age Concern local groups and the rest senior citizens' fora, or consortia. By 2007, two of these fora had collapsed, although there are current attempts to revive one of these and one other has since been started. With a single exception, which will be discussed in greater detail below, those that employ staff are finding it very difficult to secure reliable funding and are heavily reliant on the Big Lottery Fund for their survival.

The ad hoc way in which they have developed has meant that there is considerable variety in the basis on which they have been organised. Some reflect the administrative boundaries of local health and social services trusts that existed until April 2007; others the boundaries of district councils. Some have had extremely close relationships with statutory bodies and others very weak and oppositional relationships. The Help the Aged report commented: 'The development of the sub-regional level is fragmented and inconsistent in terms of function and form. The involvement of statutory agencies and other bodies (from the age sector) and their absence in the development of others is central to this inconsistency' (Help the Aged, 2003, pp. 8–9).

Matters have not changed very much since then, notwithstanding an attempt by members of the fora to address these issues, and in many areas these organisations remain vulnerable. Where they do operate, they tend to share certain features. Each has a membership base of local older people's groups and pensioners' clubs. The fora meet on a periodic basis, usually monthly, with each local member group sending one or two delegates to the meetings. The focus of the fora varies, depending on the interest and circumstances of their members; some develop campaigns on local issues, such as the future of a local hospital, while others see their role more in terms of developing and maintaining networks among older people locally, through organising a calendar of social events. The activities of most contain elements of both.

In early 2007, the subregional network organisations were as follows:

- Armagh and Dungannon Senior Citizens' Forum
- Castlereagh Lifestyle Forum
- East Belfast Senior Citizens' Forum
- South Belfast Senior Citizens' Forum
- North Belfast Senior Citizens' Forum

- Newry and Mourne Senior Citizens' Consortium
- Sperrin Lakeland Senior Citizens' Consortium
- Forever Young Coleraine.

In addition, the six larger local Age Concern organisations fulfil some of the same functions as these, although they are constituted as affiliated members of Age Concern and have an individual as opposed to a group membership structure. These are:

- Derry
- Larne
- Coleraine
- Cookstown
- Newcastle
- North Down.

There was also one hybrid organisation, Engage with Age, a statutory/ voluntary-sector partnership body in south and east Belfast, constituted as an independent entity. It is discussed below.

First, two contrasting network organisations will be considered in more detail, to illustrate a range of ways in which these relate to local health and social care structures. As a further contrast, Engage with Age is described. A formally independent not-for-profit entity, it was set up by the relevant health and social care trust and operates as a formal statutory/voluntary-sector partnership.

The Sperrin Lakeland Senior Citizens' Consortium

Based in Omagh, the consortium brings together local older people's organisations from a large rural area covering the whole of County Fermanagh and West Tyrone, matching the administrative boundaries of the former Sperrin Lakeland Health and Social Services Trust. At the end of 2006, it had eighty-two member groups, although the organisation felt that there was probably a greater number than this in the area.

The consortium was established in 1998 by a small group of activists who believed that it was necessary to create a stronger voice for older people in the area. They initially identified thirty-two local older people's groups or clubs, half of which were affiliated to Age Concern. Through contacting the local district councils, a total of fifty-five local organisations were identified altogether, and these were invited into the consortium.

The consortium received funding from the Community Development and Positive Ageing project, a joint initiative of Age Concern and the health and social services trust at the time, and a development worker was appointed in 1998. Because it covers such a large rural area, the consortium is organised around seven clusters, each of which meets twice a year. Each local affiliate sends one or two delegates to its own cluster meetings. At the spring meeting, each cluster elects one of its members to sit on the consortium board of directors. Because of their size, two clusters have two representatives each, so there are nine cluster representatives on the Board altogether.

The consortium is unusual in Northern Ireland in that like the impetus to set it up, its continuing management is completely controlled by older people themselves. In the view of the consortium chair:

> Prior to the setting up of the consortium, older people were regarded as not able to make decisions for themselves; they didn't go out, they had no voice — you had to be kind and bring them out. That missed a point that today's older people can talk for themselves; they can say what they want and can spell out their needs.[15]

In his view, there remained cultural problems in statutory agencies, which meant that they tended not to take sufficiently seriously what older people themselves identified as their priority problems. 'At that point comes the conflict, because while they (older people) can spell out their needs, they are not on the agenda that the Boards have, to such an extent that the Western Health and Social Services Board (WHSSB) has not yet budgeted for older people — we exist on slippage money.'

The lack of strategic investment in the work of the consortium by the health and social services agencies in the area has enabled it to retain a great deal of autonomy, but at the cost of living on precarious sources of funds. The consortium has two full-time and one part-time member of staff. Its annual budget of about £60,000 has been supported by the Big Lottery Fund, but the future of the organisation is very uncertain. Relationships with health and social services have remained poor as a result. The consortium sees itself as having a central role to play in what it defines as a central government objective, targeting social need and tackling isolation. Yet in its view the partnerships that have been established in the area to address these issues, in particular the Investing for Health initiative and the Health Action Zone, have failed to deliver for older people. At the time of the interviews, the consortium had withdrawn from both partnerships, feeling that its agenda had not been taken seriously and that it was never treated as an equal partner in the arrangements. The consortium chair put the matter thus: 'If you're reading the vibes, it is: older people don't matter two balls of blue.'[16]

---

15   Interview with Paddy Joe McClean, 28 November 2006
16   Interview with Paddy Joe McClean, 28 November 2006

Newry and Mourne Senior Citizens' Consortium

The Newry and Mourne consortium presents a marked contrast to the Sperrin Lakeland consortium. It was established as a result of an initiative taken by the local health and social services trust during the European Year of Older People in 1993. It promoted a conference in 1994 that brought the local older people's groups and pensioners' clubs together to identify a common agenda and the need for a coordinating body locally. By 1996, the trust had secured funding to employ a development worker, and this was followed the next year by a grant from the local district partnership through the first EU Programme for Peace and Reconciliation, matched by funding from the trust.

The European money sustained the consortium for two years, but when this ended in 1999, the trust continued its funding. The consortium has been 100 per cent funded by the trust, with a service-level agreement to the end of 2007 of £52,000 a year. In addition, the trust has provided a further £50,000 a year to support the activities of the fifty-four local groups in the area. The consortium has thus been integrated into a partnership strategy developed by the trust in which it works very closely with local voluntary organisations, a strategy coordinated by the trust's community development team. The service-level agreement between the trust and the consortium specifies that a trust staff member sits on the management committee and that the development worker receives professional supervision from the Director of the Newry Volunteer Bureau where the consortium has its office base. There have also been three elected councillors from Newry and Mourne District Council on the committee.

The consortium structure is similar to that adopted by the Sperrin Lakeland consortium. The territory covered by the consortium is divided into areas and the local clubs and groups in each elect an area representative to sit on the consortium management committee. The area representatives are responsible for supporting the groups locally and carry out support visits, as well as being contactable by telephone. The consortium's development worker organises a monthly mailshot and keeps in weekly telephone contact.

This insider strategy developed in the context of a strong, and in the Northern Ireland context unusual, tradition of investing in community development by the local health and social services trust and has resulted in an organisation that has some interesting core features. Firstly, it is treated as an integrated part of a government-led strategy towards meeting the needs of older people locally, and this has given it the financial security needed to take a more long-term view of the development of local voluntary action among older people. While there is a trade-off with the principle of independence, in that it is hard to see how it could successfully adopt and act on policies and plans that directly opposed the trust's policies, it has at the same time provided a secure platform for older people to participate in campaigning on wider issues for which the trust has no direct responsibility, such as the availability of free transport, free personal care outside hospitals and the linking of pensions to earnings, all issues about which local people have been enabled to campaign through the actions of the consortium.

The chair of the consortium has played a prominent role in the work of the Age Sector Reference Group discussed above and she has also been active nationally in the UK, attending the Pensioners' Convention parliament in Blackpool. In addition, she attended the Second World Conference on Ageing, in Madrid. However, she feels that the establishment of the consortium was a breakthrough, not because of the platform it has given older people for campaigning, but because of the support and structure it has given to local groups.[17]

Evidence of cross-border contacts

These two case-study organisations together cover a large part of the border region, and thus provide a useful vantage point from which to examine the links at local level between older people's organisations on both sides of the border. In general, the evidence suggests that there is little contact and that it is a low priority, although practice varies. In both areas, there is a certain amount of ad hoc social contact between local groups on either side of the border, but there is little evidence of a more strategic approach to developing joint work over common issues.

The Newry and Mourne consortium has links with Age Action Ireland and with Rehab in Dundalk and has worked with Cavan Over 50s Forum on age discrimination. Through the Newry and Mourne Community Safety Partnership, it has also participated in a programme on a fear of crime and dealing with the fear of crime, in a cross-border initiative funded through the second EU Peace and Reconciliation Programme. The Sperrin Lakeland consortium freely admitted that cross-border work was not a priority and that it had no time to devote to it. There have been cross-border exchanges between local groups, particularly in Fermanagh, and groups in Roscommon and Leitrim, but the evidence suggests that there is little energy behind these initiatives that tend to be developed on an ad hoc basis. The border area between these two is covered by the territory of the Armagh and Dungannon Senior Citizens' Forum. Interviews with members, carried out by Acheson in early 2006, showed that this smaller and newer organisation focused mainly on sustaining a programme of social events and that this had extended to the maintenance of regular social

---

17   Interview with Phil Evans, 18 January 2007

contact with older people's organisations in Monaghan and Cavan. This was sustained by a joint cross-border committee.

Engage with Age

This is a partnership body in east and south Belfast and Castlereagh, bringing together local older people's organisations and clubs, and the relevant statutory bodies. Although it is formally constituted as a charity and operates as an independent limited liability company, it is clearly structured as an inter-agency partnership, made up mostly of statutory bodies, although with a strong input from Age Concern, Help the Aged and the three senior citizens' fora in the area covered. Established in 2000, Engage with Age emerged from a partnership initiative in Castlereagh that had created the Castlereagh Lifestyle Forum in the mid-1990s, as a pilot response to what were seen as growing problems of social isolation and poverty among older people in the area. The partnership initially brought together the following organisations:

- Age Concern
- Belfast City Council
- Belfast Health and Social Care Trust
- Castlereagh Borough Council
- Castlereagh Lifestyle Forum
- East Belfast Partnership Board
- Help the Aged
- South Belfast Partnership Board.

Its establishment was driven by the then South and East Belfast Health and Social Services Trust (since April 2007 subsumed into the new Belfast Health and Social Care Trust), which saw the need to use a community development approach to addressing problems that it identified through soaring referrals for the home-help service and for day-centre places. Using the policy framework provided by Investing for Health (discussed in Chapter 2), it was able to mobilise an overarching partnership focusing on the needs of older people in the part of Belfast for which it had responsibility.

An important feature has been its ability to draw into its Board people at a sufficiently senior level in each of the partners. Thus the current chair is the director of planning for older people's services in the Belfast Health and Social Care Trust. The chief executives of South and East Belfast Regeneration Partnership Boards and the director of environmental health at Belfast City Council, who is also chair of Belfast Healthy Cities, are among the other Board directors. It thus has close structural ties both with regeneration partnerships and with the healthy cities initiative.

Funding initially came from the Belfast Regeneration Office to support a team of five staff — a manager, three community-development workers and an administrator. These posts are now supported by a portfolio of funding, including a central Investing for Health budget, the Big Lottery Fund, Castlereagh Borough Council, Castlereagh Community Safety Partnership and a Northern Ireland Office initiative, the Community Safety Challenge Project.

The organisation has worked to increase and encourage networking among older people themselves through providing local organisation support and capacity-building training for those involved. It now knows of, and provides information to, 230 local organisations in south and east Belfast and Castlereagh. In addition, it believes that there may be as many as another 100 of these in the area, many associated with local church congregations, and it is now working to develop links with congregation-based groups that traditionally have been poorly networked into other community resources. It has also encouraged partnerships between local service-providers in, for example, specific housing estates, bringing together local voluntary and community-based organisations with statutory agencies to address local needs.

Engage with Age represents an emergent form of hybrid partnership organisation, formally constituted outside the statutory sector but nevertheless functioning as a strategic inter-agency partnership around ageing as a cross-cutting issue. It has two central features. The first is that it is an inter-agency partnership, driven largely by the need for statutory and voluntary bodies to work together, and its constituted status as a charity serves as a vehicle for this. Partnerships of this kind can restrict themselves to a strategic planning and coordination function, but that is not the case here. Its second feature is that it runs a community-development programme that links civic activism among older people themselves directly to the goal of more effective planning among service and infrastructure-providers. It is likely that this is the reason why it is constituted independently, as without this status, it would not be possible to include representatives of older people as partnership members directly contributing to its governance.

The newly established Northern Ireland executive has opted for eleven new local councils to replace the twenty-six that have existed since 1972. These new bodies will have enhanced powers particularly over community planning. In this context, there is a view both in government and within the voluntary sector that Engage with Age represents a model that should be rolled out across Northern Ireland and that there should be one strategic partnership on ageing for each of the new council areas, constituted on a basis similar to Engage with Age. This would create a strategic tier between the individual statutory agencies with specific responsibilities impacting on older people and the service-provider voluntary organisations and older people's civic groups.

The local organisations — strengths and weaknesses
The quantitative evidence presented shows that there are hundreds of local older people's organisations and pensioners' organisations in Northern Ireland and that their numbers have increased rapidly since the early 1990s. Typically they operate on a club basis, meeting weekly for social contact, recreational activities such as bingo and often offering a meal for those who attend. Others may meet for physical exercise and fitness. For some older people, they have been the centre of their social lives. Yet there is a perception that members are ageing and that membership may be falling. Younger older people may not be participating in those activities as much as their older peers and, as a consequence, this form of voluntary action may be in decline.

If this is the case, the trends are not yet very evident. Club members interviewed for this and other research by the authors are aware that as they age, younger people are not joining. In many clubs, the majority of members are over the age of seventy-five and frequently well over eighty. The issue has been addressed by the Newry and Mourne consortium where the evidence of a relative decline has become apparent through under-spending of the funds set aside for club support by the health and social services trust. The formula for allocating funds was established in 1993 and depends on numbers attending club meetings and is thus sensitive to falls in numbers. The consortium acknowledges that the club culture may be in decline and that many of the local organisations may be experiencing problems in replenishing their members.

The evidence for this decline is not, however, conclusive. The consortium commissioned a survey of club members in 2006, which found a net increase in membership since 2003 of 10 per cent. Of the thirty-five clubs that participated in the survey, sixteen increased numbers by a total of 151 people, eight reported no change, and in eleven clubs numbers fell by thirty-six. Furthermore, the evidence also shows that the clubs were meeting a very clearly felt need for company and friendship, and that fear of isolation and loneliness remained important motivators for joining.

The consultant who conducted the research was the retired former manager of the local health and social services trust older people's programme and had been responsible for establishing its strategy. In his view, two trends were evident. On the one hand, problems of rural isolation meant that in rural areas clubs that were based on traditional social structures like churches remained an important aspect of social life.

Yet, at the same time, there were increasing choices for older people, as with the rest of the population, as to how to spend leisure time, and traditional clubs were experiencing too much competition for the active older citizens who were available.[18] In the Newry and Mourne district, there has been a boom in educational opportunities for older people, and membership of organisations such as the University of the Third Age has grown substantially. The Newry University of the Third Age now has 300 members. But as yet these numbers have not been replenishing leadership roles in other organisations.

In urban areas, club structures are also closely related to existing organisations with strong community roots, particularly the churches. With ageing congregations, it is possible that the support of clubs and activities for older people may be an important residual social function for churches.

Building the independent voice of older people in Northern Ireland

The development of the Age Sector Reference Group presents a good case study of the way independent civic action by a relatively disempowered group intersects with political opportunities created by the policy environment. The evidence of grass-roots organisation shows that at the local level small membership-based groups built around the need for social contact are a self-sustaining phenomenon embedded in existing local social structures, although they can be strengthened by funded community-development initiatives. We suggest that the rapid growth in their numbers that is evidenced here is driven by broader processes of social change felt locally. These are likely to be linked to changes in the labour market, drawing ever greater numbers of women into the workforce, coupled with cultural and social changes impacting on family life. There is evidence of increasing levels of social isolation among older people.

A policy context is required to turn this kind of civic action into a collective voice. At the most general level, the salience of collective voices of identifiable groups such as older people has grown in importance in both policy analysis and implementation, based on the recognition given to group rights. While there may be differences of opinion on whether this recognition goes far enough, nevertheless it has created a set of political opportunities that has generated a need to create a set of intermediary institutions between government and the grass roots that can act as the voice of older people in the processes of policy and governance.

The evidence suggests that the leadership that has emerged from the grass-roots level in the context of the development of the Age Sector

---

18   Interview with Colm Fitzpatrick, 18 January 2007

Reference Group has been a healthy and welcome challenge to any tendencies there might have been within the existing regional bodies, Age Concern and Help the Aged, to act as this voice alone. The chair of the Sperrin Lakeland senior citizens' consortium put the matter like this:[19]

> One of the great difficulties that we had is that the people who should be our greatest ally such as Age Concern and Help the Aged are all younger people who have no hands-on experience of working in older people's groups. They are doing the very same thing as the Boards; they are talking for older people without letting older people talk themselves.

Whilst the work of Age Concern and Help the Aged has been a crucial part of the changes under way, in this view, as organisations, their interests have not always coincided with the interests of those who wanted a vehicle that would directly express the voice of older people. There has been a tension between the demands of grass-roots voluntary action and elite insider organisations that have nevertheless actively pursued a strategy of promoting just that grass-roots challenge. It is doubtless to the credit of those involved that this tension has been largely creative and productive.

A further important catalyst for change has been the evolving role of a private foundation, Atlantic Philanthropies, which has been developing a proactive and, in the Northern Ireland context, very well funded programme on ageing. The programme priority emerged in 2004 during a process in which the foundation reassessed its priorities. It had its origins in an initiative in the US, two years earlier. Ageing as one of four new programme priorities was then, in addition, rolled out to both jurisdictions in Ireland and in Bermuda. In Northern Ireland, the programme has to date committed about $20 million, spent on activities organised around three themes: strengthening the voice of older adults to improve attitudes and policy; supporting the creation of effective models of services for older people, particularly in the field of dementia; and expanding opportunities for active social and community engagement by older people.[20]

The impact of this initiative was immediate. Initially the foundation funded the research programme at Queen's University Belfast into the circumstances of older people in Northern Ireland (Evason et al., 2004, 2005), data that were drawn on extensively in Chapter 2. Based on that evidence, it established the 'Changing Ageing Partnership', drawing together Age Concern, Help the Aged, the Workers' Educational

---

19   Interview with Paddy Joe McClean, 28 November 2006
20   http://www.theatlanticphilanthropies.org/ageing/northern_ireland, accessed 18 May 2007

Association and the Institute for Governance at Queen's University, to work on a single strategy to strengthen the voice of older people and improve advocacy and lobbying. As a result, both Age Concern and Help the Aged have had their ability to develop policy on ageing and to build capacity among older people's organisations significantly enhanced, supported by an improved university-based research function and an educational and training programme targeted at older people.

It should come as no surprise that relationships between the foundation and some of the established voluntary organisations in the field have sometimes been rather strained. The foundation's objectives are outcome-focused and it values strongly its ability to act independently to achieve those outcomes. It does not accept as valid any assumption on the part of particular voluntary organisations that they are entitled to its support. The foundation's position may not always be understood by people in these organisations who, although they would welcome any investment of foundation funding, may not appreciate the involvement, or what they may see as the intrusion, of a relative newcomer to this policy environment.

The immediate impact of this intervention may, at the time of writing, be a matter of some dispute. The view from within Age Concern and Help the Aged is that the additional resources have helped to strengthen their existing work to improve levels of co-operation and coordination between them. It may also have helped to accelerate the movement of the Age Sector Reference Group towards independent status, a process already under-way at the time when the Changing Ageing Partnership was established. However, it may be that the investment in the research and policy analysis capacity of the voluntary sector will in the long run prove more significant.

Conclusions

This chapter has sought to highlight the main dimensions of voluntary action and ageing in Northern Ireland. It began with an outline of the way the policy context has evolved and suggested that this context now contains three different thematic elements that are, to an extent, in conflict with one another. The first is the view that voluntary organisations can provide innovative and flexible delivery of public services that can at the same time be 'closer' to the users of those services than can relatively sclerotic and rule-bound public bureaucracies. Policies to move public service delivery from public to voluntary and private agencies have been a consistent feature of the policy environment in the UK since the early 1990s and have set in train a process that may accelerate in the years to come. Although there is still no clear evidence from Northern Ireland, the pattern of large public contracts being concentrated in a small number of larger organisations seems likely to follow the pattern found elsewhere in the UK.

Based on the so-called 'new public management' (Clarke and Newman, 1997; Lewis, 1999), this policy frame has tended to emphasise a strong means–ends logic, target setting and measurement by results. Its apotheosis can be found in a recent example from England where the Learning and Skills Council spent £155,000 on lawyers' fees, pursuing a small voluntary organisation with assets of £4,500 for breach of a contract worth £115,000.[21] It stands in contrast with the second theme, which emphasises complexity, iterative learning, and interdependent horizontal relationships between different arms of government and civil society (Newman, 2001). The aim here is on building relationships across agency boundaries to facilitate complex problem-solving. This tendency has drawn voluntary organisations into a complex array of vertical and horizontal policy communities on the understanding that they can bring good information on what works as well as enhancing the perceived legitimacy of emerging policy solutions. In Northern Ireland, the structures established to implement the 'Investing for Health' public health strategy discussed in Chapter 2 provide an excellent example.

These developments have been a particular feature of public administration of the UK government under the Prime Ministership of Tony Blair. They have often been underpinned by centrally driven strategies that have then to be implemented by different government departments and agencies in collaboration with other bodies. The value they have placed on engaging directly with the voice of public service users has varied depending on the field in question, but this has been an important element of the strategies on ageing, both in the formulation of the strategy itself and in the implementation of measures that have flowed from it. This trend has created a new set of opportunities and challenges that has not only shaped the nature of relations between government and the voluntary sector, but has also profoundly influenced the emergence and development of voluntary organisations themselves.

The third trend has been the increasing emphasis on the recognition of group rights to the extent that it has now come to rival redistribution as a core function of the welfare state (Banting and Kymlicka, 2006). Whilst this trend is by no means to be found only in Northern Ireland, it has been particularly influential there, shaping both the institutions of government and the legal basis under which they operate. The 1998 Northern Ireland Act formally instituted the recognition of group rights into the structure of government and, as has been documented in this chapter, this has had profound practical implications for the structuring of voluntary action

---

21 *Third Sector Daily*, 18 June 2007

around group identities. In the case of older people, it has reinforced structures that have given them a collective voice. But because of the compliance regime that now underpins public administration, it has given this voice an explicit job to do in holding public agencies to account regarding their legal obligations.

The nature of the political settlement in Northern Ireland has perhaps given this trend a particular importance, but it reflects developments elsewhere, particularly the growing importance, both in Europe and elsewhere, of antidiscrimination laws. UK antidiscrimination legislation now covers older people and the labour market, but it may be that the provisions of the 1995 Disability Discrimination Act and the 2006 Disability Discrimination Order will in the end have a more profound impact on the lives of older people, many of whom will fall within the legal definitions of disability. In particular, the 2006 Order contains a strong duty of equality on public bodies reinforcing the provisions of the Northern Ireland Act, providing additional powers of scrutiny for the Northern Ireland Equality Commission. This changing legal and structural framework is likely to reinforce the opportunities for the expression of a collective voice for older people alongside other marginal groups.

Several features in the evidence we have presented here stand out. The first is the number and density of local older people's clubs and associations. Although we have no evidence of the numbers of those that have died out, those that responded to the survey in the second half of 2006 mostly date from 1990 onwards, since when there has continued to be a rapid growth in numbers. In addition to those that we know about, there are likely to be more, particularly ones embedded in church congregations as these appear to be less well networked, and sporting associations such as bowling clubs whose members are predominantly older people. The evidence we have suggests that an important motivator for joining is social isolation or fear of social isolation, and one consequence of this is the dominance of social activities as the main activity of these associations.

Second, it is apparent that the main regional or Northern Ireland-wide organisations all emerged in the space of two years, between 1984 and 1986. Age Concern, Help the Aged and the Pensioners' Convention all date from that period in Northern Ireland, and this raises questions as to why this should be. In contrast, it has taken more than twenty years since then for an independent regional organisation of older people themselves to mature and emerge. One reason for this time difference may simply be that most of the local older people's clubs and associations are much younger than these three regional bodies, but this observation begs the further question as to why they tend to be more recent. It is likely that other explanations are needed.

5

Community and Voluntary Action: Ireland

This chapter looks at voluntary action for older people in Ireland. First, it looks at policy for voluntary and community action generally, followed by policy for voluntary and community action for older people. It then goes on to look at the emergence of voluntary and community organisations for older people in Ireland, before attempting to construct a map of the current field. Analysis and observations are offered and conclusions drawn.

Policy for voluntary and community action

The development of policy for voluntary and community action in the Free State proved to be a difficult challenge, indeed one that the Irish state may not have proven its ability to meet. Voluntary and community action in Ireland can be dated back to the eighteenth century and a significant voluntary and community sector was in existence when the Free State was formed in 1922. The sector developed, for the next seventy-eight years, in an environment in which there was no official, formally articulated governmental position on the relationship between the two or their mutual expectations. The state followed a conservative, minimalist social policy, eschewing the development of a welfare state that was a feature in Northern Ireland and Britain from 1945 onward. The favourable predisposition of the state toward Catholic social teaching which emphasised subsidiarity meant that the Irish state welcomed voluntary and community action in providing social services that it was unwilling or unable to provide itself. While this gave voluntary action scope for development, the state did not feel the need to support voluntary action in a proactive way, whether through appropriately supportive policies, structures or funding. The level of civic participation was low by European standards and remains so to this day (Dimas and Almunia, 2004). Compared to Northern Ireland, the density of voluntary and community organisations in Ireland is about half that of the north, investment in the sector considerably lower and the number of volunteers about half the level of the north.

The new state first provided modest subventions for voluntary action when section 65 of the Health Act, 1953, stated that health authorities 'may, with the approval of the minister, give assistance to any body which provides or proposes to provide a service similar or ancillary to a service which the health authority may provide'. In reality, such grants do not appear to have been made available in a significant way until the 1960s. From then and from the establishment of the health boards in 1970, voluntary and community organisations providing services for older people were among the early and main beneficiaries of section 65 grants. The health boards followed broadly similar structures: care of the elderly was a priority field of work in all of them. Working with voluntary and community organisations providing services for older people was a definable aspect of the work of each health board. In the Southern Health Board, for example, in 1992, 40 per cent of the organisations it funded were for older people (O'Sullivan, 1994).

Faughnan (1997) believes that the discretionary nature of funding for voluntary and community organisations was not unconnected to the failure by the state to develop a coherent national policy. Funding — whether for organisations working with older people with section 65 grants, or elsewhere — was a problem for two reasons. First, the level of funding was, until recent times, so low as to make development and quality of service difficult. Second, the process under which funding was negotiated was inimical to development, being discretionary, ad hoc, uncertain and even chaotic.

Section 65 grants attracted considerable ire from voluntary and community organisations until their abolition in 2004. They were often allocated as a result of informal discussion, rather than objective criteria. Voluntary and community organisations felt that they had to win such grants by means of their personal communication skills with health board managers, rather than because of the intrinsic quality of their work. Many groups felt obliged to approach county councillors or people with connections to politics as intermediaries who would support their applications. New organisations found it hard to break into section 65 funding, while stale organisations could continue to get the same level of support as before (funding appears to have been withdrawn only in rare cases of financial impropriety, but never for poor performance). Section 65 was often provided to plug end-of-year deficits, rewarding financially undisciplined organisations at the expense of those which raised more money themselves and which kept within their budgets.

During the 1960s, there was a growth of social service councils, up to forty being established, and hopes were entertained that these would become the basis of integrated, planned social services, with voluntary and statutory bodies working in partnership. Services for older people were to the fore and the *Care of the Aged* report encouraged local authorities (then the health authorities) to give them financial support (McKeown, 2004). Many social service councils were initiated as a joint enterprise between the county manager and church leaders. A small number proactively developed services for older people over the years, Clare Social Services Council (now Clarecare) being a prominent example, providing services such as home help, outings, chiropody, social gatherings, holidays and housing repairs. Others maintained a steady level of service for many years, especially in the midlands. These were the exception, for, in the event, the social service council movement as a whole withered, although a number still exist, principally in the western half of the state (Galway being the other, aside from Clare, with the highest profile).

Services for older people provided the context in which the state made its first, but abortive, attempt to build a structure for the development for voluntary-sector activity in Ireland. The interdepartmental committee on older people, which led to the *Care of the Aged* report (Department of Health, 1968) persuaded the Minister for Health that there should be a national body to promote voluntary and community-based activities. The National Social Service Council (NSSC) was duly set up in 1971. It was subsequently renamed four times, restructured twice, survived one government decision to abolish it and now, as the Citizens' Information Board, provides a valued range of information services, but does not fulfil the development role originally envisaged. Faughnan's classic under-statement is that it was not given the scope to fulfil the role originally envisaged for it (Faughnan, 1997).

The institutional problems experienced by the NSSC were later reflected in the excruciating difficulties experienced by the government in developing and implementing a national policy toward the voluntary and community sector. The legal basis for the operation of charities dated to 1601 and, although the legislation governing charities was reviewed in 1990, an outline of planned legislation was not given until 2006 (O'Brien, 2006a). Commitments to develop a formal policy for voluntary orga-nisations were made in 1976 and 1981, a white paper being promised in 1990. This took ten years to birth, being eventually published in 2000 as *Supporting Voluntary Activity*. Interestingly, in the face of the policy vacuum at central government level until then, some parts of the health service had already attempted to fill the gap. *Enhancing the Partnership* (Department of Health and Children, undated) tried to put the relationship between health boards and voluntary and community organisations on a more formal basis, as will be seen below.

Supporting Voluntary Activity set down three core statements. First, that the state valued the contribution that the voluntary and community sector made to society, especially to building a more inclusive society, and affirmed its independence. Second, that relationships with government should be put on a more formal, structured basis, a set of mechanisms being agreed to ensure that this would be done (Voluntary Activity Units in each government department). Third, that there would be an improved financial environment for the sector, with multi-annual funding and an immediate injection of funding for federations, training and support, and research.

Although *Supporting Voluntary Activity* remains government policy, few of the decisions contained within the white paper have been implemented. Of the financial package, only 47 per cent was delivered in the period promised, and the research programme was cancelled. None of the new structures to improve dialogue between voluntary and community organisations were created to add to the small number already in existence. Multi-annual funding was not introduced. Worryingly, a prominent voluntary and community organisation which criticised government policy had its funding removed, the government making it clear that there were limits to the degree to which dissent would be permitted. The failure to implement the white paper was doubly disappointing in the light of the government's endorsement of measures to increase the level of social capital in the country, following a study on the topic by the National Economic and Social Forum (National Economic and Social Forum, 2003b).

The publication of the white paper coincided with the approach, in 2001, the United Nations International Year of Volunteers. The government established a national committee on volunteering, which published a landmark policy, *Tipping the Balance* (National Committee on Volunteering, 2002). The government experienced considerable difficulty in forming a view on its extensive proposals for a national policy on volunteering, eventually announcing a package of funding to support local volunteering in 2005.

The only identifiable area of progress in the area of voluntary statutory relationships was in legislation to make charitable organisations accountable, a new Charities Bill being eventually published in 2007. The Taoiseach established a task force on active citizenship; this reported in 2007, the new government elected later that year giving a commitment to implement its extensive recommendations for volunteering and engaged citizenship.

An important interface between the state and the voluntary sector was social partnership. From the 1960s, the government had worked with employers, trades unions and farmers to set wage and price levels, with a view to achieving industrial peace and economic stability and the results of their negotiations were called the national agreements. In 1987, under the *Programme for National Recovery*, the scope of these agreements was extended to much broader policy areas, with the trade union movement trading wage moderation for an influence on a broader range of economic and social policy. In 1994, the Irish National Organisation of the Unemployed was admitted to national social partnership, and the following three years saw considerable space being opened for civil society organisations in the social partnership process. Voluntary and community organisations participated in the subsequent national agreements (*Programme for Competitiveness and Work, Partnership 2000, Sustaining Progress, Toward 2016*) and were also given seats on the National Economic and Social Council (established in its original form in 1961) and the broader National Economic and Social Forum (established 1994).

An important feature of voluntary-sector development has been the process of contracting whereby voluntary and community organisations providing social services work in formal contract with statutory bodies (originally the health boards), contracts which stipulate the rights and responsibilities of each partner, in line with social policy practice in the Atlantic countries (Boyle and Butler, 2003). Services for older people are very much in the middle of this contracting process, called in Ireland service-level agreements or service agreements. Two features distinguish service-level agreements in Ireland. First is the oblique nature of their introduction. *Shaping a Healthier Future* (Department of Health, 1994) announced, almost in passing, that 'larger voluntary agencies will have service agreements with the health authorities which will link funding by the authorities to agreed levels of service to be provided by the agencies', pledging that the identity and autonomy of the voluntary agencies would be fully respected and that they would continue to have a direct input into the overall development of national policy. Contracting would not be applied to smaller organisations. The announcement was made in the context of the Department of Health's struggle to divest itself of direct funding of fourteen large mental-handicap services and make them a health board responsibility. The subsequent battle continued to be played out in two subsequent policy statements, *Enhancing the Partnership* and *Widening the Partnership* (Department of Health, both undated). The first service-level agreements were introduced in 1997. Voluntary and community organisations not acquainted with the high politics of mental-handicap services would have been familiar with neither these impending developments nor their significance.

Second, the practice of service-level agreements broke the commitments given in *Shaping a Healthier Future*. They were applied to small organisations as much as large ones, contrary to the 1994 statement, and in all fields, not just that of learning difficulties. The rigours required of large organisations were extended to small ones as well. No arrangements appear to have been put in place to improve the direct input into policy-making promised. Although *Enhancing the Partnership* provided a model service-level agreement, examination of the actual terms of agreement in the different health boards found that the boards extended, sometimes enormously, the responsibilities placed on voluntary and community organisations, while minimising their own. For voluntary and community organisations working with older people, the outcome will have been an increase in responsibilities, duties and paperwork without any commensurate access to the policy-making process in return. Having said that, ten years later not all local health offices in the Health Service Executive (HSE) operate service-level agreements. Ad hoc arrangements are still made with small local organisations working with older people on a 'Come in and talk and we'll see what we can do for you' basis.

Can policies for voluntary and community action be discerned at local level? Some evidence is available from the health boards before they were closed at the end of 2004. The North Eastern Health Board (2001) expressed its recognition of the value of voluntary and community action, especially in the areas of day care, social centres, transport, meals-on-wheels, home visiting and social projects, and committed itself to developing partnership with these organisations through service agreements. The Eastern Health Board's ten-year plan (1999), in a section called 'Partnership with voluntary organisations', cited the work of the Alzheimer Society, the Society of St Vincent de Paul, Age Action Ireland, Friends of the Elderly, ALONE, Simon and the Salvation Army. The board accepted that it was incumbent on it to develop systems of consultation through such methods as written submissions, meetings, workshops and study days. Several boards, such as the South Eastern (2000), reported that they had increased grants to voluntary and community organisations, and the Western Health Board (2001b) noted how it would 'develop and enhance partnership' with voluntary and community organisations. The North Western Health Board emphasised how it worked closely with, and would continue to work with, voluntary organisations. The East Coast Area Board recorded as a significant development the agreement of care plans with groups such as the Alzheimer Society, Carers Association and Rehabcare.

From these reports, one derives an impression that the health boards valued voluntary and community services, that they saw the relationship in terms of partnership and wished to increase funding levels, but remarkably little is articulated about the quality of that relationship, or the involvement of voluntary and community groups in policy.

Several years following the introduction of social partnership in 1987, the government established twelve local social partnership companies as part of area-based responses to unemployment in areas of disadvantage.

These were coordinated by Area Development Management, since renamed Pobal and built up to a total of thirty-eight partnerships. In recent years, the area partnerships have become more aware of their responsibilities toward older people. Several have now developed older people's networks, and three partnerships have followed a dedicated community-development process with older people: Bray Partnership (County Wicklow), Eirí Corca Baiscinn (West Clare), and Inishowen (County Donegal) (Lynch, 2005).

Policy for voluntary and community action for older people

Supporting Voluntary Activity was a policy document that concerned all voluntary and community organisations. No separate policy has been published dedicated solely to the role of voluntary and community organisations for older people. Nevertheless, the growing emphasis by the state on community-based services for older people inevitably obliged the government to consider, at closer quarters, the role of voluntary action in such provision. *Care of the Aged* (Department of Health, 1968) may have been the first to do so, recommending the establishment of local social services councils to coordinate community-care services. Until then, county medical officers prompted the formation of parish committees to provide services for older people and assisted them with some funding. In 1972, the Department of Health issued circular 11/72, directing health boards to provide home-help services directly only if voluntary organisations failed to do so. By the end of the century, a third of all home-help services came from voluntary providers, but this concealed great regional variations. *The Years Ahead* (Department of Health, 1988) paid attention to the issue of policies for voluntary and community action for older people, Chapter 11 being entitled 'Partnership between carers, volunteers and state agencies'. *The Years Ahead* identified fourteen areas of voluntary and community action for older people (care in nursing homes; residential care; housing (special and sheltered); homes; shelter; material aid; day care; transport; home help, meals and laundry; support (Alzheimer's, carers); information and advice; security; visiting; social clubs). It found an abundance of problems in the voluntary–statutory relationship: lack of recognition of the voluntary and community sector; shortage, even absence, of money for its work; lack of coordination; a disproportionate burden on the sector; unevenness of service; enormous variations in funding patterns; funding-led services and a lack of influence, with voluntary and community organisations being kept at arm's length, without access to information or planning. *The Years Ahead* put forward recommendations and these issues are now addressed.

Judging by *The Years Ahead*, the voluntary–statutory relationship appears to have come well adrift. This was strikingly evident not just at national but also at local level (Browne, 1992). Despite the early promise of the 1960s when the state encouraged and funded voluntary and community action for older people, now their relationship appeared to be mired in difficulty. Mulvihill (1993) found that structured relationships between voluntary organisations providing for older people and statutory bodies were limited. Although there might be good casework liaison, only a small proportion of services (11 per cent overall) contributed to policy-making or the planning of services — from 7 per cent of agencies in the North Eastern Health Board area to 21 per cent in the southern. There was little pressure on health boards and other statutory providers to engage with voluntary and community organisations, and few had actually done so.

The National Council for the Elderly (1994) found considerable variations between health boards as to how they approached the balance of provision of services for older people between voluntary or statutory services. In the case of home-help services, for example, most health boards devolved responsibility to superintendent public health nursing staff. In the largest health board areas, the eastern and in parts of the mid-western, voluntary organisations had responsibility. In other board areas, a mixture was used. In the case of day centres, most health boards provided these directly, the exception again being the Eastern Health Board, where provision was undertaken by voluntary organisations. In the case of meals-on-wheel services, these were provided by voluntary organisations (90 per cent in the former Eastern Health Board area, for example (Haslett, Ruddle and Hennessy, 1998).

In its observations on services for older people, the National Council for the Elderly did not take a particular view on whether services for older people should be provided by statutory or by voluntary bodies, or on what the optimum mixture of the two was. Its principal comment was that the present mixture had grown up in such an ad hoc, unplanned manner as to lead to uneven, poorly coordinated services of variable quality, which was hardly the optimum outcome for older people (Browne, 1992). The National Council for the Aged was extremely critical of the failure or refusal of the state to map out a vision for the development of voluntary services for older people. Mulvihill (1993) referred to the 'policy vacuum' in the area. *The Years Ahead* pointed to the many negative consequences of the continuing policy vacuum, such as poor coordination, lack of recognition of the voluntary and community sector working with older people, excessive responsibilities thrust on volunteers, unevenness of service, underinvestment, lack of dialogue between organisations and health boards and exclusion from decision-making.

As noted earlier, older people feature as a distinct strand within national health framework strategy documents, which is the main area where policies for older people are made by the state. In the fundamental revision of health service management in 2005, no explicit policy was set down to govern the relationship between voluntary and community organisations, on the one hand, and the state and statutory services on the other. The lack of a clear policy, one that spells out the appropriate structures and funding relationships and the appropriate welfare mix, is considered by many to be a problem in the voluntary and community sector, though the government side seems less aware of it as a problem. The HSE published a *National Service Plan 2005*, which included a six-page section 'Services for older people', but this gave few clues as to an overarching strategy, beyond committing the HSE to providing services 'in partnership with service users, their families and carers and a range of statutory, voluntary and community groups'. The present health strategy, *Quality and Fairness — A Health System for You* (Department of Health and Children, 2001), for example, gives commitments to the expansion of community, residential and hospital services for older people in approximately equal measure. The strategy states, in its section 'Actions for older people':

- 'Community groups will be funded to facilitate volunteers in providing support services such as shopping, visiting and transport for older people';
- 'Community and voluntary activity will be supported [by] programmes to support informal caregivers through the development of informal networks, provision of basic training, and greater availability of short-term respite care will be developed and implemented; programmes to foster voluntarism and community responsiveness to local needs will be undertaken'.

The balance of what is to be provided by voluntary and what is to be provided by statutory services is not stated, though the voluntary sector is identified as having a clear role in shopping, visiting and transport. McGiven (2004) has also drawn attention to the characteristic of the state approach to services for the elderly of enunciating the need for a service, but not making it clear who should have the responsibility for initiating or providing it.

By contrast, the first framework strategy, *Shaping a Healthier Future* (Department of Health, 1994), had a section entitled 'Role of the voluntary sector', which covered all voluntary and community services in the health field. *Shaping a Healthier Future* described voluntary and community organisations as 'to the forefront' in identifying needs in the community and developing responses to them, complementing statutory services in an innovative and flexible manner. It promised a statutory framework to recognise the role and responsibilities of both parties, and service agreements for large voluntary agencies. In its section, 'Ill and dependent elderly', the framework strategy stated that voluntary organisations had 'played an important part in reorienting services for older people and in pioneering innovative ways of caring for older people and supporting their care' and reiterated the policy articulated in *The Years Ahead* of supporting the care of older people in their own community by family, neighbours and voluntary bodies.

The National Economic and Social Forum (NESF), in its *Care for Older People* report (2005) has a short section on the role of voluntary organisations working with older people. Unusually for a government report, it identified those that it considers to be the main national organisations representing older people.[1] This stated that it was important that the voice of older people be included in planning and development at a local and national level: 'This involves investing in the capacity of older people and older people's organisations to be involved, for example, through training and also that local and national bodies actively involve older people in planning which affects them.' Older people do not have a strong customer voice, says NESF, there is a lack of advocacy for vulnerable older people and there is a lack of coordination between the voluntary groups.

A few other policy documents have indicated how the Irish state sees the scope of voluntary action for older people. In the area of housing, for example, the Department of the Environment's *Plan for Social Housing* (Department of the Environment, 1991) envisaged an expansion of voluntary housing in which older people were named beneficiaries.

Statutory bodies accept that there is no explicit policy to guide voluntary and community action for older people. In the debate on the 'mixed economy of welfare', the state does not have a view as to what that mixture should be. Opinion is divided, though, as to whether or not this is a problem. Some take the view that services have suffered, sometimes badly, from the ensuing lack of clarity of roles and from lack of investment.

Nor do most voluntary organisations seem to have a view either. The Hospice Foundation, when it made its in-depth review of the development and current state of hospice and palliative care services (2006), identified the voluntary–statutory funding mix for such services as chaotic, but

---

1   These were: Age Action Ireland; Age and Opportunity; ALONE; the Federation of Active Retirement Associations; the Irish Senior Citizens Parliament; the Older Women's Network; and the Irish Association of Older People. Two are a surprise here: ALONE, whose work is limited to Dublin; and Age and Opportunity, which is a derivative of a state agency, the National Council on Ageing and Older People.

offered no commentary on how this situation had arisen, nor on how the voluntary–statutory relationship should evolve in the future. Even though several hospices had made remarkable use of volunteer services, the foundation had little to say about how they should develop in the future, except that there should be more of them.

Formal policy or not, some assumptions are made about what that role should be. These may be summarised as:

• Values: voluntary and community action by and for older people is intrinsically desirable.
• Expertise: as a general rule, voluntary organisations have an expertise and knowledge about their clients, which no one else could match and which makes them ideal delivery agents (for example, Alzheimer services).
• Commitment: voluntary and community services attract committed people and this improves the quality of service.
• Economy: voluntary and community services are less costly to the state. The state is wary of commercial providers who may overcharge the state for services. Voluntary organisations are considered less likely to do so.

As such, there is a predisposition by the state to favour voluntary and community action, but the predisposition is not sufficiently developed to consider the full implications for either funding or structures.

The Department of Health and Children, together with the Department of Social and Family Affairs, concluded work in 2005 on the report of an interdepartmental group on long-term funding for services for older people. This was expected to outline the respective roles, expectations and responsibilities of statutory bodies and voluntary and community bodies in these services, but publication, which had been expected by the end of 2005, was delayed indefinitely and is now unlikely to happen.

Next, we look at the funding of voluntary and community organisations working with older people. Funding is, in its own way, an expression of policy, and these funding patterns are informative of governmental priorities. Traditionally, government funding for voluntary and community organisations working with older people was limited, and the section 65 system was strongly criticised for the inadequate levels of support provided. Voluntary and community organisations found themselves having to rely on their own fundraising through such methods as street collections, raffles, table quizzes, special events, bankers' orders and so on, supplemented by requests for grants from small companies. There is evidence that in the 1990s, the level of government investment in voluntary and community organisations increased substantially, to the point where government became the main funder (Harvey, 2002).

The principal funder for voluntary and community organisations working with older people is the health service. Funding occurred, from 1953 to 2004, under section 65 of the Health Act, which provided for the funding of voluntary and community organisations offering health and related services, a definition that has been followed suitably broadly. From 1970, these funds were provided through health boards. Section 65 grants constituted the bulk of funding for voluntary and community organisations from 1953 to 2004, as delivered by the eight health boards (eleven in the final period). From 2005, these became known as section 39 grants and they are now allocated by the thirty-two Local Health Offices (LHOs).

A small number of organisations received national grants. These took two forms. First, several national organisations, because they functioned nationally, were allocated grants for their national work, but these were distributed, for payment purposes and convenience, through one of the eight, later eleven, health boards. These separate 'national' grants have proven impossible to separate from health board funding, so their overall size is impossible to gauge. One leading voluntary organisation described the whole process as a 'fog'. From 2005, such grants were routed through the HSE but the precise method by which they will be determined and by whom remains unclear. Second, the Department of Health and Children has had at its discretion, since the introduction of the National Lottery in 1987, a national grant, currently in the order of €4 million. In contrast to the aforementioned system, this grant is advertised nationally, with clear criteria, and the outcomes are given to the Oireachtas. In 2005, 107 such grants were distributed, to the value of €3.7273 million, of which ten can be identified as groups working with older people. Although a national fund, only two of these grants appear to be grants for national organisations (Irish Senior Citizens Parliament, and Alzheimer Society conference) and most were quite small grants for local groups (for example, €5,000 for the Finglas Senior Helpline).

What funding is now supplied to voluntary and community organisations working with older people? Table 5.1 below provides details of all HSE funding to voluntary and community organisations working with older people, where that information is available. As part of this research, the HSE asked all LHOs to supply such information and four reminders were issued. Of the thirty-two LHOs, information is available for twenty-one. The grants comprise a mixture of section 39 grants (the main part, sometimes still referred to as 'section 65 grants'), national lottery grants, meals-on-wheels grants and miscellaneous grants, but all are distinctly earmarked as being for older people.

Table 5.1: Pattern of distribution of HSE grants for voluntary and community organisations working with older people

LHO	No. of organisations funded	Total funding (€)	Average grant (€)
Ballinasloe	2	2,500	1,250
Cork — West Cork	33	574,956	17,422
Cork — North Cork	47	604,265	12,856
Cork — North Lee	54	999,260	18,504
Cork — South Lee	34	927,575	27,281
Dublin — north central	19	2,485,350	130,807
Dublin — west	6	3,035,078	505,846
Dublin — north west	12	2,155,500	179,625
Dublin — south west	12	3,133,326	261,105
Donegal	47	771,890	16,423
Galway	119	735,800	6,183
Kerry	84	589,986	7,023
Mayo	65	136,596	2,101
Offaly	29	49,340	1,701
Roscommon	31	1,166,255	37,621
Sligo	8	548,224	68,528
Tipperary — south	22	801,241	36,420
Tipperary — north	30	1,223,824	40,794
Waterford	20	1,027,522	51,376
Wexford	25	601,327	24,053
Wicklow	20	3,715,107	185,755
	719	**25,284,922**	**35,167**

This gives us a national level of health service support for voluntary and community organisations working with older people of a little over €25 million. Granted that this listing covers only two-thirds of the LHOs, the actual national figure will be higher, probably in the order of €35 million to €40 million, but that is a very rough estimate. As may be seen, the funding pattern varies quite widely. In some LHOs, funding is concentrated on a small number of organisations (for example, Dublin and Sligo), whereas in other parts of the country, funding is distributed to a large number of organisations, most of which receive small grants, figures in the range €1,000–€5,000 being quite common. As a result, the average grant ranges from €505,846 in West Dublin to less than €2,000 in Offaly and Ballinasloe, giving quite a range. In some LHOs, there is a mixture of large, medium and small grants, but in many of the rural areas, there is a strong trend toward a large number of small grants, Galway and Kerry being classic examples.

Although the average grant is €35,167, that figure would be much lower if we were to remove the Dublin LHOs, in which case it would be €21,605. The precise basis for such an approach is not known and, although a number of LHOs were asked to explain the philosophy behind their funding policies, none appeared to be in a position to do so. The concentration of grants in Dublin on a small number of organisations is remarkable and it is unclear from this whether the LHO has chosen to back a small number of strategic organisations with large grants, or whether small organisations working with older people do not exist, or are not considered appropriate for support.

The other principal governmental funders of voluntary and community organisations working with older people are:

- The Department of the Environment, Heritage and Local Government, which funds social housing organisations, of which voluntary and co-operative housing organisations working with older people are the largest element. At present, there are 18,600 voluntary or co-operative housing units managed by 613 voluntary bodies, with a significant proportion for older people.[2]
- The Department of Community, Rural and Gaeltacht Affairs, which, through the Dormant Accounts Fund, funds organisations providing alarm and security systems; the Community Development Programme (here, several groups work with older people, the best known being An Siol); and groups working with older people. The security scheme provided grants to 450 organisations in 2005, to the value of €2.36 million.[3]

There are few formal nongovernmental funders of voluntary and community organisations working with older people. The dominant one is Atlantic Philanthropies, which in 2002 decided that work with older people

---

2   Dáil Éireann, *Debates*, 7 December 2006, 1734
3   Dáil Éireann, *Debates*, 29 March 2006, 740

should be one of its four principal themes of work, called 'Strengthening the Voice', which will run to 2018. Its programme is subdivided into combating ageism, strengthening health and care services, end of life and NGOs. Atlantic Philanthropies hopes, over the next number of years, to provide grants to strengthen the capacity and support the strategic development of a number of leading Irish NGOs and agencies working with older people (for example, Age Action Ireland, Irish Senior Citizens Parliament, Age & Opportunity) and will, all agree, 'raise their game'.

In summary, the main funders of voluntary and community organisations are the Health Service Executive and the Department of Health and Children (for services); the Department of the Environment, Heritage and Local Government (for housing); the Department of Community, Rural and Gaeltacht Affairs (for alarm systems) and Atlantic Philanthropies (for organisational development). The HSE is the most important funder for generic services for older people, but here we are left with an unsatisfactory conclusion, which is that the general basis of funding policy for voluntary organisations working with the elderly is unknown. Does the HSE believe in funding a proliferation of small organisations? Or is this pattern of allocation a quasi-political decision to spread funding as broadly — or thinly — as possible, so as to create the highest level of community contentment?

Voluntary and community action for older people: emergence

We know something of the emergence of voluntary and community action for older people. No history of this strand has yet been written, although some histories of individual organisations have been published. These histories are confined to Protestant Aid, the longest (Milne, 1986), a short account of the active retirement movement (Carey, 2004) and ALONE (undated). Mulvihill (1993) suggests that most voluntary and community organisations are comparatively recent. Using the broad categories suggested in Chapter 1, he found the establishment dates shown in Table 5.2.

Table 5.2: Establishment of voluntary and community organisations

Date of establishment	Percentage established
Nineteenth century	3 per cent
First half of twentieth century (1900–1967)	17 per cent
Second half of twentieth century (1968–1991)	64 per cent (16 per cent not available)

The historical record suggests that voluntary action followed state action for older people, the reverse of the normal pattern. O'Loughlin (2005) traced a series of governmental measures to assist destitute older people in the eighteenth century, such as the houses of industry, and it is unlikely that there was significant charitable action to assist older people until the emergence in the nineteenth century of Catholic orders dedicated to social action. One of the most documented groups is the Association for the Relief of Distressed Protestants, founded in 1836, which, from the end of the nineteenth century, began to refocus its work as an organisation to assist older people (Milne, 1986). In 1898, it began an old-age pension scheme for impoverished older people 'too respectable' for admission to the workhouse, providing deserving cases of over sixty-fives with 2s/6d a week from money collected from sermons. Of its four funds, one was devoted to 'aged and destitute ladies' and, as the twentieth century progressed, it became a housing association for older people.

Most of the hospital services developed over the eighteenth and nineteenth centuries were generic services, open to all age groups in the population. Some, such as the Royal Hospital, focused on older people. Most services were run by Catholic religious orders, while others from the minority religious tradition had lay committees affiliated to the Protestant churches. In the course of time, some came to specialise in hospital and nursing services for older people. Examples of nursing-home services for older people developed by religious orders were those provided by the Sisters of Charity, the Daughters of Charity and the Little Sisters of the Poor. Some of the religious-based services operate from ageing facilities with ever-smaller staff, and their ability to continue to do so in the medium term must be in question. Some religious orders have already handed some of their facilities over to the health services. Their work as a provider of services for old people is little publicised, they do not participate in the national networks of older persons' organisations and they can be less than visible as a result. Some have developed volunteering services. For example, the Royal Hospital continues to have a committee to encourage voluntary workers, as does the Orchard, formerly the Friends of Clonskeagh Hospital. From 1922, the Free State and then Ireland brought a broad range of formerly voluntary hospitals into state provision, a process subsequently charted by Barrington (2000) and O'Ferrall (2000), but volunteer-based services do not seem to have been a significant part of this process of integration.

The origins of recent voluntary action for older people have been traced by Convery (1987). She relates how Red Cross workers set up the Dublin Old People's Committee over 1950–52. They began with two houses for older people, one in Terenure and one in Harold's Cross, with a visiting service in Sandymount. A club was established in 1963, a meals-on-wheels service in 1967, and a day centre soon thereafter. Over 1965–66, county medical officers in Dublin proactively approached parish priests and clergy to encourage the formation of 'old people's committees' in each parish, suggesting that they provide social clubs, dinners and social outings. Encouraged by grants, these services spread rapidly in the late 1960s. Their most visible manifestation was the day centre, and, by the 1980s, the Eastern Health Board had twenty-nine day centres, of which twenty-three were provided by voluntary and community organisations, probably all derived from these parish committees. Convery described these services as ad hoc, personality-driven, some even idiosyncratic, with a limited model of care and unprogrammatic in their approach. Whatever about money to start them up, they received little government support at this later stage.

We can get an intuitive idea of the density of this kind of service from county studies. Duignan (1996), in her profile of County Roscommon, found three day centres there and ten active-age groups. The North Eastern Health Board (2001) recorded voluntary and community organisations active within its jurisdiction carrying out services in the following areas: day care, social centres, transport, meals-on-wheels and home visiting. The voluntary and community services listed by the board are illustrated in Table 5.3.

Table 5.3: Voluntary and community services operating within the North Eastern Health Board area

Type of service	Meath	Cavan/Monaghan	Louth
Social clubs	14	14	3
Social centres	–	21	3
Day-care centres	2	4	5

Source: North Eastern Health Board, 2001

We do not know the degree to which these developments were matched in other parts of the country, but what information we have suggests that they fell far short of what was needed. Athlone Social Services Council (1973) determined that there was a big need for voluntary action in the town to provide meals-on-wheels, day centres, clubs, paramedical services, laundry, shopping help, visiting, home help and redecoration assistance, leaving the impression that such voluntary services did not yet exist there. Power (1978) confirms the relatively undeveloped state of services for older people in the 1970s, finding that only 10 per cent of older people living alone were being assisted by voluntary organisations (the Society of St Vincent de Paul and the Legion of Mary) and that they were more likely to be assisted by statutory services, nurses, priests or ministers of religion. Fogarty (1986), in his examination of assistance to older people a decade later, found that there was a high rate of informal caring for older people and a disposition by young people to help older people, but he described the organisational environment for voluntary and community action for older people as chaotic. The most recent examination of the level of service provision indicates that the proportion of older people receiving a service from a voluntary organisation remains low, well in single figures (O'Hanlon et al., 2005).

What is the voluntary sector working with older people now? The Irish Republic's voluntary and community sector comprises several thousand voluntary and community organisations. In 2005, the number of voluntary and community organisations formed as limited companies and recognised by the Revenue Commissioners as operating for charitable purposes numbered 5,106. The proportion of these organisations working with older people is not identifiable, though the names of some provide clues. To these must be added a small number of voluntary and community organisations that take legal form other than companies (several hundred), and possibly hundreds that either do not have legal form or have not sought recognition by the Revenue Commissioners. There is no known means of identifying them.

Most people would agree intuitively with the assertions by O'Sullivan (1994) and Brown (1996) that the role of voluntary and community organisations working with older people in Ireland is very important. Despite this, there is no official system whereby voluntary and community organisations are categorised under fields of work. There is no national system for the registration of voluntary and community organisations. The landmark research study of the voluntary and community sector, done under the auspices of the Johns Hopkins University, has categories for 'health' and 'social services' but none that will specifically isolate 'older people' (Donoghue, Anheier and Salamon, 1999).

The lack of a national database of voluntary and community organisations presents us with many problems. It makes it difficult for us to assess the size and scope of the sector working with older people, as well as presenting methodological difficulties granted that we wish to survey that subsector. Haslett (undated), attempting to examine services for older people provided in day centres, found it impossible to locate or come to a national figure for the numbers of such places and the numbers catered for, eventually giving up the unequal struggle.

However, some useful sources are available. For example, Age Action (1999) published a directory of services for older people in both parts of Ireland. This found 342 local organisations, fifty-one national organisations, eighty active-retirement associations and fifty-nine Alzheimer societies. Whilst this is probably only a fraction of the total number, the directory may give a useful indicator of the balance of organisational types.

Individual health boards had, until their abolition in 2004, some fragmentary information on voluntary services provided within their geographical areas. Annual reports and service plans for all the health boards for 2001 were studied for this research. Some reports had only passing references to voluntary and community services for older people or were otherwise uninformative. The North Eastern Health Board (2001), for example, recorded thirty-one social clubs, twenty-four social centres and eleven day-care centres, and assisted the Alzheimer's Association, social housing, older women and transport services. The Eastern Health Board (1995) identified a hundred and seventy-six voluntary and community organisations within its areas, providing day centres, clubs, visiting and transport. Four years later, the board (1999) noted sixty-five day centres, a hundred and one clubs, thirty-seven home help organisations and a hundred and thirty-eight meals-on-wheels services. The board (2001) assisted over a hundred and forty organisations to provide care, home helps, meals-on-wheels, day centres and clubs. The Western Health Board (2001a) provided grants to ninety-nine organisations worth IR£502,340. The North Western Health Board (2001a) 'worked closely' with voluntary groups such as Sligo Social Services, care of the aged committees and the Society of St Vincent de Paul to provide home-based services. Grant aid was provided to the Alzheimer Society and carers' support network.

The Southern Health Board (2001) also identified the Alzheimer Society, supporting other groups to provide day care, meals-on-wheels and support services. The Mid-Western Health Board funded services to provide respite care, day care, housing-related and community day centres.

From these reports, we get an impression of the range and type of voluntary and community action for older people, albeit little detail. Some older people may be found in the more institutional part of the voluntary sector. As noted earlier, about 5 per cent of older people are in nursing-home or long-term care (about 17,000 people). This proportion has barely changed over the years and is divided into those in private, for-profit nursing homes (the largest group), with small proportions in health board geriatric hospitals, geriatric homes and public district hospitals. The important group for this research is the proportion in voluntary-sector nursing homes: 18 per cent of older people in long-term care (O'Shea, 1993), 14 per cent according to slightly more recent figures (Silke, 1996). Most of these facilities are thought to be provided by religious organisations. Figures collected by the National Council for the Elderly for 1988, the last year for which details are available, found that there were fifty-nine such nursing homes with 3,509 beds.[4] Over half, thirty-one, were in the Eastern Health Board region.

The most substantial change in nursing-home provision is its composition. Although the religious group has remained static or even contracted, the change is that whereas in 1968 the state provided 90 per cent of nursing-home beds, this had fallen to less than 50 per cent in 2001, private providers accounting for the balance. Some of the nursing homes provided by the religious orders are actually *for* the religious or the staff of their institutions over the years who have retired. Because of the decline in vocations, these numbers are likely to decline sharply and the religious orders will be faced with a choice of running quite small homes (which may not be economical), closing them and disposing of the land or opening them to people unconnected with the order.

The most detailed analysis of this voluntary and community sector, arguably the only dedicated analysis of its kind, was carried out by Mulvihill (1993). The National Council on Ageing and Older People (undated b) updated his research to suggest that the voluntary and community sector working with older people is in the order of 1,200 organisations with about 27,700 volunteers reaching out to 93,800 people. Those figures appear to be based on Mulvihill, so we must reference him in more detail. He carried out an exhaustive characterisation of these organisations and it remains the baseline study in the field, reporting on their location, objectives, staffing, volunteers, facilities, funding, management, services, clients and relationships with statutory bodies.

An important finding of Mulvihill was that only 54 per cent regarded themselves as primarily focused on older people; many organisations who worked with older people also served a range of other needy categories. Returning to the voluntary organisations, their main characteristics were as follows:

- Most were small, averaging about a dozen volunteers.
- Only a small proportion had staff.
- The main services provided were, in descending order: social events, visiting at home or in hospital, advice/information, material aid, transport and meals-on-wheels.
- They were financed, in descending order, by charitable fundraising (for example, church-gate collections), health board grants, donations and charges.

---

4   Information kindly supplied by Joe Larragy, National University of Ireland, Maynooth.

Within the voluntary and community sector working with older people, there have always been several substrands. Housing for older people is one that is immediately visible. Voluntary housing has always been a small, but significant, part of housing provision. Overall, the sector has about 13,000 homes, about 1 per cent of the total national housing stock (Mullins, Rhodes and Williamson, 2003). Philanthropic housing services date to the 1870s. The first housing project of the Association for the Relief of Distressed Protestants began in 1899 (Brabazon House) and although the association helped people of all age groups, older people were the prime beneficiaries. Its second home was Albert Retreat (1923), followed by Albert House in 1964. Government grants assisted the association to build Pax House (1967) and two more homes in 1983, by which time the association had retitled itself as Protestant Aid (Milne, 1986). Protestant Aid, through its various charities, now provides homes or nursing-home care for over 150 older people (Protestant Aid, 2005).

Older people have been the largest single beneficiary group of voluntary housing and accounted for two-thirds of the 1,850 voluntary units in existence in 1984. Twenty years later, older people are still the largest single beneficiary group, accounting for 48 per cent of such housing, about 7,000 units. Of the 240 voluntary and community organisations affiliated to the Irish Council for Social Housing, 127 provide and manage services for older people (Irish Council for Social Housing, 2005) (about ninety more organisations exist and are unaffiliated, but they are likely to be either small or inactive). These are dominated by six large providers, the rest providing very small numbers of units in single figures. They may be divided into group housing schemes and sheltered housing schemes with, in the latter case, care services, social facilities and on-site services such as caretaker or warden.

Of the 7,000 or so units for older people, between 800 and 1,200 are estimated to be provided by the Society of St Vincent de Paul, the largest single provider for older people. The next largest provider is Respond! (established in 1981), which provides 3,000 units, of which about 670 are for older people. The typical providers for older people are small, local associations providing clusters of five to ten units. Recent years have seen the development of national housing associations based on a distinctive brand, ethos, approach and professionalism, many coming from Great Britain (for example, the Sue Ryder Foundation, Circle, the St Pancras Housing Association (now Clúid)) and Northern Ireland (FOLD, Oaklee, NW Housing, BIH (Belfast Improved Homes)).

Older people themselves are, of course, part of the national picture of voluntary action. Volunteering tends to peak in middle age and falls off after retirement. The role of older people as volunteers themselves has often been neglected and undervalued. Few voluntary organisations have consciously solicited older volunteers while some voluntary organisations have even expected their older volunteers to 'retire' from volunteering (Baines, Lie and Wheelock, 2004). Fahey and Russell (2001) found that 33.4 per cent of older people aged fifty-five to sixty-nine engaged in formal voluntary activity, above the national average rate, though we do not have information on the proportion active in self-help groups or organisations purpose-designed to promote the welfare of older people. Older people most likely to be active as volunteers are professionals and well-educated people now in partial retirement. Volunteering remained high among older people still working full time, leading the authors to conclude that warnings about a fall in volunteering as a result of higher participation in the labour force by older people were groundless. The National Committee on Volunteering (2002) published a figure of 27.8 per cent of sixties and over volunteering. The National Council on Ageing and Older People (2005a) further dis-aggregated this figure by age, showing a declining scale of involvement from 36 per cent among the 'young' elderly to 14 per cent among the 'old' elderly. The most recent, *Irish Times* 50+ poll gives volunteering figures for older people to confirm this picture: 24 per cent for all over fifties, falling to 14 per cent for over seventies (O'Brien, 2006c).

The National Economic and Social Forum (2003b) explored the level of participation of older people in voluntary activity and those parts of community activity that comprise the building of social capital. The National Economic and Social Forum gives much lower rates for partici-pation in voluntary activity for sixty-fives and over, between 6 per cent and 7 per cent, compared to national levels of 17 per cent to 20 per cent. Its more detailed picture suggests that we must be careful of the definition of 'voluntary activity' used in survey work, the precise questions asked and the context in which they are asked.

Donoghue (undated b) has observed that organisations for older people in Ireland have concentrated on services and that few have been involved in advocacy or campaigning. Campaigning by older people has been rela-tively subdued. Thirty years ago, Power (1978) reflected on the appalling housing circumstances in which many older people found themselves, expressing surprise that older people expressed so little discontent with their circumstances, indeed rating their life experiences positively. The reasons, he concluded, lay in their personal histories of hardship where, having known more necessitous times earlier, they did not consider themselves poor now. Many years later, Tansey (2001) noticed that among poor older people assisted by voluntary organisations, lifestyles were simple and expectations low, an unlikely environment to prompt militancy. Brown (1996) contrasted this with Britain, where such passivity is less evident. There was little sense of old people's common interests. Eurobarometer studies showed the disposition by older people in Ireland to support a political party formed to further the interests of older people to be below the European average (16 per cent, compared to 22 per cent (EU12) (Walker, 1998)). Even the younger organisations in the elderly sector in Ireland follow a service-providing role associated with traditional voluntary organisations. This, in turn, has reflected a more general perception of older people as passive, dependent, frail, infirm recipients of services, even a drain on society, rather than an empowered group. Brown speculated that the heterogeneity of 'the elderly' made the formation of a generic campaigning voice for them intrinsically difficult. They had, she argued, made some progress in challenging negative stereotyping of older people in society, citing as evidence the growth of active-retirement associations. The image of older people, the heterogeneity of the group and the traditional model of organisation followed made this 'difficult terrain to negotiate' for potential advocacy organisations.

The National Economic and Social Forum, in *Care for Older People* (2005), recommended that older people should have an 'active role' in planning and service delivery at local level on an ongoing basis, through 'consultation and participation', and that older people should be specifically represented on HSE advisory panels, strategic planning committees, vocational educational committees and city and county development boards. The recommendations fell far short of the policy, planning and service advisory councils of older people that are the norm in continental European countries. Nor did it recommend any changes in the way in which policies for older people should be planned at national level. Although NESF recommended a widened and strengthened role for the interdepartmental group on the needs of older people, such a widened, strengthened role did not encompass voluntary or community organisations. By contrast, the Equality Authority (2002) recommended that ways be found to involve older people much more in policy strategies.

Health board figures and other research give a broad picture of the nature and density of voluntary and community activity for older people. Their data, though, tends to be of a snapshot nature, static and poor at capturing trends. Here, the interview group was able to assist in identifying changing patterns of development and the following are the principal dynamics identified:

• The emergence, in the past ten years, of generic national organisations working for older people and articulating their needs. These were identified as Age Action Ireland and the Irish Senior Citizens Parliament.

- The emergence of national organisations concerned with specific aspects of ageing. Examples are the Alzheimer Society, the Federation of Active Retirement Associations and the Hospice Foundation. Related to this are a number of disability organisations that have increasingly assisted older people with disabilities.
- The emergence of carers' organisations. Whilst carers' organisations are, by definition, about carers, they are also concerned with the welfare of the cared-for, which have two main constituency groups: older people and people with disabilities.
- Professionalisation of the sector. The term 'professionalisation' is one with a number of connotations and is sometimes used disparagingly by people committed to pure notions of volunteering. Here, it is used to refer to two developments: the employment of greater numbers of paid and qualified staff; and the formal driving up of standards in such areas as governance, management, employment and services.
- The contraction of the religious sector. With the sharp fall in vocations, religious communities no longer have the staffing to manage such services. Some staffing levels are now quite low. Some appear to have adapted their work to provide hospice care.
- Services in frontier areas of care for older people. These are palliative care, home-care packages, helplines, elder abuse and the new technologies.

Change has caused perhaps the greatest difficulty for the small, parish-based services, 'old folk's committees' established in the 1960s and 1970s. Essentially, they have followed three types of trajectory:

- Entrepreneurial: exponential expansion under entrepreneurial leadership
- Modest expansion
- No expansion – flat-lining.

The first — and smallest — group has expanded rapidly under entrepreneurial leadership and management, developing a broad range of new services, better adapted to the changing circumstances of older people (for example, telephone advice lines). The organisation may own its own centre, will have modernised the facility and will have operating budgets in millions. A significant number of health and social services will be run from there and it will have service agreements from the health boards to provide a range of services, including the new health packages. The largest may have ninety to a hundred salaried employees, budgets over €1 million and serve over a thousand old people, doing so almost 365 days a year.

At the other extreme, a substantial part of the local voluntary and community sector working with older people has developed little since the 1960s and 1970s and still provides a similar type of service in a similar manner. It still relies on voluntary contribution for funding, personnel and the provision of services. Some have struggled along with small section 65 grants, in the order of €500 to €1,000 a year. Their services are rarely comprehensive and may be limited to several mornings a week. Some close for three weeks at Christmas. New food-safety rules will oblige them to make considerable improvements in their kitchens and food-distribution systems. Some operate in considerable isolation, with little contact with health services or other voluntary organisations. Many predict that this strand within voluntary and community action will become extinct.

In between, a few have modified and developed services, upgraded services, attracted funding for repairs, the roof or a minibus, and may have taken on one, two or three staff (for example, coordinator/organiser, care attendant). Committees have taken financial risks and renewed their memberships. The quality of the service will have improved, but the numbers served may not have increased significantly.

Voluntary and community action for older people: map

There is no up-to-date national directory of voluntary and community organisations working with older people, so we must rely on a number of different information sources. For example, Age Action Ireland published a now-dated directory of services (1998), while one sectoral list exists, in the hospice sector (Hospice Foundation, 2004).

In mapping voluntary and community organisations working with older people, several data sources were used. National and regional organisations were identified through the principal national data source on voluntary and community organisations, the Institute of Public Administration's annual *Administration Yearbook & Diary* (2007). The typology that emerges is as follows:

- National organisations working for older people
- National organisations with a specialised role that is focused on or includes older people (but also addresses other groups)
- Regional organisations
- Local organisations.

We identified the following national organisations working for older people: Age Action, the Irish Senior Citizens Parliament, the Older Women's Network, the Irish Association for Older People, the National

Federation of Pensioners' Associations and the Federation of Active Retirement Associations. We identified a number of national organisations with specialised roles: the Carer's Association, Hospice Foundation, Alzheimer Society, the Irish Council for Social Housing, and the Society of St Vincent de Paul. We identified a number of regional organisations: ALONE, CareLocal and Friends of the Elderly. These national and regional organisations are profiled in some detail in Appendix A.2. Their activities in influencing policy will be examined in more detail in Chapter 6.

Local organisations

The identification of locally based organisations working with older people presents serious problems. As already noted, unlike other European countries, there is no national register of voluntary and community organisations in Ireland that will readily identify organisations working with older people. Despite this, there is strong evidence of the continued existence of a large number of local organisations working with older people. This is apparent in the Revenue Commissioners list and the details of voluntary and community organisations working with older people funded by the health service, as well as other miscellaneous services.

Small, parish-based services, old folk's committees, day centres, with a foundation date in the 1960s or 1970s — these remain the prototypical form of voluntary activity for older people today. An examination of just one part of Ireland finds that the small, local, care of the aged/senior citizen/meals-on-wheels type service remains the dominant model. Here, Dún Laoghaire was chosen: although not the local authority with the highest population of old people, it is approaching this position and, by 2021, will have the largest proportion of older people, if current demographic trends continue. The area currently has nine meals-on-wheels services, seven active-retirement associations, four clubs for older people and two befriending services (Southside Partnership, 1999). The meals-on-wheels services date as far back as the 1950s, while the active-retirement associations are more recent. Only a few of these organisations have any professional staff or publicise their work in any way. Comparison with previous directories indicates that some small organisations would become defunct but that others would spring up to take their place, but would also remain small. The picture formed was that although there was plenty of voluntary activity in Dún Laoghaire, it was highly localised, small in scale, fragmented in nature, not substantially resourced, poorly documented and uncoordinated. Only one had undergone substantial expansion in the past ten years.

Many of those interviewed in the course of this research believed that there were, in the country, many small organisations working with older people, often covering a parish or a group of parishes. Typically driven by three or four activists, they would attract small grants (€500 to €1,000) for a limited range of social activities, participate in the Bealtaine programme, and organise a Christmas party, but they would not have a development plan or be challenging of the situation facing older people. It is very difficult to rise from this level to attain a critical mass to provide a significant or professional range of services (for example, chiropody) or confront many of the practical difficulties faced by older people (for example, a minibus to deal with the lack of rural transport).

The level of local activity for older people appears to be variable. Despite the impression of an abundant, but small-scale level of activity, there may be parts of the country that have a low level of services for older people. Research by Respond! (2005), carried out in anticipation of planned voluntary housing development, sheds light on the level of voluntary activity in Baldoyle, north Dublin where there is an older local population. Here, Respond! found the numbers participating in the active retirement association to be low, compared to a similar group on the more affluent south side of Dublin.

Voluntary and community action for older people: profiles

In the course of this study, research was carried out to draw a national map of voluntary and community organisations working with older people, with a view to obtaining an up-to-date picture of their current work, especially of those working at the local level. It was decided to survey organisations working with older people funded by the HSE in 2005. The HSE list had three particular advantages: first, it was up to date, comprising organisations known to be operating in 2005; second, it came from a strand of funding dedicated to older people, ensuring that there were no groups in the sample not working with older people, and, third, the HSE has requirements for accountability, legality and organisation, and to reach these an organisation must achieve a level of formality and maturity. There are two potential disadvantages with such a listing. The first is that it does not include organisations working with older people that did not seek health-service funding in 2005, or those that were unsuccessful. The second is that the organisations funded may reflect health-service preferences for the type of organisation it wishes to fund. As Table 5.1 above shows, there is a wide range of funding strategies, some LHOs funding as few as two organisations, others as many as 119.

The HSE supplied the identities and addresses of 438 organisations working with older people and they were surveyed in May 2006. These lists were supplied by individual Local Health Offices, of which there are thirty-two. Of this group, only twenty supplied lists and twelve failed to do so, despite four subsequent reminders from the HSE. Geographically, the listing is uneven, being strongest in Munster, with significant parts of the country, including parts of Dublin, unrepresented.[5] Nevertheless, the sample does include large rural areas, provincial towns, urban areas (for example, Cork city), so the mixture is a good one. Although respondents were not required to identify themselves, a number did so, showing the counties most represented to be, in descending order, Cork, Donegal, Galway and Mayo. The survey worked on an eventual frame of 348 valid names and addresses. Of these, 186 responded, a return rate of 53.4 per cent, which is a high return rate for a postal survey. Not all answered every question and the full details are given in the methodological note. Where questions were answered, this was done with great precision, especially in the area of income, sometimes to the second decimal place.

Age of formation
First, the organisations were asked about their year of formation. The responses are shown in Table 5.4.

Table 5.4: Age of formation of organisations working with older people, May 2006

Year of formation	Percentage
Up to 1899	0.5
1900–49	0
1950s	0.5
1960s	8
1970s	10
1980s	22
1990s	30
2000s	28

This gives a strong impression of recent formation, with 58 per cent being formed since 1990 and 80 per cent being formed since 1980. This raises interesting questions about the wave of organisations working with older

---

5   The LHOs for which useable lists were available in time for the survey were Cavan/Monaghan, Dublin NW, Dublin SW, Dublin W, Kerry, Donegal, Mayo, Wexford, Wicklow, Waterford, Cork S Lee, Cork N Lee, Cork W, Cork N, Tipperary S, Tipperary N, Sligo, Roscommon and Galway.

people set up in the 1960s and 1970s (only 18 per cent). Were their
numbers quite small, compared to the larger numbers that have followed?
Or have many disappeared? Or were they located mainly in Dublin, which
is underrepresented in this sample?

Old people served
These organisations served a total of 17,028 people, or an average of
ninety-eight people each. One large organisation stated that it served no
fewer than 3,000 people, with the next largest at 300, so a more representative average would be obtained by removing this one exceptionally
large organisation, in which case the average would be 87.6 people. In
reality, most organisations serve relatively small numbers of older people,
as the breakdown in Table 5.5 shows.

Table 5.5: Number of older people served by organisations

	Number of organisations
Serving more than 100	40
Serving more than 50 but fewer than 100	47
Serving fewer than 50 older people	86

Staffing, human and financial resources
These organisations had 425 full-time staff, 832 part-time staff and 309
Community Employment staff. This works out as an average of 2.44 full-
time staff, 4.75 part-time staff and 1.8 Community Employment staff. In
reality, the picture is more complicated, because many organisations had
no staff at all, as can be seen in Table 5.6.

**Table 5.6: Organisations with no full-time salaried, part-time salaried
or Community Employment staff**

	Proportion of organisations
No full-time salaried staff	73 per cent
No part-time salaried staff	69 per cent
No Community Employment staff	57 per cent

What is useful here is to look at the staffing complement of those
organisations that *do* have staff. Table 5.7 shows the picture that emerges.

Table 5.7: Average number of staff in organisations with full-time salaried, part-time salaried or Community Employment staff

	Average staff
Organisation with full-time salaried staff	9.2
Organisation with part-time salaried staff	15.4
Organisation with Community Employment staff	4.1

Although average of CE staff is the smallest of the three categories (4.1 per organisation), it is actually the most *intensively* used form of employment. Only 57 per cent of organisations did not have CE staff: conversely, 43 per cent did.

Asked about their office premises, 42 per cent said that they worked from home, 25 per cent shared an office and 32 per cent had their own office.

These organisations had a total of 3,022 volunteers, or an average of 18.7 volunteers per organisation. The spread is quite uneven, for the majority of organisations actually have a small number of volunteers, as Table 5.8 shows.

Table 5.8: Organisations and volunteers

Number of volunteers	Number of organisations
100 or more	4
More than 10 but fewer than 100	57
Fewer than 10	100

The income of these organisations came to €17,325,966. This figure must be treated carefully, for most organisations actually had a low income with, at the top extreme, three over the €1 million mark (one received €6.017 million). The average income was €108,968, but if we take out the three 'millionaires' we get a truer picture, with an average of €57,943. The prototypical voluntary organisation working with older people actually has a small income, as Table 5.9 indicates.

The interesting feature here is the dip in organisations in the €5,000 to €10,000 range (only sixteen), with large numbers below this level (eighty-one) but larger numbers above €10,000 (thirty-one). This could be a function of those organisations with staffing (or without).

Table 5.9: Organisations and income

Income	Number of organisations*
€1 million or more	3
More than €500,000 (but less than €1 million)	3
More than €100,000 (but less than €500,000)	11
More than €50,000 (but less than €100,000)	14
More than €10,000 (but less than €100,000)	31
More than €5,000 (but less than €10,000)	16
Less than €5,000	81

*(N=159)

The sources of the funding, illustrated in Table 5.10, mark a change with Mulvihill (1993), where the main sources were fundraising, health board grants and charges, in that order. We must be cautious in our treatment of the HSE as the main funder, granted that the sampling frame was drawn from a list of organisations funded by the HSE.

Table 5.10: Sources of funding

Source	Percentage
Health Service Executive	55
Donations, legacies, fundraising, other grants	27
Charges	18

Federation and co-operation
All the organisations were asked if they belonged to national federations. Fewer than half did, 43 per cent. Of those who belonged to national federations, by far the greatest proportion belonged to the Federation of Active Retirement Associations (36 per cent), followed, in descending order, by the Irish Council for Social Housing (8 per cent), Age Action (7 per cent) and the Irish Senior Citizens Parliament (5 per cent). Almost all the rest belonged to different, individual groups, some working for older people, others not.

All the organisations were asked if they had contact with organisations working with older people in Northern Ireland. Only 8.6 per cent had such contact. Those that did were asked to indicate the intensity of that contact.

For 66 per cent it was occasional, for 27 per cent regular and for 7 per cent it was formal, but the numbers for this sample are small.

Involvement in policy-making
All the organisations were asked if they felt that they had a say in policies affecting older people and were given the option of ticking one option that best described their situation. The results are shown in Table 5.11.

Table 5.11: How organisations felt about the say they were given in policies affecting older people

	Percentage of organisations
Represented on policy-making bodies	15
Consulted informally and regularly	14
Consulted informally but occasionally	34
Never consulted	37

Clearly, most fall into the middle range of informal consultation, 48 per cent. Overall, though, this is not a picture of consultation, for only 27 per cent are consulted formally or regularly, with 71 per cent consulted either occasionally or not at all.

Future work
Finally, all were asked about how they expected their work to develop over the next three to five years. Table 5.12 shows the responses.

Table 5.12: How organisations expected their work to develop over the next 3–5 years

Expectation regarding work	Percentage of organisations
Expected to expand substantially	22
Expected to expand modestly	34
Expected to stay about the same	37
Expected to decline	4
Expected to come to an end	3

Put another way, 56 per cent expect to expand to a greater or lesser degree, 7 per cent expect to contract or disappear and over a third expect stability.

The picture emerging of local voluntary and community organisations working with older people is as follows:

- Most were formed relatively recently.
- Although there are some large organisations and a small number of very large organisations, the prototypical voluntary organisation working with older people is small, has no office, works from home, has fewer than ten volunteers, serves fewer than fifty older people and has an income less than €5,000.
- For those organisations that do have staff, there is a reliance on part-time staff. Community Employment is the most intensively used form of employment.
- The HSE is the main funder of groups working with older people, providing just over half their income, the balance being found by charges, fundraising and grants.
- Fewer than half the organisations belonged to national federations. For those that did, the proportion belonging to the Federation of Active Retirement Associations is striking and it is now clearly a major player in the field. The proportion belonging to Age Action Ireland and the Senior Citizens Parliament is small. The level of cooperation with Northern Ireland is low, only 8.6 per cent having any form of cross-border contact at all, and that tends to be occasional. Overall, this is not an environment that develops learning.
- Over half expect to expand their work, either modestly or substantially, while only 7 per cent expect to decline or disappear, with over a third expecting stability.
- Only 15 per cent of organisations working with older people are represented on decision-making bodies. Overall, the picture of consultation is a poor one, with 71 per cent either never consulted or consulted only occasionally.

Case studies

In addition to making a vertical analysis of voluntary and community action for older people, at national, regional and local level, we also made a horizontal cross-section: a number of case studies of voluntary and community organisations which, we hoped, could tell us more about the sector along the lines required of the terms of reference, especially in the areas of new organisational formation, leadership, innovation and pathways of development. These organisations were identified with the assistance of experts on the sector, identified in the acknowledgements. The following case studies were made: Senior Help Line, Summerhill,

County Meath; Positive Age, Cavan; Westgate Foundation, Ballincollig, County Cork; the EQUAL project, Carlow; Sligo Alzheimer Association; Dublin Central Mission; Sue Ryder Foundation, Ballyroan, County Laois; and St Francis Hospice, Raheny, Dublin. The detailed profiles are provided in Appendix A.3.

So what did they tell us about the role of voluntary and community organisations working with older people? First, the role of a founder-entrepreneur appears to have been crucial in the development of a new service. Almost all the services here had such a leader or driving force. In most cases, the founders tend to downplay their own roles out of natural modesty, but it is doubtful if many of the services described here could have developed without the energy, motivation and passion of these individuals concerned. These individuals were also driven by ideas such as positive age, palliative care, integrated housing, telephone help and respect-based services.

Second, it is evident that there were points of innovation of services for older people in Ireland. These profiles looked at a number of points where forward-looking services were in development, around such concepts as social gain, appropriate housing and support and the combating of discrimination. For example, the Dublin Central Mission made an important statement that for older people, architecture and the physical environment are important.

Third, these case studies appeared to draw from foreign example in a number of cases. The Senior Citizens' Helpline was inspired by a service developed in Italy, while others were derived from Britain. Although this might be expected in the case of the Dublin Central Mission, which has a religious orientation toward a larger congregation in Britain, it is noticeable that other services drew on examples from Britain: the hospice service and the Sue Ryder Foundation. The others appeared to be indigenous, with no obvious reference points outside the state. The sophisticated approach to volunteering by St Francis Hospice has no obvious origin, source or inspiration.

Fourth, the experience of state support was a mixed one. Several of the organisations expressed frustration at their dealings with state services, be that over the nature of funding for care provided (Westgate), the understanding of social gain (Positive Age) or the criteria for funding nursing assistance in housing projects (Dublin Central Mission). None of these complaints actually relates to the *level* of funding. Rather, they relate to the issues of principles of service, professionalism of approach, or inability to resolve departmental boundaries on the part of the authorities.

Fifth, staying with the issue of funding, it is also apparent that many of the organisations managed to develop despite a difficult funding environment.

In the case of the Sue Ryder Foundation and the Senior Citizens' Helpline, the directors provided their services free of charge for many years. The funding efforts expected of the hospice in providing a frontline service are enormous. There is still an expectation of voluntary organisations of a very high level of fundraising, certainly in comparison to continental Europe. One of the projects (Westgate) has confronted the health service, in a systematic way, for its inadequate approach to the funding of services, but such questioning appears to have been considered inappropriate and strongly resented. Others have, it appears, avoided such conflict only by accepting the diversion of a considerable effort into their own fundraising.

The case studies show that new services for older people are in development. The Senior Help Line has a number of appealing features: the adaptation of a model from another country (Italy); the high level of involvement of volunteers; the confrontation of the problem of technophobia that is supposed to afflict older people. The service is run at low cost, a feature open to two interpretations. At one level, the use of volunteers is praiseworthy, but whether all its functions are appropriately carried out by volunteers could be questioned (for example, service coordinators) and the question arises as to whether too much of a virtue is made of its Spartan approach. The development of the helpline as a joint initiative of the health board and a voluntary organisation is another appealing feature, but an unusual one since the 1960s. The helpline may be a harbinger of future developments, for several of those interviewed in the course of the research pointed to a future in which older people would make increasing use of new technologies, personal computers, assistive devices, webcams, 'the smart home'.

Finally, we can learn about leadership and voluntary-sector formation. Three, sometimes overlapping, patterns of formation appear to be in evidence. Although those interviewed were asked about the characteristics of their leadership, most appeared not to have given the matter much thought or attention, so the pattern here is extracted from quite limited data and impressions and should be treated with caution. Some even played down the role of individual leaders (unless they were deceased), self-effacement perhaps standing in the way of organisational analysis.

First, relatives or carers of older people appear to play an important role. Alzheimer branches, for example, are typically formed by eight to ten carers who may be current or, more likely, past carers of a person with dementia. They could be a partner, son or daughter of the cared-for person who may have been looked after for a decade, or might now be in residential care. They are interested to give their personal experience an organisational expression. This can arise from different types of experiences: positively, the desire to ensure that others benefit from positive models of care;

negatively, out of frustration with the lack of support that they experienced in caring roles and a desire that the situation should be better for future generations.

Second, organisations may be formed by what might be called 'concerned professionals' coming together to form an organisation. Typically and especially in rural or provincial areas, such a group may include a doctor, solicitor, business person, engineer, manager or teacher — people with organising skills, networks, or connections to funders or who know others who will smooth their paths to such groups. Several groups disputed the image that they were middle class and pointed to the broad range of socioeconomic backgrounds involved, although, interestingly, they sometimes identified leaders drawn from professional backgrounds with known organising skills, such as the gardaí and trade union organisers.

The third type of leader is what may be called 'the social entrepreneur'. Several organisations working with older people come together on the initiative of charismatic (in the traditional sense) founders who gather around them like-minded people to build a movement or to bring a foreign concept into the country. This is evident if we look at groups like ALONE, CareLocal, or the Carers Association and the case studies. The Sue Ryder Foundation, for example, was developed in the midlands by a local social activist who was also a successful public representative (Senator Charles McDonald). With his wife, he applied the Sue Ryder model, which was considered to provide a good example of high-support, independent living that valued the dignity of the older people as well as being an identifiable brand. The Westgate Foundation, though it lacked a foreign model, was built from nothing to a large social-service provider through the managerial, fundraising, organisation-building talents of Noel Byrne. Most of the services described here may be attributed to a 'founder-entrepreneur' who had the vision of a model and applied it relentlessly over the years. The role of the social entrepreneur appears to be significant and important here. There has been little study in Ireland of issues of social entrepreneurship or the ways in which it can be incentivised in the future.

Conclusions

This chapter has reviewed the voluntary and community sector working with older people in Ireland. First, it examined the environment in which the voluntary and community sector as a whole works and then went on to explore the voluntary and community sector working with older people. This environment presents a range of problems, difficulties and challenges. The emergence of the voluntary and community sector was traced from the nineteenth century onward. Next, the chapter constructed a map of the sector. At national level, it found that there were six national representative organisations for older people, five specialised national organisations whose work dealt mainly with older people but also dealt with other groups. Three regional organisations were identified, all in Dublin. Turning to the local level, the survey found that although there were some large organisations and a small number of very large organisations, the prototypical voluntary organisation working with older people was small, had no office, worked from home, had fewer than ten volunteers, no staff, served fewer than fifty older people and had an income less than €5,000. Eight organisations were profiled, illustrating innovation, inspiration and the role of the social entrepreneur in the development of the voluntary and community sector working with older people.

State action to respond to the needs of older people in the eighteenth century was followed by voluntary action in the nineteenth century. Modern voluntary action for older people in Ireland can be traced to the Red Cross in Dublin in the 1950s and the initiative of county medical officers in establishing parish committees in the mid- to late 1960s. Today, although there is a significant voluntary and community sector in Ireland, it is impossible, because of inadequate investment in registration and data-recording systems, to identify and locate the precise proportion that works with older people. Evidence from health boards and directories leads us to the conclusion that organisations working with older people constitute a significant strand of the voluntary and community sector, working in such areas as day centres, active retirement, meals-on-wheels, home helps, specific medical conditions (for example, Alzheimer's), transport, social clubs, visiting, caring and housing. Most organisations are local, although some national ones also exist.

The development of policies for the support of the voluntary and community sector has presented acute difficulties for Ireland. From the 1950s, health authorities were permitted to provide financial support for voluntary and community organisations, and groups working with older people were early beneficiaries. From the 1980s, observers commented on the unsatisfactory nature of funding, the funding relationship and the lack of access by these organisations to dialogue with the authorities on policy matters. No specific policy for voluntary action for older people has ever been articulated in a dedicated policy document by government, but issues in that relationship were addressed by *The Years Ahead*. Experts in the field regard the state's failure to resolve its relationship with the voluntary and community sector working with older people as being as serious a problem as those with the sector as a whole. It does matter, they say, leading to uneven, inconsistent services of doubtful standard, which are poorly planned and badly coordinated — and older people lose as a result. This research indicates that voluntary action for older people is abundant, but localised, small-scale and variable from place to place, underpinned by funding policies that support a proliferation of small groups.

Several writers have turned their attention to the problem of policy implementation in the area of older people in general and the voluntary and community sector working with older people in particular. They have pointed to the lack of quality of the public debate, the relative lack of influence of community interests compared to hospital interests within the health policy field, lack of departmental leadership and the political culture of discretion rather than rights. It would be difficult to contest the validity of these interpretations. The most recent writers have focused on the problem of lack of empowerment of groups working with older people and their non-involvement in the policy chain, especially within the health services where those public services that are most relevant to them are designed, planned and delivered. Students of politics might term this the lack of 'voice'. Here issues of who can make a contribution to the policy, at what point and in what way, become important. The addition of new voices to the policy chain can sometimes bring profound changes in the nature of those policies, which is one of the reasons why change is so often stoutly resisted. Although the issue of 'voice' has intruded into the literature and into the work of the National Council on Ageing and Older People, it has made remarkably little further progress, even though, as we saw in Chapter 1, it is a core issue in continental European services for older people. The discourse on older people in Ireland, at most official levels, has excluded this important issue. A discourse in which important issues are shut out is a phenomenon familiar to political scientists as 'cognitive lock' and there would appear to be an instance of it in Ireland (Connolly, 2007). Because of its importance, we return to this theme in Chapter 6.

We now know a little of the origins of many of the voluntary organisations working with older people, described here. A few were brought to Ireland using ideas and concepts developed in other countries (for example, the hospice movement, individual housing associations (Britain); Friends of the Elderly, Society of St Vincent de Paul (France)) or were part of a European project (for example, Irish Senior Citizens Parliament, Older Women's Association). In each case, though, they depended on one or a number of indigenous citizens to develop these ideas and help them to take root.

Apart from the leadership, the committees of these groups have often been filled by people from a professional background with a sense of public concern and duty. Such personnel have proved important in establishing the connections necessary with the political system for funding to be obtained. Some groups, though, have consciously reached out to the very large number of less advantaged older people who have not benefited from expanded educational opportunities, but who have a wide range of different skills, knowledge and experience.

The lingering impression is that the voluntary and community sector working with older people comprises a small number of national organisations, some vying with each other to be 'the voice' of the sector with a definable but low level of national support; a number of specialised organisations working mainly but not exclusively with older people; a number of medium-sized service-providers who limit their role to services and do not offer a commentary on policy issues; and the vast bulk of small organisations providing local, parish, social services. In some parts of the country (for example, Dún Laoghaire), little has changed in forty years. The emergence of retirement associations is striking.

Voluntary and community organisations working with older people are well linked internationally. The leading national bodies all belong to European umbrella bodies, in some cases more than one, and play an active role therein. Some services in Ireland have developed on foot of models pioneered in Britain and continental Europe. It is not clear to what degree different European thinking on older people's place in society has permeated.

Two features of the voluntary and community sector are dramatically absent: first, there seems to be no strategy for its development, either on the part of the state or within the sector itself; and second, there are few structured channels for policy engagement at regional or local level, in sharp contrast to the picture in continental Europe. Dealing with the first, there seems to be no view, either within the sector or on the part of the state as to whether the proliferation of small organisations is desirable or not, or the most useful path of development — indeed, the question seems never to have been considered. In the area of consultation, the survey found that only 27 per cent of groups are consulted formally or regularly, 71 per cent either occasionally or not at all. This is not an environment likely to promote good service development or to empower older people. It is to this political question that we turn next (Chapter 6).

6

Older People's Organisation and Policy-Making

This chapter focuses on the role of voluntary and community action in policy-making on ageing in both Northern Ireland and Ireland. Chapters 2 and 3 examined the current set of policies for older people in each jurisdiction, and Chapters 4 and 5 mapped the voluntary and community sectors working with older people, including groupings with an interest in policy matters. Here, we look at their role in policy-making. First, we need to examine the current policy architecture before we look at the policy-focused organisations that participate in this process and then their experience of contributing to policy-making. Conclusions are then drawn.

Before doing so, a context should be set. So far, there has been only limited analysis of the manner in which voluntary and community organisations address Ireland's political system, although Murphy (2005) was the most recent to describe and contextualise their activities. In Northern Ireland, there are several important descriptive accounts of how the interface between the voluntary sector and government has developed since the earliest days of the welfare state (Kearney, 1995; Birrell and Williamson, 2001; Kearney and Williamson, 2001). In neither case has there been very much analytical literature.

There is a very large literature on the ways in which the political system interfaces with social movements and pressure groups, how these ways structure the fields of voluntary action, and their relative effectiveness. Two issues raised in this literature are particularly pertinent to our discussion here. The first concerns the relationship that exists between the nature of the constituency seeking to exert influence, the forms of engagement that are on offer and the operation of power in these engagements. The second focuses more on the question of strategy. To what extent do older people's organisations operate within the political system and to what extent outside it?

The options open to movements and interest groups to influence the political process are subject to a complex matrix of factors, some to do with these movements and groups themselves such as their ability to

thers to do with the variety
ı government are managed.
ay be said to offer broadly
to movements and interest

y pressure groups gather
for example, government
ıstem arbitrating between
range from adversarial
ınnected to the decision-

model in which political
_ _ˌ ᴜ ᴏᴍᴀᴎᴇɪ grouping of key organisations which
gather around the same points of political influence and work together
with government to achieve consensual outcomes, usually under the
name of social partnership. Here, groups wishing to influence the
political system must work through larger entities (for example, trades
unions, social partners) to present their case and influence policy.

- *Policy community*: This approach repositions the players thematically.
  Here, there is a vertical group of interests representing a generally stable
  set of groups, from government departments through state agencies down to small and local organisations, all pursuing a common set of
  interests and resources (for example, agriculture, energy). Governments,
  pressure groups and interested parties generally take a broad set of views
  in common, share common assumptions and network together and their
  policy circle or community can be quite hard for outsider groups to break
  into. The theme they share in common is more important that the
  organisational differences that set them apart.
- *Rational scientific managerialism*: this approach is based on a strong
  means-end orientation and has become the leading approach in the
  management of large public programmes such as health and social care
  in many countries across the world. It emphasises the role of audit as
  the primary means of control and values professional and technical
  knowledge over experiential knowledge. Political issues over matters
  such as resource allocation decisions tend to be reframed as technical,
  with the consequence that it discounts alternative viewpoints and very
  often provides very few points of access to the policy process for
  interests outside a charmed circle of auditors and consultants.

These correspond in turn with a variety of approaches open to government
in the management of social problems. In contrast to hierarchical systems

of command and control, exemplified by state-run industries and welfare institutions, governance in the contemporary environment has modulated between three competing approaches (Newman, 2001). On the one hand, there is a rational goal orientation, typified by the new public management that emerged in the 1990s in the UK in particular, with its attention to ends and means, targets and performance review. On the other hand are open systems and self-governance models, where the emphasis is switched to experimentation and innovation, iterative learning and interdependent horizontal relationships, and on the self-sustaining engagement of citizens in solving social problems. These models sustain conflicting goals and processes, with the result that policy can often be an uneasy mixture of all three, with governments mixing and matching even within particular policy fields.

In practice, the ways in which social movements and interest groups interact with the process of governance will consist in an amalgamation of these two sets of dimensions. Rational goal orientation in policy-making and implementation will tend to push those organisations involved towards contractual relationships in which a great deal of emphasis is laid on the 'Three Es' — economy, efficiency and effectiveness — in the delivery of public services on behalf of the state. Both corporatist and policy community approaches will favour a more iterative and open approach to problem-solving in which interest groups will be invited to the table either on the grounds that they can further the legitimacy of decisions by representing a constituency and bringing it on board, or because of their specialist knowledge, or for a combination of these reasons.

In principle, movements and interest groups may adopt either insider or outsider strategies (Grant, 2000). Insider groups may succeed in getting a seat at the table and come to be regarded as the legitimate voice of a particular interest group. But they will be expected to abide by the rules of the game (Taylor, 2003). In contrast, outsider groups, whether through choice or because they lack the contacts with government agencies and departments, or because they have been deliberately excluded, seek to influence policy from outside the policy process. In reality, the distinction may not be so clear-cut in that sometimes organisations can pursue insider and outsider strategies simultaneously (Coxall, 2001). In fact, many would seek to do so. Furthermore, it tends to leave unexamined the extent to which insider groups are actually influential. Thus Maloney, Jordan and McLaughlin (1994) suggest that there should be a third category, peripheral insiders. They see the key boundary as lying between outsiders, peripheral insiders and core insiders (Taylor, 2003). Peripheral insiders are organisations that ostensibly sit inside the policy process in that they are regularly consulted or attend meetings of partnership boards, but have little influence in practice. Maloney et al. (1994, p. 32) comment that it often causes officials more trouble to ignore them than to accord them polite recognition. They are an important category for our discussion.

The switch in governance towards a greater use of partnerships, policy communities and other more open mechanisms has led to an increase in opportunities for organisations to move inside. In both Northern Ireland and Ireland, older people's organisations have been drawn into corporatist and policy community arrangements, although as we shall show this has not been consistent. In some cases, structures have been created within the voluntary sector specifically to mirror structures in government and to facilitate access to those structures. It is less clear, however, how effective organisations have been in influencing policy, and this raises in an acute form the question of how power is distributed in these new forms of governance.

Power in policy operates at a number of different levels. In his seminal paper, Lukes (1974) distinguishes between three faces of power: first, the direct exercise of power by one over another; second, the exercise of power to fix the agenda of discussion; and third and most subtly, the ability to modify or fix the assumptions underlying the policies and social problems under discussion. The consequences of the exercise of power for the role of voluntary and community organisations in policy-making are not trivial. In practice, they often do not 'decide the game that is being played; they do not determine the rules of play, the system of refereeing, or, indeed, who plays; and the cards are stacked in favour of the more powerful players. In fact, many find that they are in the wrong game altogether' (Taylor, 2003, p. 123).

What then is the policy game in which older people's organisations participate, who gets to participate and on what terms, and what are the similarities and differences in Ireland, North and South? This chapter describes policy-making and the role and experience of older people's organisations in those processes in each of Northern Ireland and Ireland, before offering some conclusions.

Policy-making: Northern Ireland

Policy architecture for older people
As was discussed in Chapter 2, the policy environment in Northern Ireland is a complex mixture of EU-derived policy, national UK-led policy-making and policy that is the responsibility of the administration in Belfast. But there is no clear-cut division between them. Policies that are a local responsibility are set in a context that is often set nationally, but the impact of this relationship may vary from policy area to policy area.

Furthermore, political instability over the past forty years has meant that a clear pattern in the relationship between the two is often difficult to discern. During the decades of direct rule by junior ministers in the Northern Ireland office, a general lack of political commitment and competence led to a sclerotic system of public administration, in which a great deal of power and authority was vested in the civil service and numerous unelected public bodies, which were simultaneously conservative and vulnerable to influence by single-issue lobbies. Social legislation covering the areas of policy that were the responsibility of this administration generally copied legislation passed previously in the national parliament in Westminster.

Since the devolution settlement of 1998, the reserved powers of the national parliament at Westminster have been restated as being substantially about taxation and redistribution through the social security system. Whilst the amount of money available for public administration remains subject to the application of the 'Barnett formula', decisions over priorities and the detailed shape of policy in health and social care, housing and education, as well as aspects of economic policy, are now more clearly the responsibility of the devolved administrations. The administration of justice, including the police, courts and prisons, together with the social security budget, remain outside the 'Barnett' process. The promise of elected assemblies in Northern Ireland, Scotland and Wales suggested that a greater divergence in policy between the different parts of the UK would emerge, even if unevenly, as each of the devolved administrations had differing degrees of autonomy and was open to influence from contrasting local political contexts. So far as Northern Ireland is concerned, the instability of the institutions established by the 'Good Friday' agreement between 1998 and 2007 has probably meant that divergence with the rest of the UK has been delayed.

This chapter will describe the overall system of public administration that existed at the time of devolution in 1998 and identify the changes being introduced through the Review of Public Administration of 2005. It will then focus on the institutional arrangements for determining and delivering policy on ageing and old people, before discussing the extent to which this has been open to influence from the bodies representing the interests of older people.

Public administration in Northern Ireland under direct rule was once memorably described as: an 'excuse for administrative intransigence' which resulted

in a subjugated population acquiescing in a system, which is seriously lacking in both political and administrative accountability. The assumption that no changes can be made to public service delivery in the absence of progress on the constitutional front has created and embedded a plethora of boards, trusts, quangos and civil service departments characterised by administrative indifference' (Hughes, Knox, Murray and Greer, 1998, p. 20).

Initially the devolution settlement made the mixture even more complex as the number of government departments was increased from six to eleven without the loss of any other bodies. To these should be added departmental executive oversight committees

Figure 6.1, reproduced from Knox and Carmichael (2007, p. 204), sets out the structure as it existed in 1998. The Northern Ireland Assembly and its associated structures at the top of the diagram replaced the Secretary of State for Northern Ireland and four junior ministers. The bodies towards the bottom of the diagram were inherited from the prior direct-rule administration. These arrangements had emerged over the years as responses to political crises of the time and, as a result, had little overall coherence, were inefficient and were 'disastrously fragmented' (Dowdall, 2004, cited in Knox and Carmichael, 2007, p. 204).

The nature of the devolution settlement tended to make fragmentation even worse as the Executive did not incorporate the principle of collective responsibility and, as a consequence, the eleven Ministers ran their departments as quasi-independent satrapies. This was exacerbated by the dysfunctional relationships between political parties and personalities in the first period of devolution before the institutions were suspended in 2002. At the time of writing, it remains to be seen whether the political performance of the Executive elected in 2007 will be an improvement, although the formal levels of joint accountability remain weak.

The Review of Public Administration, which reported in 2005, was a priority of the devolved government between 1998 and 2002, based upon a general acknowledgement of the unsatisfactory status quo. Because their number had been negotiated between the political parties, a major omission in its remit was the eleven government departments, with the consequence that a number of non-departmental public bodies that were particularly close to their home departments were excluded also (Knox and Carmichael, 2007).

The Review proposed three major changes. First, a reorganisation of strategic policy-making at the centre, clarifying the role of departments as policy-making only, and creating new regional strategic authorities for each of health and social care, and for education in particular. Second, it proposed the creation of a delivery tier at subregional level, around seven coterminous areas; and third, the reduction in the numbers of local councils from twenty-six to those same seven areas. Lack of agreement among the political parties about the future of local government — only Sinn Féin has expressed enthusiasm for seven new councils, with the other parties preferring twelve or fifteen — has meant that the Northern Ireland Executive has finally settled on eleven. But by the first half of 2008, only the proposed changes to health and social care structures had been put in place, with the formerly eighteen trusts reduced in number to five. The four Health and Social Services Boards will disappear in April 2009, to be replaced by a single regional health and social care commissioning body and a number of 'local commissioning groups'. These changes will be discussed in greater detail below.

Figure 6.1: Government structures in Northern Ireland in 1998

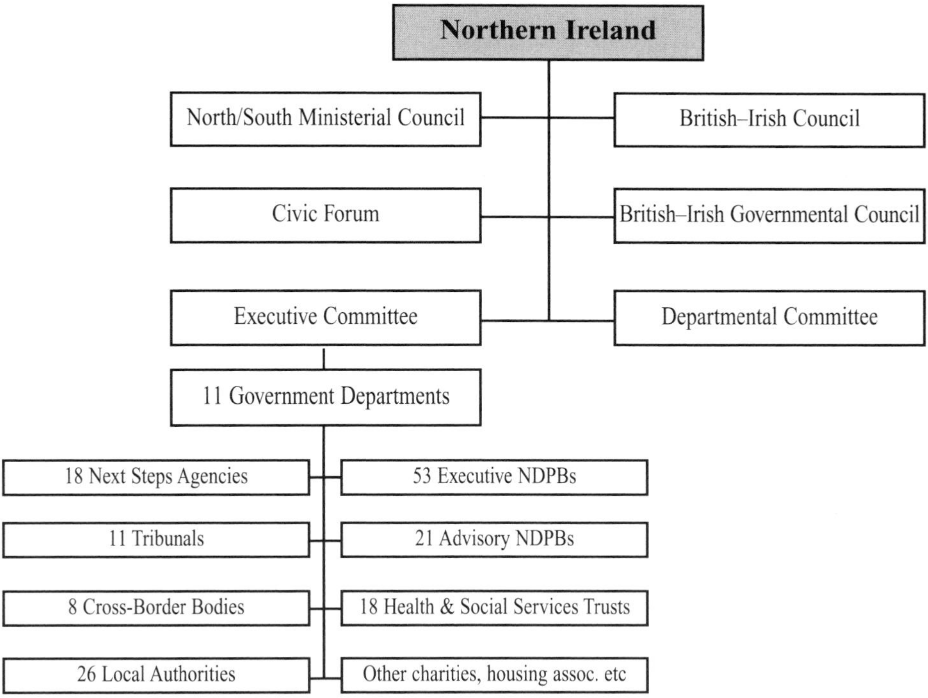

Source: Reproduced from Knox and Carmichael, 2007 (p. 204)

So far as policy and services specifically addressing older people are concerned, the two most important departments are the Department of Health, Social Services and Public Safety (DHSSPS) and the Office of First and Deputy First Minister (OFMDFM), which has responsibility for equality and social exclusion policies. In addition, the Department for Social Development (DSD) has important relevant responsibilities for social security and housing, looking after both the Northern Ireland Housing Executive and the Social Security Agency, as well as leading government strategic policy on the voluntary sector as a whole.

The DHSSPS remains the single most important source of funds for voluntary organisations concerned with older people, reflecting its lead role in administering health and social care policies. Its budget of £4,476.9 million for 2007/08 dwarfs that of all other departments with the exception of the DSD where the total includes social-security expenditure (Knox and Carmichael, 2007). As a group, older people are the main beneficiaries of health and social care services, but neither the department nor its agencies have structures that are specifically aimed at enabling organisations representing older people to discuss policy issues in a structured way with either civil servants or politicians. In fact, the system of health and social care delivery is notable for the degree to which it is a closed system, difficult for any group aside from professional interests to access policy decision-making.

If anything, the reforms to the structures adumbrated above will increase the imperviousness of the system. Table 6.1 compares the old and the new structures.

Table 6.1: Changes in the administrative structures for health and social care in Northern Ireland, 2007–2008

Old structures	New structures
4 Health and Social Services Boards	1 Strategic Health and Social Services commissioning body
1 Ambulance Trust	1 Ambulance Trust
18 Health and Social Services Trusts	5 Health and Social Care Trusts
15 Local Health and Social Care Groups	(7) Local Commissioning Groups
8 Support Agencies	3 Support Agencies
4 Health and Social Services Councils	1 Patient and Client Council

Civic participation in health and social care structures has always tended to be consumerist in tone, reserved for qualified people in non-executive director roles, or constructed as a technical matter of good professional practice by HPSC staff. The new structures preserve all these features and, indeed, perhaps exacerbate them, possibly reflecting the absence of voluntary and community-sector interests in the departmental working groups responsible for implementing the reforms.

Under the department which will continue to set broad policy, commissioning of services will be the responsibility of the new strategic authority for the whole of Northern Ireland, although this will be delegated to one of the seven proposed local commissioning groups. These will be dominated by primary health-care professionals, with only two of the fifteen places reserved for lay community input. They will be advised in turn by local community commissioning associations (there will be several to each of the seven local commissioning groups). These associations will have delegated powers and budgets and are envisaged as partnerships between GPs and other health and social care professionals and representatives of the local community and voluntary sector. But the advice that is emerging from the DHSSPS on the constitution of these bodies clearly indicates that the community representation preferred is people with professional experience of health and social care delivery — for example, retired GPs. There is thus little evidence of room in the structure for the representation or recognition of group rights, and the intention seems to be to keep such groups at a distance from decisions over resource allocation and priorities, with a clear preference for professional rather than lay knowledge. Although at the time of writing the exact make-up of the commissioning structures had still to be determined, there is little indication that they will leave much room for direct representation from the many local older people's organisations, let alone their regional or subregional representatives.

At departmental level, structures to enable engagement with the voluntary sector as a whole, set up in the mid-1980s in the wake of the *Wolfenden Report on the Voluntary Sector*, still operate. As discussed in Chapter 4, these include the Central Personal Social Services Advisory Committee, currently chaired by the Chief Executive of the Simon Community with a membership drawn from departmental officials and representatives of the community and voluntary sector with an interest in social care. It receives reports on policy developments and can make recommendations, but has little power to insist that its recommendations be followed. It is expected that the committee will continue after reorganisation is complete.

During the first period of devolved government up to 2002, in addition, a cross-party group of Assembly members on ageing was established, which began to work with the nascent Age Sector Reference Group

(ASRG), providing a direct route to MLAs on ageing issues. The suspension of the Assembly in 2002 meant that these relationships had insufficient time to mature and it is a matter for speculation what impact they might have had on policy-making in the area in the longer term. However, the invitation from the MLAs to the ASRG was undoubtedly a boost to its status and legitimacy as a representative body.

The regulation of social care has become an increasingly important theme in policy throughout the UK, and regulatory structures in Northern Ireland tend to be closely modelled on their equivalent bodies elsewhere in the country. These bodies tend to be more open to lay input than the administrative structures put in place for health and social care delivery. An important non-departmental public body in this respect is the Northern Ireland Social Care Council (NISCC), which has responsibility for training and professional development of social care staff throughout the social care system, whether in the public, private or voluntary sectors, through the professional registration of social care staff.

Members of the Council are appointed by the Minister to represent stakeholders — that is to say, social care agencies in the public, private and voluntary sectors (although there are currently none of the latter), registrants and users. The latter include a number of carers and disabled people, although at present no representatives of older people's organisations in particular, although the structures would allow for this and the situation could therefore change in the future. The NISCC supports a service users' and a carers' reference group, whose members include individual carers and users, including older people, but there is not a strong representation from organised groups, none of whom have a right to representation.

Apart from the regulatory systems, other policy initiatives within the broad responsibility of the DHSSPS have opened avenues of influence. Promulgated in 2002, 'Investing for Health' is a health promotion strategy adopted by the Northern Ireland Executive and prepared by the DHSSPS. The strategy 'seeks to shift that emphasis (on treatment of ill-health) by taking action to tackle the factors which adversely affect health and perpetuate health inequalities' (DHSSPS, 2002b, p. 7). Its background is the World Health Organisation policy framework, 'Health 21', adopted in Copenhagen, in 1998, by all fifty-one member states of the WHO European region, and it thus follows developments elsewhere in Europe and in other parts of the UK. Interestingly, the consultation document produced in 2000 had proposed *incorporating* a group rights focus by building its targets around identified groups of people, including elderly people, but this approach was in the end rejected in favour of an approach that focused on health inequalities across groups. Its targets are consequently wide-ranging and at a high level, and focus on redistribution of health outcomes across income bands, for example seeking to improve life expectancy and halve the gap in life expectancy between the poorest and the wealthiest areas, and reduce the gap in ill-health between the poorest and the wealthiest areas.

Focusing on the causes of ill-health and of inequalities in health, the strategy crosses departmental boundaries and seeks to create a framework 'which is based on partnership working amongst departments, public bodies, local communities, voluntary bodies, District Councils and the social partners' (ibid, p. 7). A regional Investing for Health forum has been established with voluntary and community-sector representation, and the current four health and social services boards have established area Investing for Health partnerships, themselves linked to existing partnership initiatives such as the Belfast and Derry Healthy Cities and the health action zones where they have been established. These partnerships comprise 'key voluntary, community and statutory organisations in the area' (DHSSPS, 2002b, p. 145).

Built on different principles from those underpinning the delivery of social care, this framework is providing a separate set of opportunities for policy influence of older people's voluntary organisations, is beginning to have a profound impact on the ways in which these organisations relate to state agencies at the local level, and is starting to influence the resources to which they can have access. It is also beginning to change the way in which social care is understood at the local level by the health and social care trusts, with more emphasis being given to community development as a method of intervention.

The open-ended 'what works' approach of Investing for Health has opened up new opportunities for group rights recognition in ways that are quite different from the formal governance of health and social care, although the opportunities have to be exploited by (usually) entrepreneurially minded middle management staff in health and social care trusts who gain support from their senior managers. Our evidence suggests that without such internal 'fixing', it remains very hard for identity groups outside the system to move inside.

A good example of how this policy frame has opened up avenues for influence is in the participation of older people's organisations in the Engage with Age Partnership in Belfast, described and discussed in Chapter 4. However, the relationship between Investing for Health and the management of the delivery of core social care services remains underdeveloped with the consequence that the level of engagement in policy processes it offers older people's organisations varies widely from one part of Northern Ireland to another and appears very dependent upon insider support.

The Office of First Minister and Deputy First Minister (OFMDFM) works jointly to the First Minister and Deputy First Minister in the Assembly and has overall responsibility for many thematic issues that stretch across the individual remits of the other ten departments. It has no equivalent in Ireland. It covers diverse matters from administering the UK honours system in Northern Ireland and managing the Northern Ireland government bureaux in Washington and Brussels to coordinating government policy and the review of public administration. It also has responsibility for external relations, including the North–South Ministerial Council and the Northern Ireland government input to the British Irish Council, thus replicating some of the functions of the Department for Foreign Affairs in Ireland.

So far as policy on ageing and older people is concerned, the OFMDFM's core responsibility for equality policy and antipoverty policy has given it an important leadership role. In both these policy areas it has sought to create policy communities that directly involve relevant elements of the voluntary and community sector, and this has been a particular feature of its equality-policy work. This reflects a trend in UK policy-making as a whole since 1997.

The Equality, Rights and Social Inclusion Division of OFMDFM is broadly responsible for equality policy (operationally delegated to the Northern Ireland Equality Commission), and social inclusion and antipoverty policy. This means that it has responsibility for equality legislation and for monitoring the performance of the Equality Commission itself. Thus it was responsible for the implementation of the regulations on age discrimination on employment, in line with the EU Employment Framework Directive (2000/78/EC), and is currently leading work on single equality legislation for Northern Ireland.

As was described in Chapters 2 and 4, an important impact of the equality duty of Section 75 of the 1998 Northern Ireland Act was to create a legally based equality-monitoring system into which representatives of the groups of people covered by the legislation were drawn. This was the process that led to the emergence of the Age Sector Reference Group being a point of reference on ageing issues for the Equality Commission as it fulfilled its legal requirements under the Act. Furthermore, it has created a very close relationship between the Commission and Age Concern, whose Chief Executive Officer also serves as Deputy Equality Commissioner and whose current chair of the board of trustees was, until 2007, Chief Equality Commissioner. Her predecessor as Chair was a Commission staff member.

The central antipoverty unit sits within the Equality, Rights and Social Inclusion Division to manage the antipoverty strategy, which is thematically organised through interdepartmental 'promoting social inclusion

(PSI)' working groups. The theme on ageing emerged in the second tranche of themes identified under the 'New Targeting Social Need' initiative, the government's antipoverty strategy in the years immediately following 1998. As discussed in Chapter 2, the consultation on a strategy of ageing was launched in this context. A core feature of the government's approach to social inclusion policy has been its use of insider policy communities for each theme. Voluntary-sector representatives along with other stakeholders participate as full members of these strategy working groups, which jointly work on policy recommendations. Ministers are free to accept or reject the recommendations, but it does serve to give an equal seat at the table for relevant voluntary-sector representatives. The process of setting strategic policy on ageing in Northern Ireland was described and discussed in Chapter 2.

In parallel with the strategy on ageing, a similar process was undertaken in respect to carers. A carers' working group was established and a separate strategy developed, led by the DHSSPS.

The Civic Forum

The Civic Forum was agreed in the 'Good Friday' agreement and legislated for in the 1998 Northern Ireland Act and is thus part of the formal governance arrangements in Northern Ireland. It was established at the insistence of the Women's Coalition who argued that there was a need for a more deliberative approach to government than would be offered by elected representatives in the Assembly and there should be a recognition of the important role that voluntary and community groups had played in Northern Ireland since the early 1970s (Bell, 2004). Modelled loosely on the National Social and Economic Forum in Ireland (see below), it was established as a 'consultative mechanism on economic, social and cultural issues' (Strand One, section 34, April 1998, cited in Bell, 2004, p. 567). Of the sixty members of the Forum, eighteen were from the voluntary and community sector. These were selected as a result of a process proposed by the leading intermediary bodies in the voluntary and community sector; one of the eighteen seats was reserved for a representative from the 'age sector'. As described in Chapter 2, the necessity of finding a mechanism to select this individual provided an important additional role to the new Age Sector Reference Group.

The Civic Forum met regularly between 2000 and 2002, but it never satisfactorily resolved problems over what its consultative brief amounted to (Bell, 2004). Additionally, there was considerable opposition to its remit and role among some elected politicians, particularly members of the DUP (McCall and Williamson, 2001). It is unclear what it achieved and it is perhaps significant that with the reinstatement of the devolved assembly in

2007 there were no moves to resurrect it and no demands from among voluntary and community organisations that it should be resurrected.

A feature of government relations with the Northern Ireland voluntary sector has been the high degree of formal acknowledgement of the sector as an entity in itself and the existence of formal structures to manage the relationship. This first emerged in its current shape in the aftermath of the publication in 1993 of the government strategy on voluntary action and community development, but developed further after 1998 with the adoption of the Northern Ireland compact. Policies towards the sector as a whole are led by the Voluntary and Community Unit, housed in the Department for Social Development, which serviced the 'partners for change' task force on government/voluntary-sector relations, referred to in Chapter 2. The task-force membership was drawn equally from the civil service and the sector itself. It is important to bear in mind that these structures do not provide for representation on policy by particular sectional interests within the voluntary sector. Thus an important voluntary-sector participant in the task force's work had a long-standing interest in policy on ageing and subsequently became chief executive of Age Concern, but the task force was not designed to be a vehicle for representation of these issues.

In addition, a joint government/voluntary-sector forum was established in 1998 as a result of the compact. It brings together representatives of voluntary organisations with the civil servants in each of the eleven government departments with lead responsibility for relations with the voluntary sector. It has an important monitoring and feedback role, in theory enabling civil servants to engage with their opposite numbers in the voluntary sector on the effectiveness of the relationship between the sector and individual government departments, although as will be discussed there have been disagreements between the two sides as to how far the forum's remit extends.

The experience of participation in policy-making

It is important to bear in mind that the ability of older people's organisations inside Northern Ireland to affect policy will be limited to matters for which the devolved administration has responsibility and, even then, within funding and taxation policies set centrally at Westminster. With a population of just 1.7 million people in a nation of over 60 million people, the influence that Northern Ireland can exert over major decisions on taxation and government expenditure is likely to be tiny. Thus a core demand of older people's organisations, shared throughout the UK, is for the restoration of the link between the old-age pension and earnings to reverse the relative decline of older people's incomes. Lobbying activities within Northern Ireland itself will have no impact whatsoever on this issue, and organisations like Age Concern in Northern Ireland and the Northern Ireland Pensioners' Convention can add their relatively small weight to national campaigns only through formal and informal links with their counterparts in Britain.

In addition, the lack of devolved powers over taxation, coupled with the large gap between public expenditure and income from taxation, can limit what the local Assembly can do. The indefinite delay to the decision in principle of the Assembly to fund personal care outside hospitals, described in Chapter 2, is an indication of the difficulties the devolved administration may have in funding its priorities.

This is not to say that there are no significant areas of policy that are subject to local control, although the extent of these may not have been tested as far as they might be, as a result of the instability in the devolved institutions of government since 1998. Indeed, within the parameters set by the political relationship between Northern Ireland and the rest of the UK, the overall picture provided by the Northern Ireland case is of a structured and well-developed formal relationship between relevant elements within the voluntary sector and government at various levels. As reported in Chapter 4, there is evidence that many older people's organisations are involved in these arrangements, and, for many, the experience is reasonably satisfactory.

Satisfaction depends, however, on the level of expectation, and there is evidence that organisations have been satisfied by participation (the invitation to the table) and have been less put out by the difficulties that there have been in exerting influence.

It is notable how little influence organisations have been able to exert over health and social care policy, the administration of which has been predicated on a strong rational ends-means managerially led process, in which control is exercised through target and contract setting and monitoring by means of narrowly defined criteria. In this system, the primary relationship between older people's voluntary organisations and government has been by contract or service agreement. Organisations caught in this system have found it hard to influence the policies behind the budgets that fund their work. We know that very large sums of money have flowed to voluntary organisations from government by this route, and the organisation case studies in Chapter 4 illustrate their impact. But the extent to which this has been accompanied by an opening up of the health and social care policy environment to influence from the outside is much less clear. As we have suggested, the administrative structures seem designed to exclude this possibility.

Policy-making through vertically integrated policy communities is largely absent from health and social care, with the exception of the health promotion strategy where a more open-ended iterative approach has been adopted. But as we have shown, even there, insider access is subject to gate-keeping by middle managers within the administrative system. The structure of the review of community care that reported in 2002 is illustrative of an approach that privileges professional knowledge and casts other interests as providers of information for professional appraisal, rather than as full participants (DHSSPS, 2002a). The review project board was chaired by the chief executive of Fold Housing Association. Its members included the chief executive of the Law Centre, Northern Ireland, and a staff member from Carers Northern Ireland, but it otherwise comprised senior managers from both social care trusts and the relevant parts of the Department of Health, Social Services and Public Safety. The Project team that conducted the review was led by a manager from within a social care trust and was staffed entirely by professional staff within the Department itself. The team conducted 'an extensive consultation exercise with a wide range of service users and providers . . . a very worthwhile exercise as the service-providers and users gave the review team a great deal of useful information' (ibid., p. 1). Whilst this included two focus groups with older people's groups, most information came from a variety of service-providers and professional staff.

The contrast in approach by the OFMDFM in the development of social inclusion and antipoverty policy is notable. The use of working groups with a remit that crosses departmental boundaries and involving outside expertise from relevant voluntary and community organisations has become well established. This has provided a platform for organisations to argue their case and has been an important determinant in the development of representative structures within the 'age sector' in particular.

However, it has a number of limitations. First, it tends to lock lobby organisations into advisory structures that develop consensus views within given budgetary limits. One civil servant involved in this process commented to the authors that an important part of the civil service role was to 'manage expectations'. Working groups may advise government ministers, but the latter may reject or modify that advice. Organisations may find themselves committed to consensus positions that they can hardly argue against subsequently.

Second, action on strategies that emerges from the working-group process can be delegated to individual lead departments where implementation is not subject to influence to the same extent. For example, carers' organisations have complained that the carers' strategy, which they had helped to develop, has resulted in little or no change once it was given back to the DHSSPS to implement. In their view, there has been insufficient linking between the carers' and the older people's strategies, with the former vulnerable to being pulled into other agendas within the

DHSSPS in a process that paid too little attention to the need for interdepartmental co-operation.

Third, it raises the question of capacity. Even the largest of the voluntary organisations in the age sector with an interest in influencing policy, Age Concern, has until recently lacked a research and policy function capable of generating change in policy. Work has, as a result, tended to be reactive to agendas coming from government departments, through consultation responses and similar routine inputs. Even here there is a danger of consultation burnout, particularly in the backwash of consultations over the public-body equality schemes that followed the implementation of section 75 of the 1998 Northern Ireland Act.

The recent investment by Atlantic Philanthropies in this capacity indicates that there is recognition of this weakness. It remains to be seen what impact this has on policy input in the future. Apart from Age Concern, the biggest organisations typified by Extra Care for the Elderly do not have the resources or brief to lobby on matters beyond their immediate operational concerns. At grass-roots level, notwithstanding the emergence of subregional and regional network organisations, the capacity of older people as an organised group remains limited.

The experience of those organisations that have participated in workinggroup structures has been mixed. The voluntary sector representatives on the joint forum reviewed experience of the whole process and concluded that whilst there were examples of good practice, this had not been embraced everywhere, with particular problems of interdepartmental collaboration around the strategic themes. For example, there is evidence that interdepartmental blocks have slowed down the implementation of measures in the older people's strategy. The problem is structural as well as cultural. The OFMDFM lacks the mechanism to make the departments act on their strategic commitments, even with the authority of the first and deputy first ministers behind it, as a result of the weakness in collective responsibility in the Executive.

The initiative for the review was taken by the voluntary-sector joint forum members alone, but their civil servant counterparts appear to have been initially reluctant to allow the forum to be used as a review mechanism of this sort, suggesting a divergence of views on the function and remit of the forum.

Policy-making: Ireland

Policy architecture for older people
In Ireland, the government department responsible for policy for older people has traditionally been and remains the Department for Health and

Children, a department established in its original form in 1947. The department has, at the direction of the Minister for Health, followed the practice in recent years of publishing framework policy documents for health policy, the first being *Shaping a Healthier Future* (1994), followed by *A Plan for Women's Health 1997–99* (Department of Health, 1997), the most recent being *Quality and Fairness — A Health System for You* (Department of Health and Children, 2001).

Dedicated policies for the welfare of older people are the *Care of the Aged* report (Department of Health, 1968) and *The Years Ahead — A Policy for the Elderly* (Department of Health, 1988), and these remain the two main milestones of policy development. These policies were put into effect through the health board system, which operated from 1970 to 2004, the country being divided into eight health boards (eleven at the very end of the period). Although practices for older people and other groups varied within these boards, the policies generally followed the national parameters laid down by the department. When the boards were replaced by the Health Service Executive in 2005, the government stressed that policy-making would remain the function of the department — indeed, that would be its sole function — and that the task of the HSE would be, by definition, to execute such policies. The health vote in the public estimates would go to the executive, and the role of the department would be exclusively a policy-focused one. The HSE published a *National Service Plan 2005*, which included a six-page section 'Services for older people'.

Older people's services in the department come under the aegis of one of the department's assistant secretaries general and are the exclusive concern of a unit comprising a principal officer, assistant principal, two executive officers and three clerical officers. At political level, a minister of state has, for a number of years, been assigned responsibility for older people's issues, and in the Dáil has fielded questions and issues on policy for older people. Sometimes this responsibility is formally indicated in the Minister of State's title (for example, 'Minister of state with special responsibility for services for older people') and the formula and its use can vary. In order to ensure a coordinated and joined-up approach, the 2002–07 government established an interdepartmental group on the needs of older people.

These developments indicate that the policy for older people is politically sufficiently important to attract the status of at least part of the time of a junior minister. Despite this, voluntary and community organisations have found the calibre of several such ministers of state to be poor and the persons chosen to be political lightweights (a phrase frequently used). Age Action Ireland, for example, described minister of state Ivor Callely as not understanding or engaged with issues of older people, difficult to deal with, compounded by his disappointing performance, with older people losing out as a result.[1]

Whether the separation of policy from execution between the Department of Health, on the one hand, and the Health Service Executive, on the other, will remain clinically absolute is doubtful. Most commentators take the view that the development of services and practice will inevitably draw the HSE into a policy-making role. The Prospectus report (2003), which devised the Health Service Executive, proposed the establishment of consumer panels. Various expert groups have since been set in train by the new executive, and the Chief Executive Officer is now establishing a series of consultative fora. One of these is responsible for older people, and the first meeting was held in late 2005. Its purpose is to provide ground truth, give advice, make suggestions and contribute to policy. The Carers Association is the principal voluntary organisation represented. The Chief Executive Officer established in 2005 more than twelve expert advisory groups, one of which will deal with older people and is to include voluntary and community representation. These developments suggest that the policy/execution dividing line between the department and the executive will be far from sharp.

From the early 1980s, policy-making for the welfare of older people became the function of a specialised body formed in 1981, the National Council for the Aged, since renamed the National Council for the Elderly (1990), and finally, in its present manifestation, the National Council on Ageing and Older People (1997). Its two main functions are to carry out policy-focused research into issues concerning older people, and to advise the department. The Council is the principal policy formulator and agenda driver for older people in the state. The National Council itself is selected and appointed by the Minister for Health and Children for four-year terms at a time. It has twenty-seven members, drawn from the health services, leading health-service professionals, doctors, geriatricians, public health and voluntary and community organisations, some national and some local.

It has a strong research and policy development record, with no fewer than ninety-four reports published to date. The Council may also have the unstated, but important, function of building a consensus within leading actors in the health field on policies for the elderly before they become officially endorsed and recommended. The role of the National Council on Ageing and Older People has drawn mixed comments. The Council is appraised strongly for its research work, coherent policies and informing role. For some voluntary organisations, it has done the research legwork

---

1 Dáil Éireann, *Debates*, 7 December 2005, 1429–1430

that has enabled other organisations to make the case for improved services. It is criticised, though, for its lack of success in ensuring that its recommendations are implemented and for being insufficiently challenging of government, and it is compared unfavourably with bodies like the Equality Authority. It attracts a low buy-in from those on whom it is dependent for the implementation of its recommendations. Having said that, critics do not seem to be aware of the frustration level that may exist within the Council itself at its own difficulty in making an impact. The Council's terms of reference give it an advisory role only, not an implementing one. Some specific recommendations have been implemented and the Council may be more successful in pressing for a more systematic government approach to ageing.

The National Council of the Aged was important for its establishment of spin-off bodies. During the 1980s, the Council sponsored an annual day for older people, to encourage the participation of older people in civic life. To undertake this specialised role, an organisation, Age and Opportunity, was formed and, following *1993: European Year of older people and solidarity between the generations*, it became a permanent body with regular funding from the Department of Health, and now plays an important role in encouraging civic participation. The Council attempted to establish a national body to represent older people and this emerged as the Irish Association of Older People (see Chapter 5). The Council's documents and research are widely used by government, the state sector, voluntary and community organisations and the academic community.

Other state agencies concerned with policy-making have, from time to time, addressed issues concerning older people. The Equality Authority adopted a dedicated policy for older people, *Implementing Equality for Older People* (Equality Authority, 2002), and this is considered to be important in reshaping policies for older people around a rights-based, antidiscrimination agenda.

These are the two main advisory committees to government, the National Economic and Social Council (NESC), which dates in its original form to 1961, and the National Economic and Social Forum (NESF), which was established in 1994. Both are corporatist bodies, drawing their membership from the leading organisations involved in social partnership (employers, trades unions, farmers, voluntary and community groups). Elected representatives from the main political parties sit on the NESF, but not on the NESC. Their remit takes in all areas of economic and social policy and, as we shall see, NESF has specifically interested itself in older people. Other bodies with a relevance to policy-making here are the National Pensions Board, the National Retirement Planning Council and the Medico-Social Research Board.

Older people fall within the remit of the local authorities insofar as they are responsible for physical planning, recreation, community facilities and housing. With the reform of local government in 2000, city and county development boards were established in each local authority area to plan for economic, cultural and social development. The boards were enjoined to consult with their communities and pursue policies for social inclusion. Delaney, Cullen and Duff (2005) found that in the case of older people, the consultation process had been problematical, the first reason being the lack of organisations able to present the views of older people. Some city and county areas had no organisations, challenging conventional wisdom that such organisations were numerous at local level.

Policy-making is also a dynamic process, with a set of systems and actors in place for the ongoing modification of policies over time. Government policy is defined in the five-year programmes for government, drawn up either before a general election, or shortly thereafter by the successful combination of parties that enter government. This may, or may not, include reference to policies for older people. In addition to policy determined by the electoral cycle, policies for older people may be evident in the national partnership agreement, an arrangement that is central to the corporatist understanding of political interaction. National agreements are three-year contracts between government and social partners that operate independently of, and may span, the electoral cycle. National partnership agreements date from 1987 (*Programme for National Recovery*) to the present. The current programme is *Toward 2016* (2006–16). National partnership agreements are generally more detailed than programmes for government. They are also monitored more intensively, the social partners meeting four times a year to review them, supplemented, in some agreements, by working groups. The nature and structures of these agreements have differed, but agreements have typically outlined the range of government commitments to economic and social policy across a broad range of fronts for the periods concerned, including policy for older people.

Toward 2016, the ten-year framework agreement covering 2006–2016, included six pages of commitments to improve the situation of older people, covering pensions and income support, long-term care services, housing, accommodation, mobility, health care, home-support packages and, breaking new ground, a series of polices for older people in employment (Department of the Taoiseach, 2006). The policy trends evident in *Toward 2016* were extended in the subsequent *Programme for Government* agreed between the three-party coalition of June 2007, where there was a two-page section, 'Better supports for older people', giving commitments regarding the improvement of pensions (€300 a week by 2012); the retraining of older workers; services to enable older people to stay in their own home; a national positive ageing strategy; consideration of an ombudsman for older people; and making the minister of state responsible for older people part of the cabinet subcommittee on social inclusion (Department of the Taoiseach, 2007).

The question 'Who are the social partners?' has been key in social policy in Ireland in recent years and this is especially pertinent in the case of older people. In Chapter 5, we noted how social partnership had been extended from the traditional groups of employers and trades unions to voluntary and community organisations. Those participating in the pillar were determined by a mixture of application and government selection and approval. *Partnership 2000*, which operated from 1996 to 1999, included as a pillar member the Community Platform, a coalition of twenty or more voluntary and community organisations, and these included Age Action Ireland and the Irish Association of Older People. Following the rejection of *Sustaining Progress* by a majority of the members of the Community Platform, the government reconstituted the voluntary and community platform with six individual members (for example, Society of St Vincent de Paul) and six strands. One of the strands was designated 'older people' and this comprised both Age Action Ireland and the Irish Senior Citizens Parliament. Both Age Action Ireland and the Irish Association of Older People also remained as members of the Community Platform, although the platform was now outside the national social partnership structure.[2]

The voluntary and community sector also has places on the National Economic and Social Forum (NESF). In the first NESF, a seat was allocated to the Irish Senior Citizens Parliament, and in the second NESF, a seat was shared between the Irish Senior Citizens Parliament and Age Action Ireland. The National Economic and Social Forum published a policy document specific to the needs of older people, *Equality Policies for Older People — Implementation Issues*, NESF, 2003a) and, following a wide consultation, presented a wide-ranging review of policies for older people, *Care for Older People* (NESF, 2005). Here, a project team of twelve, representative of NESF, was formed to guide the project. Three seats were allocated to the voluntary and community sector and these went to Age Action Ireland, the Conference of Religious in Ireland and a leading disability organisation. The sector had what was, in effect, a fourth seat, because the Irish Senior Citizens Parliament took a trade union seat. The National Council on Ageing and Older People was also invited to join the project team. NESF appealed for submissions for the policy report, receiving 140, double the normal number for such an exercise, and these

---

2   For a detailed discussion of the role of the voluntary and community 'pillar' in the Irish national partnership, see Larragy (2006).

had a strong influence in shaping the draft policy report. NESF invited submissions from the sector and also invited some organisations to make oral submissions (for example, Age Action Ireland, Age and Opportunity). The draft was shared at a plenary meeting of NESF, to which those who had made submissions were invited, along with government departments, the Health Service Executive and the research community. Some groups working with older people were also met separately, for example those working in social housing for older people.

The NESF report, *Care for Older People* (2006), not only provided an opportunity for policies for older people to be reshaped, but was a test for the corporatist model of policy-making and an opportunity for voluntary and community organisations to show how they could contribute to policy. Commentators on the NESF process believe that the older people's organisations made a highly effective contribution there, arguing their case successfully. From a policy-development perspective, NESF had several advantages. First, it had the advantage of including many government departments, broadening older people's issues outside its traditional home in the Department of Health. This, in turn, broadened policy on older people to wider national social policy values, objectives and visions, as well as the mechanisms of government and public administration. Second, it engaged a dialogue of not just government departments and NGOs, but members of the Oireachtas as well, and several contributed actively. There were, of course, some disadvantages to the NESF approach. Procedures required that the draft report be circulated to government departments for comment. Whilst this might improve the 'buy-in' to the report, it also gives these departments the opportunity to dilute the report and gave self-protective departments the opportunities to avoid criticism.

In the Oireachtas, there is neither a parliamentary group nor a committee responsible for older people. Oireachtas committees tend to follow departmental dividing lines. Policy for older people accordingly falls under the aegis of the joint committee on health and children. Each party has a health spokesperson and that brief normally covers policy for older people. In practice, the number of deputies and senators prominent on issues affecting older people is limited to these spokespersons and a small number of others, including independent members (one, Jerry Cowley, had an association with older people's issues in the west and was a deputy for 2002–07).

Returning to our model at the start of our chapter, we can therefore construct:

- A pluralist model, in which national voluntary organisations compete around the principal policy-making body, the Department of Health,

and the ancillary bodies concerned with the welfare of older people (for example, the National Council on Ageing and Older People)
- A corporatist model, in which national organisations representing older people work through national social partnership (*Toward 2016*) and its ancillary institutions (for example, NESF)
- A policy community, defined vertically from the Department of Health through state and advisory agencies, the professions and services, through the voluntary and community groups, a stable community sharing a common view of the welfare of the elderly, marked only by occasional disputes over the nature of implementation.

The model of the policy community has a special appeal in this area of policy-making. We have already noted how there is little difference in the policies promoted by government, on the one hand, and those promoted by voluntary and community organisations, on the other. Indeed, in most respects, they converge. While it is true that many voluntary and community groups would like to see a shift toward rights and systems to ensure that the voice of older people be heard, they take little exception to existing, stated policies. Many NGOs stressed that government policies for older people had, broadly speaking, the right philosophy and sentiments, but they were not resourced or implemented consistently. The main issues arise around implementation, and here the government attracts criticism for its inability or slowness actually to carry into effect its own stated values, priorities and policies. On the nongovernmental side, there is little difference in the policies advocated by the different organisations, the differences being principally in style, with Age Action Ireland being marked for its stridency.

Next, we review the experience of voluntary and community organisations in the process of policy-making, with, where appropriate, reference to these models.

The experience of participation in policy-making

How do the various individual organisations interact with the political system and what is their experience of doing so? What is the perception of observers of that experience? Here, we return to the organisations introduced in Chapter 5 and sketched in Appendix A.2, but focus entirely on their policy work.

The Department of Health and Children is regarded as the central focus for influencing national policies in respect of older people. This poses an early problem, because the department presents a remarkably small target around which groups compete, for the older persons section has only a small staff of seven (7.1), none of whom are specialists or analysts of the situation of older people. Little of their time is devoted to policy-making per se, for historically they have spent their time handling grant applications and drafting replies to parliamentary questions. This problem of low departmental policy-making capacity was identified as an issue thirty years ago by Power (1978), who recommended that experts in the welfare of older people be appointed to the Department of Health. This does not appear to have been done.

The very location of policy-making for older people within the Department of Health and Children has been questioned by Age Action Ireland. Siting the locus of policy-making in this department means that the welfare of older people is inevitably seen through a narrow, medical, health-related, social-services paradigm. Accordingly, Age Action Ireland had proposed the relocation of this policy community to the Department of the Taoiseach, where there should be a senior citizens unit to mainstream older people's issues across all government departments, with, as an enforcer, an ombudsman for services for older people (Murray, 2006).

Earlier chapters noted the convergence of policies between those advocated by voluntary and community organisations and those articulated by government policy, from *Care of the Aged* to *The Years Ahead*. Where there have been disagreements, these have been around implementation, resources and emphasis, rather than concepts, priorities or values. The existence of a policy community around the Department of Health, the nongovernmental community, the National Council on Ageing and Older People, can therefore be postulated. Evidence for this may be seen in the debate of the *Care for Older People* report of the NESF (2006), where this policy community was at one in pressing a united case against the Department of Finance, which sought restraint in public spending on the welfare of older people.

Having said that, there is abundant evidence of barriers within and around this policy community and its parts, where some of the issues around the pluralist model are relevant. Age Action Ireland fulfils Grant's classic definition of an outsider group wishing to be more inside, but still behaving as an outsider group. Age Action Ireland has asked on numerous occasions for representation on the National Council on Ageing and Older People, but this has never been accepted, a very evident case of 'access denied'. Indeed, the voluntary and community sector presence there, whilst far from absent, has always been very limited. This rejection may press Age Action into behaviour that is sometimes seen within government as 'too pushy', 'noisy', even 'aggressive'. Age Action occupies a well-worn position within the political system of being both 'in' and 'out': on the one hand, anxious to influence; on the other, desiring to assert its independence, evade capture and maintain its credibility with its constituency.

For this, it is admired, several commenting on its media profile: it 'says the things that need to be said' about older people.

The second point for influencing decision-making in the area of older people has been the health boards. As we know, the health boards did not have a structured system for making policy with voluntary and community organisations working with older people — indeed, health boards were extremely resistant to doing so, and recommendation after recommendation for fora or similar structured relationships was ignored or undermined successfully.

The main point of contact between the health boards and voluntary and community organisations was with directors of care for services for older people (other terms were also used, such as older persons service co-ordinators or service managers), and these tended to concern funding, details of services and individual cases. Informal discussions might be held concerning Section 65 grants, but few had any policy interface with these groups at all. Health boards did, from time to time, call in voluntary and community organisations to explain future developments in services, but always well after the decisions had been taken. It is fair to say that only a few local voluntary and community organisations actively sought such a dialogue, but many others may have been dissuaded from what they heard of the experience of others. In effect, the health board forced voluntary and community organisations to be, in Grant's terminology 'outsider' groups, and was not prepared to make a policy community with them at regional level. Under the Health Service Executive, voluntary and community organisations now deal with thirty-two Local Health Officers (LHOs) and it is too early to know anything significant about that relationship.

The third point of influence between voluntary and community organisations, on the one hand, and the state, on the other, has been with the broad range of agencies and institutions that deal with older people's issues from time to time, but are not specifically devoted to them. These range from other government departments to state agencies, from the state's corporatist infrastructure (for example, NESC, NESF, partnership structures) to the Oireachtas and its committees.

Finally, how are these groups perceived? Although this might come as a surprise to them, on the statutory side, the national organisations working with older people are well regarded. They are considered to be knowledgeable, mature, sharp, alert, well grounded and effective, and they make a high-quality contribution. They are considered well able to hold their ground. The two most visible are universally considered to be the Irish Senior Citizens Parliament and Age Action Ireland. In addition, the Carers Association appears to be well regarded in governmental circles for its clarity of presentation, businesslike approach and carefully thought-out proposals. The Irish Senior Citizens Parliament is perceived to have an intimate, realistic and well-grounded knowledge of income issues affecting older people, and to have excellent contacts in the political system, whereas Age Action is considered to have a broader policy interest and to be much sharper in its dealings with the media. The Parliament is considered to be well connected to the political system and able to get access to more ministers quicker than anyone else. It is omnipresent, always at conferences and events. Age Action Ireland is regarded as the most militant, and possibly overambitious in its proposals. At the same time, it is respected: 'That's the job it is supposed to do and it does it well.' Statutory bodies appear to be well aware of the differences between the various voluntary and community organisations and the issues of territory between them.

Conclusions: reaching a tipping point?

An important question to address is: how effective have these groups been in influencing the policy process? In Ireland, the question extends to the participation of voluntary and community organisations in the social partnership structures as a whole. Larragy (2006) points out that in this context, the extent of social inequality in Ireland has not noticeably narrowed since the early 1990s, before the voluntary and community pillar was established. And we have shown, in Chapter 3, the extent to which the relative position of older people in Irish society has worsened significantly in the same period, a pattern repeated nowhere else in the EU.

In Northern Ireland, where questions of taxation and income redistribution are effectively off the agenda so far as local influence is concerned, the issues appear rather different. The jurisdiction's primary legislative basis, the Northern Ireland Act 1998, which has a function analogous to a constitution in a nation state, adumbrates and defines older people as a group with claims on the fairness of public administration, and this has structured a set of legally defined structures of engagement between older people's organisations and the monitoring and review process governing the operation of these group rights. But this has little implication for other areas of policy. Even where policy communities have been established, for example the process that led to the adoption of the older people's and the carers' strategies, it has remained difficult for organisations to influence the implementation of the strategies' goals and objectives.

Measuring the effectiveness of pressure groups is notoriously difficult. Effectiveness is a function of both the capacity of movements and groups to mobilise and organise resources and the openness or otherwise of the political environment in which they seek to operate. Pressure groups must reach a critical mass of staff, resources, skills and membership mobilisation (density) in order to wield effective and sustained influence on the political system (Grant, 2000).

In Ireland, pressure groups for older people have a relatively limited density. The overall resources available for these functions, even if they are used imaginatively, are, by any objective standards, low, as Chapter 5 showed. Even making allowance for the smaller and more intimate political system compared to Britain, voluntary and community organisations in Ireland may still fall short of reaching that critical mass. Linking this discussion to the pen portraits of organisations, one is struck by how much some national organisations have done with so little.[3] National voluntary organisations working with older people have found it extremely difficult to attract resources to carry out policy work, although easier to attract funding for educational, training and service activities. An example is the National Federation of Pensioner Associations, which, although it has actively presented the situation of older people to government since the 1970s, did not attract an office grant until this century and receives funding of only €10,000 a year.

In Northern Ireland, the density of organisations is very similar, although the infrastructure would appear better funded and more formally organised. However, even here there has been a limited capacity for formal policy work. The circumstances of direct rule, coupled with the very small size of the jurisdiction, have favoured the establishment of close-knit policy communities involving civil servants and elites within the voluntary and community sector, but in the case of older people, overlapping functions among different organisations and relatively low resources have reduced their impact.

Governments in both jurisdictions have used policy communities and, to a lesser extent, corporatist structures to manage policy-making for older people, and there are examples of both in both cases. In both cases, policy communities constructed to develop policy are, however, hamstrung by the inability of older people's organisations to influence implementation. This is particularly the case with health and social care, the policy area with the biggest budget and perhaps the area in which older people have the biggest potential stake. In Ireland, there is clearly a policy community around older people's issues, revolving around a remarkably small core in the Department of Health and Children, where there is a broad agreement on values, issues and priorities with state agencies, nongovernmental organisations and elected representatives, though not necessarily around implementation. Some newer issues have gradually intruded on to this policy community's agenda, notably discrimination, but an issue that has failed to make significant progress is that of consultative systems for older

---

3   These are set out in Appendix A.2

people. A key point to note, though, is that the officials of the Department of Finance are not part of this policy community.

A striking feature of the policy-making work of voluntary and community organisations working with older people in Ireland is the permeability of the political environment at national level. All the voluntary and community organisations encountered in this study commented on the accessibility of the Department of Health and Children, its officials, members of the Oireachtas and others concerned at national level with the welfare of older people. Voluntary and community organisations had little difficulty penetrating the political system or in getting access to departmental officials (indeed, the Parliament may have developed the technique to an art form). Some, indeed, commented that there were more invitations to participate in advisory groups than they had the capacity to meet. There are some exceptions to this, where gate-keeping was very evident. First, government ministers have been remarkably slow to people the National Council on Ageing and Older People with representatives of the non-governmental sector, suggesting that it is far from the powerless body it is sometimes alleged to be. Second, the Department of Finance appears to put itself out of the orbit of engagement of the nongovernmental community, from which distance it exerts its (in the NGOs' view) baleful influence. Third, the health service at regional level has successfully resisted, for over a generation, the idea of a culture of structured engagement with the nongovernmental sector concerned with older people. Here there is no engagement at the level of policy implementation.

This pattern is quite clearly replicated in Northern Ireland. The development of overall older people's policy has been driven by an open policy community, in which the key older people's organisations played a leading role, prompting the formal adoption of a far-reaching and quite radical set of policy aspirations. A similar process could be observed in respect to carers' policies. Yet in both, the influence of these organisations has been resisted in the structures designed to implement health and social care policies, the arena where most money is spent. As we have seen, these structures appear designed to keep organised representation by stakeholder groups other than professionals out of the picture altogether.

The reason is the shift in governance paradigm between policy design and implementation. In the former, open policy communities are adopted to make maximum use of the knowledge within the voluntary and community sector, while at the same time using their participation as a means of legitimising policy. Yet delivery of policy, particularly in the case of health and social care where huge sums of public money are involved, is carried out through governance by rational operational processes valuing managerialism, audit and central control. Here voluntary organisations are constructed primarily as deliverers of services to given specifications.

If we add in the legal framework offered by Section 75 of the Northern Ireland Act, we have a fivefold typology of types of engagement. The ways in which these are deployed in both parts of Ireland are summarised in Table 6.2.

Table 6.2: A typology of government/voluntary-sector engagement on older people's issues in Ireland, north and south

Model	Example	Treatment of pensioner group rights	Influence in Ireland, north and south
Legal framework defining both group identity and group rights	Section 75 of the 1998 Northern Ireland Act	Built into the system of monitoring and review, creating group-identity structures that facilitate engagement	Northern Ireland only
Corporatist	National advisory boards for the welfare of older people — Belgium, Netherlands, Germany, France. National partnership structures in Ireland	Pensioner groups have legislated rights of access to policy-making	Present in Ireland, but weaker in Northern Ireland. Pensioner representation weak in both
'New public management', rational, operational	The governance of health and social care	Not recognised. Patients/clients/users seen either as consumers or as a matter for professional good practice	Strong in both jurisdictions
Iterative, open policy communities	Health-promotion strategy; ageing in an inclusive society (PSI working group, NI). Policy-making in Dept of Health and Children (RoI)	Not formally recognised, but space left for entrepreneurially driven engagement	Present in policy-making, but absent in implementation in both parts of Ireland

A further consideration concerns the way in which voluntary organisations working with older people in both Irish jurisdictions have bought into a deferential and, by European standards, not especially assertive culture (Age Action Ireland and Age Concern NI are perhaps the exception). In Ireland, medium-level organisations are quiescent, and several inter-viewees commented on the absence of smaller, in-your-face pioneering groups of the type represented by ALONE in the 1980s. The culture of the Irish political system rejects attitudinal assertiveness, as witnessed by repeated put-down remarks on the militancy of Age Action Ireland and the commending of organisations that follow a more deferential approach. The situation in which voluntary and community organisations find themselves is one in which the expectations of the people whom they represent are remarkably low, a feature noticed by Power a generation ago (1978).

In Northern Ireland, perhaps as a legacy of the 'troubles', where speaking out of turn might too easily be misinterpreted, and where, in a divided society, cross-community coalitions around issues like ageing have to be sustained with care, there is a strong culture of 'not being political' particularly among welfare-oriented voluntary organisations (Acheson, Cairns, Stringer and Williamson, 2007). In such societies, establishing assertive social movements around issues like ageing is very difficult. Even the disability sector has remained quiet and fairly low key in contrast with other European countries (Acheson 2003).

Here we see Lukes' (1974) third dimension of power in operation. Policy discourse on older people in Ireland excludes consideration of how to ensure a participative voice for older people in the design of those aspects of their lives that matter most to them, and this marks it as quite out of line with continental European models. Hodgins and Greve (2004a) suggest that the state's problem with voluntarism may lie at the heart of this problem. Citing the 'shopping, visiting and transport' refrain (*Quality and Fairness — A Health System for You*, 2001), they argue that the state approach to voluntarism in services for older people relies on untested assumptions about their superior quality, cost and value. Above all, they say, 'economy is never far from the minds of policy-makers, whether that be expressed as representing savings in public spending (*Care of the Aged*) or 'cost effectiveness' (*The Years Ahead*).

Furthermore, the absence of the Department of Finance from corporatist structures and policy communities populated by older people's orga-nisations simply reinforces the way policy-making is subject to underlying assumptions about taxation and preserving a climate conducive to private-sector investment. Services for the elderly have been guided by ageist assumptions about their being passive recipients of services, meaning that they are unlikely to be consulted about their needs, and are regarded as one of many 'problem' groups among a hierarchy of problem groups. Although Hodgins and Greve do not say it, such an approach would neither expect nor, probably, welcome an advocacy approach being taken by these 'cost-effective' services.

Although there are individual national voluntary organisations that are assertive, the nongovernmental sector working with older people in Ireland now contrasts dramatically with the disability sector, which has been radicalised across its broad range, notwithstanding the shared common interests (for example, services around caring). It also contrasts with the much more mature voluntary sector working with older people in continental Europe, which has the advantage of operating in a more benign political and consultative climate.

A rather similar situation is discernable in Northern Ireland. The rules of the participation game are in the end set by the UK Treasury, which has control over taxation and redistribution. In 2002, the Treasury published a cross-cutting review of the voluntary sector, which marked a distinct shift towards a discourse on voluntary action more interested in efficient delivery of public services than civic participation (Osborne and McLaughlin, 2004), further reinforcing the power of the rational means-end paradigm of government.

At the end of Chapter 1, following our examination of the voluntary sector working with older people in continental Europe, we asked whether we would find, in either part of Ireland, new social movements working with older people, a mobilisation of older people and a political engagement with the state at local and regional level. Instead we have found an abundance of largely small-scale voluntary action, variable in intensity, and a political engagement whose permeability has obscured the lack of a structured participation by an assertive social movement of older people. But as older people reach greater numbers in the population, will a tipping point be reached in which this situation changes?

7

The Comparison and Some Conclusions

At this stage, it is important to sum up and compare the similarities and differences in the voluntary and community sector working with older people in both parts of the island.

Important differences are apparent in the first instance. Voluntary and community organisations in Northern Ireland must try to influence two governments: that in Westminster, which has overall responsibility for social policy in general and older people in particular; and the administration in Belfast, which operated largely under direct rule from 1972 but intermittently under devolved government from 1998, more permanently so since 2007, and which has some administrative flexibility within the broader policy framework. In the Republic, voluntary and community organisations face a unitary political system, although, as we have seen, that has not necessarily made their task any easier. There remain clear differences in the historical development and in the administration of the two welfare regimes under which the two voluntary and community sectors must operate, Northern Ireland having a welfare state and national health service from 1949, and the Republic slowly building an incremental social policy but developing a limited, two-tier health service.

As our earlier research showed, this environment had considerable bearing on the voluntary and community sector (Acheson et al., 2004). The more formal specification of the state's role and responsibilities, particularly in social welfare in Northern Ireland, tended in the end to create a more organised environment for the growth of the voluntary sector and a clearer policy context for relationships between the state and the sector to be conducted than was the case in the Republic. Ireland's voluntary sector, accordingly, lagged behind in its size, density, maturity and organisational form. In the course of time, Ireland's welfare state grew as an imitator of that of Britain, the role of its voluntary and community sector strengthened accordingly. Still, an examination of key landmark dates is revealing. Whereas the Northern Ireland Council for Social Services dates to 1938, its comparator body in Ireland, the National Social Services Council, was not established until 1970. The Northern Ireland Council for Voluntary Action was established as a representative body for the voluntary sector there in

1984; a comparable event in Ireland has yet to happen. NICSS had a Standing Committee for Older People from the late 1940s; Ireland's National Council for the Elderly was not established until 1990.

Partly as a result of rapid economic development in Ireland, some form of parity between the two welfare states (though not the health service) may now have been reached, and 2007 saw the interesting spectacle of 'free travel' being introduced in Northern Ireland, an unusual (and possibly unique) example of the social policy from the south spilling over into the north. Both old-age pensions and carers' allowances are now more generous in Ireland than in the UK. Health services apart, the actual sets of policies of the two governments, regarding older people, appear now to be broadly similar and inspired by generally similar values and principles (Chapters 2 and 3). Trends in pension systems, possibly the most important element of public policy to affect older people, follow a similar broad trend of tilting the balance of provision from public to private. If we examine a broad range of key policy documents, there is convergence across most of them, such as positive ageing, increasing employment for older workers and emphasising care in the community in preference to institutional provision. In a European context, both Ireland and the UK share rather similar welfare regimes.

Despite their differences, though, both jurisdictions have tended to avoid the structures whereby older people's organisations have a consultative role with the state at local level, which we identified in Chapter 1 as an important feature of other European countries, such as Germany, the Netherlands and Sweden. Although both the UK and Ireland have reasonably permeable political systems, both have proven resistant to formal consultative structures for older people, the Republic especially so. This may be the result of both a common political culture and a shared model of neo-liberal socioeconomic development, a model increasingly remarked on by European commentators, which sees Britain and Ireland as quite apart from the continental model. In Chapter 1, we commented on how both countries shared, in social policy, more similarities than differences.

Nor is the situation of older people themselves that different. Although the proportions of older people over sixty-five in the population are four percentage points adrift (11 per cent in the Republic, 16 per cent in Northern Ireland), those proportions are expected to grow at a similar rate over the first half of this century. The proportion living in income poverty is similar, 27.1 per cent in the Republic (Prunty, 2007), 20 per cent in Northern Ireland (Kenway et al., 2006). Older women are disproportionately affected compared to men. Looking at non-income aspects of poverty, poor-quality housing is, in both jurisdictions, the area of life in which disadvantage impacts most severely for older people. Studies of older people in both parts of the island suggest that their social situation is broadly similar. Most report good health. Although most have reasonably good social connections, there is evidence that a distinct minority (around a fifth in both) experiences social isolation.

Whatever these similarities and differences, we can now observe a certain level of formalisation of the voluntary and community sector in both parts of the island. In Northern Ireland, three major regional voluntary organisations emerged during the 1980s: Help the Aged, the Pensioners Convention and Age Concern (1984 and 1986). In Ireland, two major national voluntary organisations emerged a decade later but also quite close in time, Age Action Ireland (which was partly modelled on the UK example of Age Concern) and the Senior Citizens Parliament. Both jurisdictions now feature two to three leading voluntary organisations of remarkably similar form, which play an important role in shaping the debate on the welfare of older people, although the northern organisations are much larger in staffing and other resources.

At the other end of the scale is the local level. Both jurisdictions appear to have large numbers of very small organisations working with older people. This is especially evident if we look at the bodies known, in the south, to have received HSE funding, but it is also a feature of the voluntary sector working with older people in the north. If we ask ourselves the question, 'What is the typical organisation working with older people in both parts of Ireland?' the answer is, in both cases, a small, local organisation, carrying out a similar range of social, recreational and positive ageing functions, with people travelling a relatively short distance to its functions. Our survey work showed that many organisations working with older people were quite recent in origin, had a small income, took advantage of a number of income sources, do not employ paid staff and do not engage in lobbying work. In this key area of voluntary-sector activity, there is little difference between the two.

If we compare our two surveys, we get the comparisons illustrated in Table 7.1.

There are some differences here, but the similarities are more evident, uncannily so in some cases. In both cases:

- Density has grown markedly from the 1990s.
- Over half the organisations are small in financial size (half less than £2,000 in Northern Ireland, half less than €5,000 in the Republic). The income distribution is broadly similar.
- Health services are a significant funder: less than half in the north, more than half in the south.
- The proportion without staff is almost identical: 73 per cent in the Republic, 73.5 per cent in Northern Ireland.

Table 7.1: Summary comparisons in voluntary action and ageing in Ireland, north and south

	Northern Ireland	Ireland
Age of formation	5 per cent prior to 1970 61.4 per cent since 1990	8.5 per cent prior to 1970 58 per cent since 1990
Income	17 per cent over £50,000 50.2 per cent less than £2,000	19 per cent more than €50,000 50.9 per cent less than €5,000
Sources of income	Health service 40 per cent	Health service 55 per cent
Staffing	73.5 per cent no staff	73 per cent no staff
Affiliated to networks	56.4 per cent	43 per cent
Consulted by government	18.3 per cent: never 27.5 per cent: occasionally 20 per cent: regularly, informally 27.3 per cent: formally represented	37 per cent: never 34 per cent: occasionally 14 per cent: regularly, informally 15 per cent: formally represented
Cross-Border networks	5 per cent	8.6 per cent

Those differences, where they exist, tend to reflect the higher level of voluntary-sector development and greater consultation with government (for example, level of affiliation, level of consultation). A significant funding source in Northern Ireland is the lottery, which in Ireland is absorbed into government funding (including the health services) and does not function as an independent fund.

We will now return to differences. A feature of the voluntary sector in Northern Ireland, which is absent in Ireland, is that of the subregional network. Northern Ireland, as Chapter 4 showed, is well endowed by networks of older people's organisations, twelve being noted, a phenomenon absent in the south. This may be a function of the different scale of the two jurisdictions, but it could also be a feature of the general preparedness of the government in Northern Ireland to invest in voluntary and community-sector infrastructure and a more fully articulated policy environment, an imperative that has been poorly understood by Irish governments. A second difference evident in the voluntary and community sector is the presence, in Northern Ireland, of the Age Sector Reference Group

(ASRG). This has no direct comparator in Ireland. The group makes possible the presentation, to government in Northern Ireland, of a coherent perspective by voluntary and community organisations working with older people. Although the objectives of equality legislation in Northern Ireland and Ireland are not that different, Section 75 of the Northern Ireland Act set down more demanding consultative requirements on how government relates to the voluntary sector. The ASRG has not only enabled that equality dialogue between the sector and government to take place at a high and structured level, but appears to have had an important secondary benefit of defusing some tensions between the leading voluntary-sector organisations clustered around government. It has also been politically effective on a number of specific issues, as the campaign on water charges illustrated. Equality legislation in Ireland has not created equivalent openings.

It is difficult to measure how effective the advocacy record of the respective voluntary and community sectors is. Looking at broader political and distributional issues, the record is discouraging. Activism in Northern Ireland has so far had little purchase on national UK concerns, notably the attempt to reinstate the link between pensions and earnings, while within Northern Ireland its impact on social care administration has also been limited. In Ireland, the income situation of older people, especially in respect of poverty and pensions, has declined markedly since 1987, despite greater mobilisation in the voluntary and community sector working with older people and despite the adoption in Ireland of European-inspired corporatist social partnership which delivered considerable gains to older Europeans.

In our earlier study, we found that the European Union was an important shaper of social policy in general and, albeit indirectly, the voluntary and community sector in particular (Acheson, Harvey, Kearney and Williamson, 2004; Acheson and Williamson, 2007). This is much less evident in the sphere of older people. There appear to be two reasons. First, European competence in the area of policy for older people is much less well developed and a relatively limited and recent field of competence (Treaties of Amsterdam, 1997 (discrimination) and Nice, 2001 (pensions)). Second, because of this, the ability of the European Union to fund organisations working with older people has been restricted. Even since then, funding has been confined to a relatively narrow band of sectors and activities, principally action against poverty and discrimination. Where this has happened, though, there is evidence of some effectiveness. Although cause and effect may be difficult to separate, EU funding for initiatives against discrimination and for a more positive role for older workers, through, for example, the EQUAL programme, coincided with increased prominence being given to issues of discrimination against older people and positive policies for the support of older people.

Whilst the European Union role has been relatively absent as a funder, this has not been the case in the area of philanthropy. Here, Atlantic Philanthropies has played an active role in supporting the voluntary and community sector working with older people, both north and south. The resources available to Atlantic Philanthropies dwarf those of other trust and philanthropic funders, and the foundation's decision, in 2004, to make older people one of four overriding priorities for ten years will have a significant effect on the evolution and development of the voluntary and community sector in both parts of the island. In the south, Atlantic Philanthropies took the decision to concentrate its support on, as we noted, a number of key organisations. Its support was important, not only for the substantial amount of funding involved, but also for the purpose for which funding was provided — in the case of Ireland, to build up and develop a small number of leading organisations.

In Chapter 6, we spoke of a tipping point, which might make voluntary and community organisations working with older people significantly more effective on the policies affecting this important part of the community. Granted the growing demographic, social and labour-market importance of older people in both jurisdictions, this is an important issue to test. It is possible that the next decade will see, along parallel paths, the growing significance of older people north and south matched by a more mobilised and effective voluntary and community sector working for them and with them.

The corporatist structures of governance in Ireland and the use of policy communities both there and in Northern Ireland are indicative of a more general move away from centralised 'command and control' systems of government in contemporary welfare states. But as our evidence suggests, the role and reach of voluntary organisations in a welfare field such as older people are subject to continuous negotiation and can expand and contract depending on the function and purpose of particular government institutions.

What does the Irish case say about the broader question of how voluntary action in a core welfare field is changing in the light of larger trends in welfare-state change? The similarities and differences between the two jurisdictions on the island are instructive. Although public health services remain remarkably underdeveloped in Ireland against European norms, reflected in the relatively very low levels of public expenditure, otherwise Ireland and Northern Ireland as an integrated part of the UK welfare state share similar welfare regimes, particularly in the extent to which they rely on private solutions to the distribution of welfare goods and the way in which they privilege wealth creation in the private sector in their respective political economies.

The similarities in the structure of voluntary action in the field of ageing are indicative of these similarities in political economies of welfare working out in practice. We speculate that the peculiar combination of a dense base of local organisations, mobilising thousands of older people in their activities, which nevertheless has a marginal impact on public policy, and the management of those public services on which old people rely is a particular feature of welfare regimes of this type. One hypothesis is that family-based welfare systems have come under increasing pressure and that this has incentivised older people into collective activity with a strong social and recreational focus. This has been aided by the increasing levels of health and, for some, wealth among retired people, both of which have helped to increase the range of activities engaged in.

Data on public attitudes to ageing throw an intriguing light on, and help to explain, this situation. Traditional social movement theory has held that mobilisation depends to a degree on the pre-existence of a perceived grievance (Smelser, 1962). In this view, objective conditions have to be accompanied by a perception of a grievance about these conditions. Smelser's approach fell out of favour for many years, but there has been a more recent revival of interest in the role of perceptions in shaping grievances and opportunities for collective action (McAdam, Tarrow and Tilly, 2001; Koopmans and Statham, 1999; Crossley, 2002). The evidence we have suggests that perceptions of older people in both Irish jurisdictions, about both how they are treated and how they view the potential for organising, would not predict a strong social movement, although there is somewhat more dissatisfaction in the north than in the south (Evason, Dowds and Devine, 2004). Thus in the north over 70 per cent of people between the ages of sixty and seventy-four feel that 'the state is not doing enough' while in the south, only just over 50 per cent of people between the ages of sixty-four and seventy-four feel the same way. People in their early sixties were reported as feeling rather more strongly. But interestingly people over sixty were no more aggrieved than were younger adults in either jurisdiction. Whilst there appears to be a generally shared feeling of dissatisfaction, it does not seem to be specific to older people themselves and thus does not appear to be related in people's minds to their age.

When we look at specific issues, however, it is apparent that, apart from a fear of crime, which was of generally high concern, older people in both jurisdictions were more likely to focus on loneliness than any other issue, including making ends meet. Fear of loneliness appeared higher in the south than the north, but only marginally so; in both cases, over 65 per cent listed it as one of the main issues facing older people (Evason, Dowds and Devine, 2004).

These data illuminate the processes that may underlie the development of voluntary action among older people in Ireland, north and south. An important strand in social movement theorising has been the view that successful mobilising is facilitated by the existence or otherwise of sets of opportunities in the political environment, sometimes referred to as political opportunity structure.

Important in this view are the relative openness of the political system and the availability of elite allies (McAdam, 1996). Not only have there to be issues that are felt to be amenable to change through collective action, but the view that they can be thus changed must be shared by at least some elite allies, and the political system must be open to pressure on the issue through such means. The one issue of this type in which action might be considered viable, in that over 50 per cent of older people in both Irish jurisdictions identified it — the inability to make ends meet — is exactly an issue to which political systems are least open and elite allies most difficult to recruit. This is partly because of the power of older people as a lobby relative to political interests wishing to keep taxation low, but also because of the perceptual gap between personal budgetary constraints and national taxation and spending policies, which is just too large to motivate people to organise (Bagguley, 1994). It is not perceived as the kind of grievance that collective action might have a realistic chance of addressing.

The result of this process can be seen in a second shared feature to which we can draw attention — the level of disconnection that there is between the mass base and political influence, which is relatively weak in both Irish jurisdictions, when compared to some other European countries. The increasing use of policy communities in both jurisdictions and the presence of older people's organisations in national corporatist partnership structures in Ireland have not translated into a strong political impact in either case. The partnership structures that have been established have, by and large, been as a result of government initiatives, albeit supported by the emergence of effective leadership organisations within the voluntary sector with roots in the grass-roots mobilisation of older people's groups.

A striking feature of the situation in Ireland is the high level of consensus around policy between elites within government and national voluntary organisations, with most disquiet being expressed around the implementation of policy. Given the decline in the relative status of older people over the past fifteen years, this is remarkable, but perhaps explicable in the light of the private nature of the motivations of those older people involved in organisations at local level, and the high levels of assent among the general population to the economic model that has secured the very high levels of growth in the economy, as evidenced by voting patterns in recent general elections.

The higher levels of development of regional infrastructure bodies in Northern Ireland and the greater array of formal mechanisms of engagement with state agencies than is the case in Ireland are indicative of the much earlier and more formal involvement of the state in health and welfare provision and a recognition from the late 1970s onwards that a more formal relationship with the voluntary and community sector would be beneficial. In the light of current trends and the clear UK national consensus, supporting a liberal welfare state that drives underlying policy on taxation and redistribution, it should perhaps be best understood as a historic effect embedded in a particular institutional and political path.

The evidence we have presented illustrates the way in which a particular political economy of welfare structures voluntary action in a particular welfare field that is embedded in a set of relations between the state, market and informal patterns of the production and distribution of welfare goods. Thus, the similarities in the structure of voluntary action in the field of older people's welfare in the two Irish jurisdictions are evidence of similarities in the political economies of welfare that apply.

Our core argument is that the ways in which the state, the market, and informal family provision interrelate in the provision of welfare goods are very similar in both jurisdictions in Ireland. Moreover, because of the ways in which we have suggested that voluntary action on issues of ageing are embedded in these structures, it is both socially pervasive and politically weak, despite the growth in the use of formal mechanisms of engagement between the sector and state institutions.

The theoretical framework we introduced in Chapter 1 suggests a way of interpreting the link between a welfare regime that not only favours market-based welfare delivery, subject to state regulation, but also favours private solutions to public welfare issues and the particular combination of voluntary organisations that was found. A dense base of local organisations, mobilising thousands of older people in their activities, which nevertheless has a marginal impact on public policy and the management of those public services upon which old people rely, may be a particular feature of welfare regimes of this type.

Drawing on the distinction between action in the public sphere and private action (Young, 2000), and the discussion provided by Evers and Laville (2004) of the mechanisms that structure systems of welfare delivery, it is possible to suggest an explanation. The structuring of the means of meeting the human needs of older people in both Irish jurisdictions privatises personal trouble and erects a set of rules that privileges wealth creation by private actors, especially large corporations.

Flexible labour markets and long working hours are inimical to family-based support, disrupting the communicative interaction upon which family-based solidarity rests; fear of loneliness becomes the core issue around which older people seek solutions through solidarity — a private solution to a private fear. The power of the state to enforce rules that favour the market as a coordinating mechanism reinforces the power of money in a process that reinterprets welfare as the servant of the market. Collective action for social contact that is largely confined to private concerns of recreation and relief of loneliness, with a minimal presence in the public sphere of political debate, is the mobilising outcome in a welfare environment of means-tested social security and fragmented state engagement in social care.

Methodological Note

In total, 765 names and addresses were supplied for the study in Ireland. Following the elimination of duplicated names and addresses, zero grants for the year in question and unsatisfactory names or addresses, there were 348 valid groups, names and addresses, as follows:

Cavan Monaghan	17
Cork — South Lee	20
Cork — North Lee	18
Cork — West	18
Cork — North	18
Dublin — north west	10
Dublin — south west	11
Dublin — west	5
Galway	43
Kerry	21
Donegal	46
Mayo	43
Roscommon	13
Sligo	4
Tipperary — south	18
Tipperary — north	7
Waterford	7
Wexford	15
Wicklow	14

Thanks are due to the following for their responses:

Ciara Brophy, Dublin south west
Adrian Charles, Dublin south west
Frances Clifford, Tipperary north
Mary Jo Corey, Clare
Mary Clare Cotter, Cork south Lee
Michael FitzGerald, Kerry

Helen Galvin, Offaly
Melissa Johnson, Dublin north west
Carmel Kavanagh, Wexford
Bernadette Kiberd, Dublin north west
Leo Kinsella, Cavan Monaghan
Frank McDonald, Mayo
Edith Mullin, Donegal
Catherine Murphy, Cork north Lee
Frank Murphy, Roscommon
Catriona Nolan, Wicklow
Margaret O'Brien, Cork north
Jacinta O'Connell, Tipperary south
Margaret O'Donovan, Cork west
Marian O'Neill-Brennan, Tipperary south
Dan Quaid, Galway
Eimear Ryan, Dublin west
Mary Sheridan, Waterford
Carmel Taheny, Sligo
Breda Turley, Ballinasloe

In the case of Clare and Offaly, information was supplied, but without addresses was unusable.

Appendices

A.1

PROFILE OF ORGANISATIONS WORKING WITH OLDER PEOPLE, NORTHERN IRELAND

Regional bodies

The principal organisations working with older people in Northern Ireland can be divided into those that have an explicit development and policy function, Age Concern, Help the Aged, the Pensioners' Convention, the Age Sector Reference Group, the Older People's Policy Forum, and those that are primarily concerned with providing housing and/or social care services, notably ExtraCare, Belfast Central Mission, the Abbeyfield Societies, the Bryson Charitable Group, the Fold Association and Carers Northern Ireland. The first group was discussed in Chapter 4. The service-providers are profiled here.

ExtraCare Northern Ireland

ExtraCare is a charity that works in partnership with health trusts in Northern Ireland and with the Health Service Executive in Ireland. It was established in 1938 as the Belfast Hospitals' After Care Committee. In 1958, its name was changed to the Extra Care Committee for the Aged and Lonely. Today it provides assistance, support and encouragement with all personal care tasks and also provides time off for carers. The organisation employs 429 staff (386 care workers and 43 managerial staff) and, in the year to March 2007, it provided over 377,000 care hours, thereby supporting some 1,300 people to live independent lives in their own homes. In Ireland, it provided over 34,000 hours of service to older people in Counties Louth and Meath during the same period. In addition, it provides about 900 hours of care each week to the Health Service

Executive in Dublin. ExtraCare's services are provided 24 hours per day and 365 days per year and fall into the following categories: Night Help Services, Dementia Services, Domiciliary Support Schemes and Mobile Night Help Services.

In the early 1990s, ExtraCare expanded very rapidly in the context of the introduction of the Government's Care in the Community policy. In 1992, it introduced dementia services in Causeway and Craigavon and Banbridge, and, in the following year, a dementia service was introduced in Newry and Mourne, as well as the extension of a Domiciliary Support Service in Newtownabbey, Larne and Carrickfergus. In 1997, a Domiciliary Carer Respite Service was introduced in the Armagh and Dungannon Trust's area with support from the National Lottery Charities Board. In 2001, ExtraCare expanded its services into Ireland. Using the organisation's charitable funds, a Carer Respite service was introduced in County Louth and, two years later, the funding for this service was taken over by the North Eastern Health Board. Following years saw an extension of ExtraCare's services in Counties Louth and Meath and, in 2005, a rehabilitation service was commenced in County Louth.

ExtraCare has recently developed some new and innovative care projects. An example is the Rapid Response Service in the Antrim/ Ballymena area of the Northern Health and Social Care Trust. Rapid Response provides a short-term (up to two weeks) swift response to prevent inappropriate hospital admission and to expedite hospital discharge. In January 2007, Rapid Response was extended to cover East Antrim, and this was further extended to Mid-Ulster in March 2007. Six hundred clients have taken up this service since its inception. The Northern Ireland Housing Executive with Supporting People monies funds other innovative projects providing care for older people. An example is ExtraCare's warden scheme in the Rathcoole area of North Belfast, which provides both a warden and assistive technology, which is managed by Fold Telecare, a division of Fold Housing Association.

ExtraCare works closely with health and social service trusts as a voluntary provider subcontracting for services on behalf of the trusts. It spends its charitable funds on innovation and on giving additional assistance to people who cannot function on the level of assistance provided by the Government. Its Annual Report for 2005/06 deplores the fact that, despite a series of Government commitments in relation to full cost recovery (HM Treasury Cross Cutting Review, 2002, and the Gershon Efficiency Review, 2004), some of its key services still run at an unsustainable loss.

Belfast Central Mission (BCM)

Belfast Central Mission is a Methodist association that has been located in the centre of Belfast since it was established in 1889. It is one of the oldest charities in Northern Ireland. The mission is closely associated with a church congregation and is an agency of the Methodist Church. Governed by a mission committee of twenty-five to thirty people, the association employs a director and three assistant directors, of whom one has special responsibility for social care. In recent times, the mission is reaching out geographically and now has programmes as far afield as Enniskillen and Omagh, Dungannon, Armagh and Banbridge.

BCM provides social care programmes for both children and young people and also for older people. Social care work with older people includes both residential and community care. Kirk House in King's Road, Belfast, a facility that provides forty-two to forty-five places in forty flatlets, is consistently full. It is the only remaining residential facility, and BCM's former home at Carrickfergus was recently closed because of low take-up of its places, and high costs. Kirk House has mixed funding from residents who are funded by income support and personal contributions from residents and families, as well as the 'Supporting People' Programme (formerly Special Needs Management Allowance) administered by the Northern Ireland Housing Executive.

BCM's work involves a significant community services programme that includes tea dances, Christmas food parcels and a lunch club for twenty-five to thirty people. It also includes holidays at Childhaven Centre, a purpose-built centre at Millisle, which is used extensively to provide a seaside holiday for older people. Most of the staff who support these holidays are volunteers. The tea dances take place on seven occasions each year and are very popular. They involve an afternoon from 1.30 to 4.00 pm. Costs are subsidised by the Mission. Two hundred and ninety food parcels were distributed to older people at Christmas 2006.

BCM engages the help of about 160 volunteers who perform a range of tasks including street collecting, work on management committees, staffing holidays, making up food parcels and befriending the residents of Kirk House who do not have relatives who can visit. Most of the volunteers are themselves fifty and over. In May 2005, BCM was one of only two teams in Northern Ireland to receive the Queen's Award for Volunteering.

BCM sees the introduction of the Supporting People initiative as a promising new funding stream to enable it to develop new services for older people and to outreach to other areas of Northern Ireland, particularly outside Belfast. The agency is also exploring the potential of Floating Support, an initiative that is funded by the Northern Ireland Housing

Executive. This innovative programme will have a cost load of forty and is designed to support people in their own homes by providing laundry services, luncheon clubs, holidays, and so on. There is a plan to develop a laundry to provide support to homes where incontinence is a problem. BCM has an annual income of some £3,000,000, of which 75 per cent is from statutory sources, with 19 per cent from fundraising, charitable trusts, and so on. Older people account for 25 per cent of expenditure and young people for 63 per cent. Rev. Eric Gallagher, who was superintendent of BCM for many years, published an account of BCM's work with the title, *Points of Need*.

The Abbeyfield Societies in Northern Ireland
The Abbeyfield movement in Northern Ireland provides supported sheltered housing for older people in family-style accommodation. The movement began in London in 1956 and operates on a volunteer and non-profit basis. Local, independently managed societies were formed throughout the United Kingdom, including Northern Ireland. In 1981, a housing association, the Abbeyfield NI Development Society, was formed to allow local Abbeyfield societies in Northern Ireland to obtain Housing Association Grant under the Housing Order of 1976.

There are now two Abbeyfield societies operating in Northern Ireland. In 2003, thirteen local Abbeyfield societies merged with the Abbeyfield Northern Ireland Development Society to form Abbeyfield UK (NI). The Abbeyfield Belfast Society has nine houses.

Abbeyfield UK (NI) Ltd is an industrial and provident society and a registered housing association and a charity. It has nineteen houses outside Belfast (with 165 bed spaces). The Abbeyfield UK (NI) Society accommodates 137 elderly residents of whom 74 per cent are aged eighty or over, and 32 per cent are ninety or older. In the first decades of Abbeyfield work, most residents were aged between sixty-five and seventy-five. The age profile has changed over the years and now more than half the residents are aged eighty-five or over.

Abbeyfield mainly provides rented accommodation in supported sheltered houses, which are either purpose built or adapted from existing buildings with added facilities. Residents live together in houses, which normally accommodate between eight and twelve older people. Each resident has his or her own room, which can be furnished with their own furniture and other items. Each house has well-equipped bathrooms, some with special adaptations for disabled residents. Most societies are able to offer rooms with *en suite* facilities. A typical house offers: a paid house manager; call alarm systems; specialist facilities, for example, assisted baths, lifts, etc; two cooked meals a day; and a network of support from local volunteers. Residents who need some help can arrange visiting services such as a home help, chiropodist or care assistant.

The nineteen houses of the Abbeyfield UK (NI) Society are located outside Belfast and all are in the east of Northern Ireland. Most are within 50km (30 miles) of Belfast and there is a concentration of houses in the Bangor and Donaghadee area. Two houses are in Ballycastle, and Ballymoney and Portstewart have one home each. There are no Abbeyfield houses in the west of the province.

Applicants to Abbeyfield apply through the Common Selection Scheme for social housing in Northern Ireland. Residents may be eligible to receive Housing benefit and/or Supporting People funding.

The Bryson Charitable Group, Belfast

Bryson House, with its headquarters in Bedford Street, Belfast, is one of the city's oldest and largest charities. Its origins are in the Belfast Charity Organisation Society (COS), founded in 1906 following a public meeting to consider how to respond to the needs of Belfast's poor. Old-age pensions and National Health Insurance legislation had not yet been introduced. There was little, apart from the Poor Law Guardians, by way of support from the state for people in need. In 1920, the COS changed its name to Belfast Council of Social Welfare (BCSW); in 1974, it became Belfast Voluntary Welfare Society; in 1986, it was restyled as Bryson House, and, in 2006, Bryson Charitable Group. The society recently celebrated its centenary.

Throughout its long history, Bryson House has been active in meeting the needs of older people in Belfast. In 1946, the BCSW established a body to meet the needs of older people and under this initiative several Old People's Welfare Clubs were established in Belfast. Today a range of programmes responds to a wide variety of needs and the society provides a number of services that it has pioneered. These include its Home from Hospital service, established in 1980. This service was piloted in Belfast and now exists in three areas, two of which are in Belfast and one in North Down and Ards. The service provides support for six weeks for older people who have been discharged from hospital. Social workers employed by the charity work closely with discharge teams in hospitals. Another example of the work of Bryson is its domiciliary long-term care service in North and West Belfast, which sees 126 clients receiving 1,450 calls per week. In 2005/06, some 61,000 hours of care were provided, particularly to vulnerable and frail older people, mainly in personal care, food preparation and domestic tasks. In the Ards Peninsula, its Neighbourly Care Service has a focus on isolated older people and provides household support, a laundry service and a shopping service. This service is supported by the Health and Social Services Trust and provides some 15,000 hours of care each year. The laundry service commenced in the 1960s and functions in conjunction with Magheraberry Prison.

Bryson's services are funded by health and social service trusts and by its development fund. The development fund is important because it allows the charity to innovate and to experiment. Most of its services, however, are provided under contract to health and social service trusts, and Bryson is a major provider of social services to older people in Belfast and the greater Belfast region. A recent innovation is the establishment of Partnership Care West in Derry/Londonderry, which is a separate company established by Bryson, and which does some work with older people and their families. In 2005/06, it provided support to 126 frail elderly people to remain at home. Bryson Charitable Group is a useful example of a Belfast-based major and long-established charity that is working closely with the statutory sector and provides services that it has pioneered and developed.

Fold Housing Association and Fold Group
Fold Housing Association was established in 1976 and was the first registered housing association in Northern Ireland under the Housing Order of that year. With over 100 sheltered and supported housing schemes in more than fifty towns and cities throughout Northern Ireland, Fold Housing Association has nearly 4,200 tenants and residents who live in sheltered accommodation, family housing and specialist care schemes.

Fold Housing Association is part of Fold Group and is one of the leading providers of housing and care services, delivered through an independent living model. It is a not-for-profit organisation that is over-seen by a cross-community voluntary board of management. The Fold Group comprises Fold Housing Association, Fold Housing Trust and Fold Help Limited. The latter is a joint venture company owned jointly by Fold and Help the Aged. The objectives of the Fold group are: 'to carry on for the benefit of the community the business of providing housing and associated amenities . . . and to provide for aged persons in need thereof housing and any associated amenities specially designed or adapted to meet the disabilities and requirements of such persons'.

Fold has four regional offices (Ballymena, Newry, Omagh and Derry/Londonderry) and a head office in Holywood. The following are its main schemes: Belfast region — thirty-eight sheltered housing schemes and eight general needs schemes; Ballymena region — fourteen sheltered housing schemes and three general needs schemes; Newry region — eight sheltered housing schemes and three general needs schemes; Omagh region — eight sheltered housing schemes and three general needs schemes; Derry/Londonderry region — thirteen sheltered housing schemes and five general needs schemes. Fold also has seven 'accommodation for purchase' schemes in the Belfast area.

In 1993, Fold formed a joint venture company (Fold Help Limited) with Help the Aged. Fold Help provides assistive technology in the form of personal alarms to some 18,000 people. Fold Help Limited provides services to every county in Ireland on a cross-border basis. The Telecare service connects to nearly 17,000 homes across Ireland, making 100,000 morning calls and handling an annual intake of 240,000 calls. Fold employs a total full-time equivalent staff of approximately 750 persons of whom 85 per cent are female and 15 per cent male.

Fold was the first Northern-based housing association to become a member of the Irish Council for Social Housing. It recently expanded into Ireland, and by summer 2007 had two sheltered housing and housing-with-care projects, one at Cherryfields, Hartstown, and the second, Anam Cara, at Glasnevin, Dublin 11.

Fold is probably the largest non-profit organisation in Northern Ireland. It is a major player in the health and social services field and works closely with the Department for Social Development, with the Northern Ireland Housing Executive and with health boards and trusts.

Carers Northern Ireland

Carers Northern Ireland is a key organisation with regard to the support of people caring for dependants, not all of whom are older people. Its contribution to the wellbeing of older people in Northern Ireland is highly significant. Carers Northern Ireland works with and for carers throughout Northern Ireland and is a branch of Carers UK. Carers UK was, until 2001, the Carers' National Association. It was formed in 1988 as the result of a merger between two existing voluntary organisations that had their roots in the 1960s. Carers Northern Ireland's main role is to support a network of local carers' groups. The numbers of these local groups fluctuates with between thirty and forty operating at any one time. Carers Northern Ireland provides information and support to carers in general, as well as to those involved in local groups, and is also involved in campaigning and providing training to workers in the voluntary and statutory sector on carers' issues and carers' assessments. Training deals with a wide range of topics related to caring, and has a particular focus on the workings of the Carers and Direct Payments Act (Northern Ireland), 2002.

Carers Northern Ireland operates an information service for carers and professionals. This deals with issues such as carers' benefits, community care and services for carers. The association also provides a range of leaflets and booklets and a regular newsletter for carers, members and professionals, and offers free internet training for carers, to enable them to access information on the web. Carers Northern Ireland also offers carers the opportunity to meet with other carers, and to share their experiences, thus helping to reduce the feeling of isolation that carers often feel. The association's campaigning role involves raising awareness of the role of carers, informing government and policy-makers of their needs and helping carers to make their voice heard.

Carers UK and Carers Northern Ireland have been active in lobbying on behalf of their often-invisible constituencies for legislative change to respond to the needs of carers. Following the introduction of the English NHS and Community Care Act of 1990, parallel provisions were introduced in Northern Ireland through the People First policy guidance that accompanied Care in the Community in 1992/93. In Northern Ireland, the provisions of the Carers (Recognition and Services Act), 1996, apply but do so by means of guidance from the Department of Health and Social Services rather than, as in England, being enshrined in law. The needs of carers were recognised in the Northern Ireland Act, 1998, under Section 75. This is the first legislation in the United Kingdom to recognise carers' vulnerability to social exclusion and to promote equality of opportunity for carers. It requires public bodies, when developing policies, to promote equality of opportunity for a range of groups, including 'persons with dependants'.

The first statutory right for employed carers (apart from rights in respect of sex discrimination) is the right to time off work for emergencies involving dependants. In May 2002, the Carers and Direct Payments Act became law in Northern Ireland. This legislation was passed by the Northern Ireland Assembly and reflected the provisions of the Carers and Disabled Children's Act (2000) in England. The Northern Ireland Assembly strengthened the legislation by placing a duty on Health and Social Services Trusts to inform carers in their area of the right to an assessment, and by amending the Children (1995) Order to make it clear that young carers should be regarded as 'children in need'. Carers Northern Ireland is an excellent example of a locally based voluntary organisation that works effectively for older people and their carers. The association draws upon the support and guidance of its parent association, which provides it with links across the United Kingdom and supports it in lobbying for the introduction of legislative change in line with the other UK jurisdictions.

A.2

PROFILE OF ORGANISATIONS WORKING WITH OLDER PEOPLE, IRELAND

National organisations

The principal national organisations working with older people are the following six: Age Action, the Irish Senior Citizens Parliament, the Older Women's Network, the Irish Association for Older People, the National Federation of Pensioners' Associations and the Federation of Active Retirement Associations. Here we sketch these organisations and, where relevant to the discussion in Chapter 5, provide a separate section on their policy work.

The profile of national organisations should be prefaced with the observation that there is no national network of older persons' organisations to which all the others give allegiance or affiliation. In a sense, both the Irish Senior Citizens Parliament and Age Action aspire to be 'the' national representative body for older people and both have now achieved a broadly equal prominence. The Wheel, which is a national umbrella body for voluntary organisations, at one stage had a section dedicated to NGOs working with older people, called the 'older persons' spoke'. Four or five meetings of the older persons' spoke were held over 2000/02, attended by such groups as the National Federation of Pensioner Associations and the Dún Laoghaire Borough Old Folk's Association. Eventually these meetings stopped, though the reasons were never formally recorded.

Age Action Ireland

Age Action Ireland is one of the best-known groups working for older people in the Republic. It was established in 1992 by Robin Webster following a study by Help the Aged, which considered that there was a need for a network of service-providers and for a body to advocate the needs of older people. Three meetings were held at this time, mixed views being expressed about the need for such an organisation. Age Action Ireland was duly established both as a network of service-providers and as an advocacy and membership body for older people. Today, Age Action Ireland has seventy volunteers, thirty staff (including shops and community employment) and a turnover of €2 million. It is funded through charity shops, donations, membership fees, company donations, community employment and sponsorship. Age Action Ireland is provided with a core grant by the Department of Health and Children as a directly funded organisation routed through the Health Service Executive (€367,000 in 2006), and some once-off funding has been received from time to time from other government departments. Age Action Ireland has its head office in Dublin but carries out activities in many other parts of the country, such as age awareness, advocacy, education, training and information work. It is best known for its advocacy work (Chapter 6).

Age Action Ireland is a member of the European Seniors Platform, AGE. Cross-border contact is maintained with Age Concern Northern Ireland (they currently participate in a joint INTERREG project) and Help the Aged Northern Ireland.

Policy work: Age Action Ireland has a high media profile, largely as a result of its decision to employ an experienced journalist as a public relations officer. Age Action Ireland has regular contact with members of the Oireachtas, work it would like to develop through a parliamentary liaison officer. Members of the Oireachtas call Age Action Ireland for information and use its library. Age Action Ireland is sometimes regarded by government as combative, 'getting up their noses', but such comments could also be considered as an unintended tribute to the organisation's effectiveness.

Age Action Ireland is one of two organisations representing the older people's strand as a social partner in the national agreement and this has considerably improved access to governmental officials. Here, Age Action Ireland raises policy issues at the four times yearly plenary meetings and participates in the consultative group for the National Antipoverty Strategy and the National Health Strategy Forum. Age Action Ireland was represented on the steering committee organising the report on policy for older people by the National Economic and Social Forum. Other points where Age Action Ireland has engaged the political system have been the Office for Social Inclusion, the annual forum of the health service and the Central Statistics Office. Age Action Ireland does an annual pre-budget submission, which goes to all members of the Oireachtas, and it has met individually with numerous deputies, both at national and local level. Representations were made to Oireachtas committees on such issues as the constitution (the status of grandparents) and the Disability Bill, 2004. Deputies are invited to events in *Positive ageing week*. Between five and ten submissions would be presented each year, covering such policy themes as long-term care, disability, pensions, employment and housing. Age Action Ireland is in regular contact with MEPs, encouraging their involvement in the European Parliament's intergroup on ageing.

Age Action Ireland has a full-time policy officer and a full-time public relations officer, making it unique among organisations working with older people in Ireland. As a result, its policy and media profile rose rapidly in a short period. It comments extensively on issues affecting older people and is frequently the first organisation to be asked by the media for its views on issues affecting older people. Age Action Ireland routinely gets one to two hits a day in the print and electronic media. Its commentaries are sharply written, critical, outspoken and challenging of injustice, discrimination and inequality (for example, Murray, 2005).

Irish Senior Citizens Parliament
The Irish Senior Citizens Parliament works to organise the voice of older people in the Republic and to ensure that their needs are presented effectively to the political system.

The Irish Senior Citizens Parliament arose from the *1993: European Year of older people and solidarity between the generations*. The European Parliament convened, in Luxembourg, a parliament of seniors, inviting each Member of the European Parliament to nominate a participant. Once there, the participants agreed that national parliaments of older people should then be formed in each member state so that they could influence the policies toward older people in each country. The fifteen participants from Ireland duly returned home and established the Irish Senior Citizens Parliament.

Organisation has been a key principle in the work of the Parliament, reflecting the trade union background of the Parliament's leader, Michael O'Halloran. At present, the Parliament has 315 member organisations whose combined membership is over 90,000 people. The Parliament functions through an annual meeting which all member organisations are encouraged to attend ('The Parliament' itself). This meeting elects an executive, which meets monthly and mandates its work. The Parliament has a number of divisions which come together to work on a common programme: Wexford, Finglas, Dún Laoghaire, the Western and Cork.

For a long period, the Parliament had a staff of two, but this has now risen to four (chief executive, development officer, two clerical staff). The budget of the Parliament is in the order of €200,000 which is largely funded through the Department of Health and Children and also grant aided by the Department of Community, Rural and Gaeltacht Affairs. There is a newsletter, *News in brief.*

Policy work: The budget is considered a key point in the political process, for the decisions of the budget have a direct and almost immediate effect on the living standards of older people. Accordingly the Parliament devotes considerable effort to preparing, disseminating and arguing for its pre-budget proposals, which are circulated to the Department of Finance and other government departments, members of the Oireachtas and

European Parliament, the social partners and other voluntary and community organisations (for 2006, this was published as *A fair deal for older people*). Local member organisations and divisions where they are so organised are encouraged to discuss the proposals with their deputies and senators. The Parliament puts a strong emphasis on personal meetings with ministers, deputies and senators. It has regular meetings with the departments of Health and Children, and Social and Family Affairs, and less frequent meetings with the Department of Finance. The Parliament also engages with Oireachtas committees (for example, the committee on the constitution) and with once-off consultations (for example, role of old people in the arts). It is represented on the Pensions Board, the Department of Transport's Public Transport Partnership Forum and its special committee on rural transport for disadvantaged people. At European level, the Parliament is affiliated to AGE and takes part in a number of its transnational projects. Election candidates for local, Oireachtas or European elections are routinely questioned about and asked to support measures to assist older people.

Among the issues pursued by the Parliament are the following:

• Improvements in income support for older people, especially those on lowest incomes, with a narrowing of the gap between gross average industrial earnings and the state pensions
• Medical cards for all older people
• Improvements in specific benefits (for example, all-Ireland travel pass, bounty at age 100).

The Irish Senior Citizens Parliament combines a mixture of approaches in its relationship with the political system:

• Focus on moderate, practical, costed arguments to improve the living standards, benefits and entitlements for older people
• A preparedness to address the 'high politics' of pensions finance
• The presentation of argument reinforced by personal access. The Parliament puts a high value on personal access to ministers and members of the Oireachtas and has an intimate knowledge of the channels necessary to secure such access (for example, programme managers, constituency organisers). The Parliament works with a broad range of politicians from all parties, believing that reaching a large number is critical in creating an imperative for change.
• Regular contact with the key decision-taking government departments
• The use of adjacent channels, which provide access to decision-making, such as national social partnership

- Use of selected channels for media influence, principally local radio but also national chat shows.

The high politics principally comes into play in dealing with the Department of Finance, where belief in the demographic apocalypse is firmly held and which is institutionally the most difficult to engage. Within the typology of Grant (2000), it would be considered much more of an 'insider' organisation.

Older Women's Network

The Older Women's Network (OWN) was formed in 1995. The network arose from the *1993: European Year of older people and solidarity between the generations* (here more colloquially called 'European year for older people'), which formed a European Older Women's Network. A number of older women, coming from different parts of the country but principally the southern border counties, felt the need for such an organisation in Ireland. The embryonic network operated for three years under the aegis of Age and Opportunity and employed a development worker.

A convening conference was held in Maynooth in 1998, with 300 people attending for three days, from both parts of the island, and with large numbers from the border counties (both sides). Many were associated with the Irish Countrywomen's Association and constituted its early leadership. Three years later, in 2001, the Combat Poverty Agency proposed that the Older Women's Network be funded as one of ten national organisations combating poverty. This required it to separate from Age and Opportunity and form a new organisational identity, but once this had been approved, it was given a core staff of three people. Eventually it obtained a self-standing office.

The reorganisation took a full year and the Older Women's Network emerged as an association of thirty-six national and local organisations and 350 individuals (aged over sixty-five), paying fees of €25 and €10 each respectively. The OWN has members throughout Ireland and some from Northern Ireland. Some are already members of the Irish Countrywomen's Association, ladies' clubs and active retirement associations. For their fee, members receive a newsletter on the situation of older women, access to workshops (for example, access training, media training, computers, driving, waste, security, educational opportunities) and an annual garden party. OWN promotes itself through its newsletter, website and stands at over-fifties shows.

Although OWN's primary focus is in the Republic, its membership is open to women throughout the island and its board includes two representatives from Northern Ireland. It ran a cross-border project over 1998–2000, 'We're talking, who's listening?' OWN is affiliated to the European seniors platform, AGE, and contributes to the European Commission's expert group on age discrimination. It has three staff.

Policy work: The Older Women's Network policy work has three aspects:

- Pressing for specific changes through other organisations
- Directly campaigning for specific policy changes
- Changed values in the way in which older women are seen in society.

First, in pressing for changes through other organisations, OWN has raised issues through the Irish Senior Citizens Parliament and through the National Women's Council of Ireland, such as discrimination in insurance, elder abuse, security and Breastcheck screening. In changed values, the network has emphasised the importance of respect for older women and the state finding ways for their participation in public life, choice in their activities and being treated with care and dignity. This is especially important for women who have, during their lifetimes, frequently been denied opportunities for education, work, career or interests, and who have normally been dependent on men through their roles as wife or carer.

In direct campaigning, the Older Women's Network has drawn up submissions on such issues as the national plan for women and the review of the National Antipoverty Strategy. Specific issues have been raised, such as entitlement for free electricity units, age discrimination, home care and hospice care. The network has met deputies (especially the relevant spokespersons), departmental officials, MEPs and the minister of state responsible for older people. Issues have been raised with the Human Rights Commission, the National Economic and Social Forum (for example, *Submission on Care for Older People*, 2005), the Equality Authority and government departments.

Irish Association of Older People

The Irish Association of Older People is an association of older people that aims to promote a modern view of and approach to ageing. Originally open to anyone over fifty-five years, it now welcomes all age groups and currently has several hundred members (the newsletter has a circulation list of 2,000). With the prompting and assistance of the National Council for the Aged, the Irish Association of Older People was formed, in 1990, by activists, mainly people in voluntary and community organisations, trades unions and the academic community. Its original name was the Forum of and for Older People, being established on foot of the first national day on ageing, 10 October 1988, called, Age is Opportunity.' Its aim is to be the direct voice of older people, representing their interests and providing them with useful information to encourage their self-help. The association believes that it involves many older people who are not active in other associations and whose voice would otherwise not be heard.

The association has two voluntary staff; publishes a newsletter, *Getting on*; and provides telephone information concerning older people. The Irish Association of Older People receives a small grant from the health service to cover rent, insurance, telephone and office costs (Community Employment staff were employed in the past).

Policy work: The Irish Association of Older People makes representations to the political and decision-making system (for example, the Oireachtas Committee on Social and Family Affairs; National Economic and Social Forum; Irish Medical Association; National Spatial Strategy; Equality Authority advisory committee on older people). Over the years, it has been in contact with a broad range of government departments, state agencies and voluntary groups (for example, Community Platform, The Wheel). The association has had meetings with the minister of state responsible for older people and was appointed to health board committees addressing such issues as the primary care strategy and chronic illness. Representations were made to the Department of the Environment about equity release schemes, the built environment, housing design and the use of public amenities.

National Federation of Pensioners' Associations
The National Federation of Pensioners' Associations was established in 1976 as a means for voicing the concerns of pensioners in the public service and private industry in such areas as income, social welfare, health, housing and taxation (Dunne, 2001). The principal founder was Garda Superintendent Tom Ryan.

The National Federation of Pensioners' Associations currently has twenty-six affiliated organisations, representing 55,000 workers. The main member organisations of the NFPA are pensions associations in the public sector (for example, Garda Síochána, CIE, RTÉ, Fáilte Ireland) and private sector (for example, Irish Distillers, insurance industry, Player Wills, Stena Line). The annual general meeting elects a committee from which an executive committee of four is drawn.

The organisation has experienced considerable difficulty in developing and maintaining its office base and was not able to attract any government funding until the past three or four years. For many years, the Irish Congress of Trade Unions provided a small office facility, but this was abruptly withdrawn in 2001. The federation now receives a small core grant from the Department of Health and Children, €10,000 in 2006.

Policy work: The association was one of the first to raise with government policy issues concerning older people, starting in the late 1970s. One of its first campaigns was for ministerial responsibility for older people, eventually achieved when a junior minister in the Department of Health was so designated. Later achievements have been the development of non-cash, universal benefits for older people (for example, medical card).

The federation has been active over the years in presenting policy sub-missions to government, and a pre-budget submission is normally made. Recent submissions cover such areas as the financing of long-term care. There is good access to ministers, the principal one being the minister of state responsible for older people. In 2005, a series of issues was raised with the ministers for Social and Family Affairs, Finance, and Health and Children, ranging from free travel passes to social welfare pensions to cancer screening services.

The association made its views known to the departments of Finance (the one they dealt with most), Health, Social Welfare and Environment. Policy submissions were often followed by meetings with the ministers concerned, and ministers were frequent speakers at the federation's annual conference. The association ensures its representation at national consultative fora, social partnership, and departmental working groups throughout the year, to ensure that the voice of pensioners is heard (for example, pre-budget forum).

Federation of Active Retirement Associations (FARA)

The Federation of Active Retirement Associations (FARA) works with older people in the field of active retirement. The first association was founded in 1978 in Dún Laoghaire on foot of the *Focus on Retirement* exhibition there by Fr Mangan, who wished to bring older people together as a self-help group where the members could meet in the parish hall, chat and organise some events together. It soon attracted 500 to 600 members, although this subsequently fell back to around 230 to 250. A second association was formed in Mount Argus, Dublin, not long afterwards, and when sixteen or seventeen had been set up by 1982/83, they formed into a national federation, the Federation of Active Retirement Associations and appointed a first president, who had just retired from Aer Lingus.

The association became more professional, drawing up a constitution, publishing a handbook for associations, attracting sponsorship (for example, from the banks) and setting up branches outside Dublin (first in Limerick). Early application was made for statutory funding, but without success (Carey, 2004). FARA eventually attracted health board grants, then a grant in 1999 from the Department of Health and Children to set up an office, and later a grant from the Department of Community, Rural and Gaeltacht Affairs for part-time development officers. Each association pays a fee according to its number of members (€1 each) and pays for a national public liability scheme (€2 per member), and there are now two staff. FARA now has 410 groups and over 23,000 individual members. It is continuing to grow rapidly and there is an expectation that membership may level off at around the 40,000 mark.

Typical active retirement associations begin when a retired person begins to organise a local group, often seeking advice on how to do so from the FARA office. Sometimes they grow out of a sporting club (for example, bowling or snooker) that wishes to extend its activities, while others grow out of senior citizens' clubs. Typical activities of an active retirement association are day trips, arts, walking, keep fit, aerobics and a book club. At national level, the association runs a number of cultural (for example, concerts), sporting, training and recreational activities, as well as exhibitions. Local branches of active retirement associations are typically formed by former public servants, generally professional and well-educated people with a strong sense of public responsibility, and used to leadership roles.

The rate of growth of membership of active retirement associations is impressive, though FARA points out that it is still only 5 per cent of the retired population as a whole. Having said that, many older people may be involved in organisations that are not specific to old age, but which provide a not dissimilar range of activities (for example, Irish Countrywomen's Association). FARA is a member of and active participant in the Irish Senior Citizens Parliament.

Policy work: FARA itself has made direct representations to government on several issues affecting the welfare of older people, but this is not done in a high-profile way, members being cautious about their level of involvement in lobbying. The main areas raised with government are the pension level; the availability of sheltered housing; and nursing homes provision, but FARA has also raised issues around women's health (Breastcheck programme), men's health (prostate cancer services), chiropody services, and the operation of the free-travel scheme. FARA has met the minister of state responsible for older persons' services on several occasions and contributed to the NESF report. Little direct lobbying of individual deputies has been done, nor have Oireachtas committees been approached, resources not yet permitting such a development.

Five other national organisations have a specialised role which mainly addresses the situation of older people, but is not limited to them: the Carers Association, Hospice Foundation, Alzheimer Society, Irish Council for Social Housing and the Society of St Vincent de Paul.

National organisations that include work with older people

Society of St Vincent de Paul

The Society of St Vincent de Paul (SVP) is the largest charity in Ireland. Although a national organisation, it works at local level through 1,000 branches or conferences, based on the parish level. Although the society has always been influential with government, only in recent years has it been visible at national policy level where it is now a forcible contributor to the debate on national social policy.

The Society of St Vincent de Paul was founded in France in May 1833 by the law student Frédéric Ozanam, to assist the poor in Paris with practical help and to contribute to a more Christian society. The society spread quickly through the world and is now in 132 countries. It was established in Ireland in 1844.

Although the society is dedicated to helping all people who are poor, a substantial part of its work has been with older people, to the extent that older people are one of the largest single groups cared for by the orga-nisation, estimated at about half of its work. Conferences attracted volunteers from the local parish churches, and their original work princi-pally involved visiting older people in their homes to combat loneliness, provide healthcare (for example, washing feet), take up issues with the public authorities (for example, lack of running water, electricity), bring material help (for example, coal) and practical assistance (for example, water), and hospital visiting.

In the early 1970s, the society opened a number of holiday homes, which were put at the disposal of older people, initially for the summer months but later during other parts of the year (Carne, Kerdiffstown, Knock, Youghal, Bundoran, Mornington, Ballybunion) and these are still in use. From 1974, on the initiative of a local solicitor, the society began housing projects for older people, starting in Ballinamore, County Leitrim, and the society now has around 800 units, mainly for older people, mainly in small, local schemes. From the 1980s, the society began to develop care centres for older people, where recreational and paramedical facilities are provided (Newbridge, Kildare, Killorglin, Carrigtwohill). The society has always been the largest provider of services for homeless people and its eighteen hostels and related services have been used mainly by older men. Although the material situation of older people has improved enormously, the SVP continues to provide both these and the one-to-one visiting services, especially in those areas where community services are poorly developed or absent (for example, warden services, public health nurses, home helps).

The manner in which the society works with older people has changed enormously. In the 1960s, the service had a strong religious drive and dimension, on the part of both the volunteer and the recipient. Such voluntary work was done very privately and the work of the society was little advertised. In the course of national reports, local conferences reported to the national office on the issues around poverty. Senior people in the society were often drawn from the ranks of public administration; they had good, quick access to government over policy issues, but such representations were made informally and quietly. The society rarely raised issues of poverty publicly but, following reports by members around problems of fuel prices, the situation of older people was the first to be brought to public attention with Brian Power's *Old and Alone in Ireland* report (1978). The society faces its own internal challenges of a greying membership (currently 9,000 volunteers) and maintaining its voluntary commitment.

The SVP has an annual income of €34.4 million, of which 38 per cent comes from government sources and the balance from donations, fund-raising and over a hundred shops in the *Vincent's* chain (Society of St Vincent de Paul, 2005).

Policy work: In the 1980s, the society was considered to take an 'insider' approach to press its case; indeed, only two copies of its pre-budget submission were ever compiled, one for the minister and one for its own files. In the 1990s, the society developed its headquarters, employing social policy staff; publicised its annual pre-budget submissions; entered social partnership; and provided frequent and outspoken commentaries on the need for more enlightened social policies. In recent years, the society has been much more outspoken and visible. Although the pre-budget submission remains the society's principal instrument of influence, it is now widely publicised and disseminated. At the same time, the Society has been a visible contributor to national social partnership and a leading member of the voluntary and community pillar.

The SVP has concentrated on relatively low-cost but important changes in the social welfare code, which it believes will, over time, lead to significant improvements in the welfare of older people. Older people have been beneficiaries, an example being the fuel allowance, where the society successfully pressed for an increase in the allowance for the 2006 budget.

Carers Association

The Carers Association arose from the Dublin Council for the Aged, an umbrella group for a number of voluntary and statutory agencies concerned with the situation of older people. The chairperson, Iris Charles, persuaded the Dublin Corporation representative to organise a seminar to highlight the realities of carers' lives and to provide an opportunity for carers to meet and discuss their situations. Over 150 people attended in the nurses' hall in St Vincent's Hospital in 1987, and more than half were carers, with many social workers, nurses and some doctors also participating. There was a high level of interest in improving information for carers, in providing care services, improving the standard of care, and in lobbying to recognise and support the important work that carers were doing. A committee of five people was formed and this led to the formation of the Carers Association.

There was much interest in the idea throughout the country and the growing work was supported by a grant from the Department of Social Welfare to employ a development officer. The emphasis of the early work was on information provision, forming support groups, lobbying and training. Now, twenty years later, the association has sixteen centres throughout the country and employs 300 staff, mostly part-time, with forty-five full-time. Core funding came from the Department of Health, delivered through two health boards, with additional funding based on service delivery contracts, FÁS and some fundraising. Now the Health Service Executive is responsible for the core and service-provision funding. Each centre has an area manager, who organises the services provided to carers, supervises staff and manages the centre's activities, providing information and training, local fundraising and lobbying. The association runs a 'Carers of the year' awards ceremony to gain publicity for carers' issues and to have a happy social event for participating carers and families.

There are about 150,000 carers in Ireland (census of 2002), providing home care for people with serious disabilities and illnesses and people suffering from extreme frailty. Carers are in all age groups, from pre-teenage through the teens and right into old age. About 42,000 carers are providing full-time care. Many older people (16,500) care for a spouse or an adult child on their own. The support groups are important focal points for carers to meet, share experiences and information, provide mutual support and receive expert advice from professional staff such as public health nurses.

In addition to the Carers Association, there is the Care Alliance, which is hosted by Age Action Ireland. This comprises a network of up to fifty organisations interested in care issues.

Policy work: The Carers Association plays an active role in bringing the issues arising from caring to the key political and administrative decision-makers. At local level, carers are encouraged to meet with their elected representatives, and many do so regularly. At national level, the association meets with ministers and officials, especially those in departments responsible for health, social services and finance. Recently, the association had the opportunity to present the issues of major concern to carers to a meeting with the Taoiseach, the Tánaiste and the Minister for Social and Family Affairs and their officials. The association has made presentations to Oireachtas committees and met with opposition parties and spokespersons. Each year, there is a pre-budget submission (in 2007, it was called *Valuing carers' contribution to the social economy*), circulated to every elected representative in the Dáil, and the association runs a day-long revolving presentation on its proposals, for the deputies. The association has been invited to participate on a number of national bodies, including the Equality Authority, the National Economic and Social Council and the community and voluntary pillar of the social partnership negotiations. The principal issues brought by the Carers Association to government are:

• The need for comprehensive support services
• A national strategy on caring
• The need to address carers' health and wellbeing
• The need for remuneration, especially for full-time carers
• Education and training for caring
• The need for policies for work–life balance for carers
• The need for access to timely and relevant information.

Hospice Foundation
The Irish Hospice Foundation is a leadership and advocacy body for Ireland's hospice movement and draws its original inspiration from the hospice movement developed by Dame Cicely Saunders, founder of St Christopher's in London. It is not formally an umbrella representative body, although it does believe that it accurately reflects the views and needs of hospice service-providers and currently includes on its board representatives of two such providers.

Most hospice service provision is organised by voluntary organisations. The first purpose-built hospice in Ireland was established by the Congregation of the Little Company of Mary, in Limerick, in 1977, and the first identifiable statutory funding for hospice services was formalised by health boards from 1989. Although the popular image of a hospice may be a purpose-built plant, hospice services may be provided in converted facilities, still or formerly run by the religious; in designated beds and wards within existing hospitals; as home-based services (the most numerous); and other forms of support. In some cases, hospice services were spun off from religious orders (for example, Sisters of Charity, Daughters of Charity), their first board appointed by the order concerned, and subsequently becoming independent. New hospice services have been developed by local groups of concerned citizens, often from a professional background, such as the Lions Clubs (for example, Mayo Roscommon Hospice Foundation). From being largely financed through private fundraising, about 75 per cent of hospice care is now state-funded. Two-thirds of hospice care is for people aged over sixty-five.

The Hospice Foundation coordinates fundraising campaigns for hospice services (for example, Sunflower Day), the money raised being directed straight into local hospice services (€5 million in 2005); engages in public information work; undertakes research on the need for hospice services; runs education and training programmes; and does advocacy work. The Foundation belongs to the European Association for Palliative Care.

Individual hospices run a number of volunteer programmes. This is at first surprising, granted the complexity and sensitivity of hospice care, and one would more likely expect volunteer programmes in simpler, less demanding organisations. One of the best-known Dublin services, Our Lady's Hospice in Harold's Cross, began its volunteer programme in 1992 and now has a volunteer department which organises activities in such areas as transport, driving, teas and lunches, internet training for patients, running the shop and library, entertainment and outings. Volunteer open days are organised but the hospice is often approach by unsolicited offers (Our Lady's Hospice, 2003). Volunteer programmes are now run by several hospice services (for example, Marymount, Cork; St Francis, Raheny); covering a broad range of activities (for example, visiting, administration, driving) and would appear to have the most sophisticated volunteer programmes of all organisations working with older people, many recruiting volunteers by the internet (for example, Galway Hospice Foundation).

Policy work: The Irish Hospice Foundation has good access to the Department of Health and Children, the department having a positive understanding around issues of palliative care, and senior officials responsive to requests for meetings. The foundation contributed to the recent NESF study. Financial co-operation with the Department of Health and Children is good, for the department co-funded a study of the needs of children for palliative care and the HSE co-funded a baseline study of palliative care needs, and the findings of the study were presented to members of the Oireachtas, from party members to independents. As is the case with other aspects of health policy, the national policy (2001) is an enlightened one, but the quality of service at local level varies enormously: while services are developing rapidly in some parts of the country, in the former Midlands Health Board area, for example, there is no plan and no palliative care beds or consultants. In the new national agreement, *Toward 2016*, The foundation received firm commitments for accelerated programme development.

Alzheimer Society

The Alzheimer Society is a national voluntary organisation established in 1982 by a small group of people, each caring for a family member with Alzheimer's disease and who found little or no information or support available to them. The society grew steadily, and today there is an extensive national network of branches and services helping people with all forms of dementia, their families and carers, with the necessary support to improve their quality of life. The Alzheimer Society is the national dementia-specific organisation for people with Alzheimer's disease and related dementias. The ethos of volunteering remains at the heart of the organisation and, in 2005, almost 300 people volunteered in a range of activities. The society employs 740 full-time and part-time staff.

There are currently 37,746 people with dementia (2006 figures), of whom 3,943 are under sixty-five and have a younger onset dementia. The national figure is set to rise to 66,610 by 2026. The society's mission is to work for and on behalf of people with Alzheimer's disease and related dementias, and their carers, to ensure that they have the necessary supports to enable them to maximise their quality of life, with the objectives of raising public awareness and providing information; providing quality dementia-specific care services; supporting carers and families of people with dementia; campaigning for better statutory services (including specialist services for younger people with dementia); representing the needs, views and concerns of all those affected by dementia; and influencing public policy for care and support services.

The Alzheimer Society's support services currently comprise twenty-six branches, a national network of thirty-one day-care centres, twenty homecare or support services, twenty-eight carer-support groups, five social clubs, one dementia advocacy pilot project and one overnight respite centre. The society also operates the Alzheimer national helpline, offering information and emotional support. Several core functions are performed by the society's national office, including information, fundraising, public relations, training, human resources, policy, social research and finance. The society has run a national awareness campaign on the early signs and symptoms of dementias, involving national television, radio and print media. There are fundraising activities at branch, regional and national level, such as the annual tea day, which is the major national fundraising event. The society provided services to 1,785 clients in 2005. The average attendance at day care was one day per week, while the average number of home-care hours per person was five hours per week. The main funding contribution comes from the Health Service Executive.

The day centres operate between one and five days a week, depending on resources. An important feature is that the society provides activity outside the home, giving stimulation and care to the person and a break for the primary carer. Depending on the person's wishes and abilities, day-care services offer a wide range of activities such as reminiscence therapy, music sessions, gentle exercises, arts, crafts and personal care. Most of the centres provide transport, and the day also includes a hot lunch.

The other principal service provided is the home-care service. The home-care or home-support service assigns a trained dementia care worker to provide support and care in a person's residence for a designated number of hours per week, offering stimulation and activity for the person with dementia and a break for the carer. The national helpline is staffed by twenty-six volunteers and receives about 300 calls a month. The society provides information packs and booklets (for example, *Understanding Alzheimer's disease*), a newsletter (*Oasis*) and education campaigns (for example, *Alzheimer hero day*).

The Alzheimer Society belongs to Alzheimer Europe, the European Neurological Alliance, and Alzheimer Disease International, based in London. The society is affiliated to the Disability Federation of Ireland, the Neurological Alliance and the Alliance for Mental Health. It participated actively in the campaign on the Disability Bill and the mainstreaming of community employment services.

Policy work: The Alzheimer Society has a policy officer and public relations officer. It has had regular meetings with the Department of Health and with the minister responsible for services for older people. The society regularly makes submissions to review groups to represent the needs of people with dementia and their carers (for example, Mercer report, nursing homes, mental health, social inclusion) and has been invited to participate on others (for example, HSE group on standards in nursing home care). It sends occasional reports to members of the Oireachtas and all are invited to participate in World Alzheimer Tea Day. Local branches are believed to have good contact with their constituency deputies and senators. The Alzheimer Society produced a *Dementia manifesto* for members to lobby politicians in the 2007 general election.

Irish Council for Social Housing

The Irish Council for Social Housing (ICSH) is the national representative federation that brings together housing organisations in the voluntary housing sector, which provide social housing. It is estimated that about 7,000 homes in the voluntary housing sector are specifically provided for older people, the largest single element, out of the total of 18,000. The Irish Council for Social Housing is the umbrella body that brings large, medium and small social housing organisations together; addresses government on the policy issues arising from their work; and works with government on the technical and financial environment for the development of social housing. Its main interface with the political system has been with the voluntary and cooperative housing unit in the Department of the Environment, Heritage and Local Government. About 300 housing associations are members of the Irish Council for Social Housing and it comprises all the significant and active associations. The total number of housing associations is larger than this, but these are most likely inactive. The ICSH has a staff of six.

The most significant issue facing the Council in respect of social housing for older people is the question of social care in housing association projects. The thrust of housing policy has been toward the provision of bricks and mortar, with little attention, still less money, given to the provision of care services for older people in housing schemes. The ICSH always argued that for voluntary housing to work successfully, arrangements must be made to put in place and fund community-care services, particularly in sheltered housing; otherwise the older people concerned would find themselves hospitalised or sent to more costly and less suitable residential or institutional care. The question of who is responsible for such care was routinely passed between the health and the housing authorities and it was not until 2005 that the Department of Health and Children made a first allocation for care services, one which has since reached €1.5 million (2007). The Council hopes that this will rise to a minimum of €2.5 million.

Although many of the newer organisations developing housing for older people have attracted the most attention, older ones are conscious of the need to deliver housing for older people in a professional, modern manner. Here, Respond! is perhaps the most useful exemplar, planning the development of small local projects (thirty to fifty units) systematically, in line with best international practice, and, more recently, larger town-extension mixed-tenure projects (160 to 350 units). In such areas as architecture, the planning of schemes, home design, community infrastructure, the development of resource centres and the provision of appropriate social support services, Respond! looks to good example in other counties, for example the Netherlands. Respond! has worked hard with government departments and departmental committees to promote and advocate more enlightened models of housing and social provision for older people, covering such issues as design, funding, carer services and technical requirements. Respond! emphasises the need to create 'vibrant, integrated, self-managed and self-reliant communities', more than just to 'provide accommodation'. The organisation continues to follow a pioneering approach, with carefully researched and planned schemes for older people (for example, Baldoyle), day-care centres (for example, Tolka Valley), intergenerational living projects (Blackpool, Cork), and supported housing on the western islands, so that vulnerable old people can live out their days in familiar surroundings, rather than be transferred to the mainland (Aran).

Regional organisations

There are three principal regional organisations working for older people: ALONE, CareLocal and Friends of the Elderly.

ALONE

ALONE was founded in Dublin in 1977 by fireman Willie Bermingham who, in the course of his work, had come across the decaying corpses of eight old people who had died alone and forgotten. He first organised a food, heating and clothing service for older people living in precarious circumstances. Mainly they were men, tenants in private flats and some quasi-homeless. The organisation was named ALONE for A Little Offering Never Ends, but most people will be unaware of the acronym. ALONE presented a number of chilling reports to draw attention to the situation of older people (see Chapter 3). It is one of the few organisations concerned with older people to write a historical account of its work (*ALONE*, undated).

ALONE now has two full-time staff. In 1986, the association became involved in social housing and now has ninety homes — they are independent-living homes, not sheltered accommodation. Residents can call ALONE and ask for assistance, which ALONE will then source for them but not provide directly, so some of the ninety receive meals-on-wheels, and have home help and care attendants. Residents — they are called guests — are asked to make a donation to ALONE of 10 per cent of their income, in lieu of rent, and this covers insurance and ALONE's other costs. Prospective residents are referred to ALONE by the city council, social workers, doctors and homeless shelters. Typical residents are men, with few personal possessions.

Apart from its housing scheme, ALONE arranges visits to older people who are lonely or isolated, generally following a referral from a doctor, social worker or friend. ALONE organises a Christmas party, outings (three or four a year) and an annual holiday to County Wexford.

The organisation is run by a board of six trustees. It has seventy-five to a hundred volunteers who have an AGM and elect a volunteer committee. Volunteers visit older people in their own homes or in nursing homes. Their role is to chat and be a friend, but they may be involved in some cooking, cleaning or light house repairs (for example, fixing the shower) or in assisting with obtaining additional services (for example, a care attendant). Most volunteers have one or two older people to visit each, but some may have up to twenty. Some of those visited live in flats in poor condition, whether rented or owned, and some are very distrustful of visitors. Most volunteers are working people.

Most volunteers come to ALONE unsolicited. Sometimes the organisation will place a newspaper advertisement called 'We don't want your money; we want your time'. There is an application form, and references are required. Following an interview and an introductory meeting (these are held fortnightly), a volunteer is then brought out by an experienced volunteer. ALONE never asks for money. Sufficient money is sent to the organisation unsolicited, sometimes anonymously. The organisation often gives talks to schools, following which the school will make a donation. The only government assistance is toward the capital cost of the housing scheme. Willie Bermingham had a rule of *No bureaucracy!* — a tradition that the organisation still honours.

ALONE has sought an increase in the electricity allowance for older people, especially at a time of steep increases in electricity prices. It is still very much aware of poor housing conditions; cramped flats as small as 3 metres by 2 metres; of people walking outdoors in winter to keep warm because they cannot afford heating indoors; and of the limits to the state pension. Right into the 1990s, ALONE (undated) continued to document harrowing stories of old people living in shocking conditions. Even at nearly €200 a week, the pension is not enough to enable people to socialise and have a good quality of life, it says. Many people do not claim their full social welfare allowances, either because of lack of knowledge or the difficulty and complexity of the procedures. ALONE campaigned for several years for a 'dirty squad' to renovate the homes of older people, and this inspired the task force established in 1982 and still operating. Another of ALONE's campaigns was to end the practice of unmarked paupers' graves used by Dublin Corporation to bury indigent citizens. In 1986, the organisation bought what is called the Millennium Plot in Glasnevin Cemetery, formerly called the 'paupers' plot'. ALONE now uses the Millennium Plot to bury, with a headstone, flowers and dignity, those who died on their own and whose bodies were not claimed subsequently by relatives (Hayes, 2006).

ALONE contributed to the 1992 initiative of Dublin Corporation, the 'Reach out — be a good neighbour' campaign, subsequently run by the Dublin local authorities, gardaí and about forty voluntary organisations. This prints information leaflets on how to help isolated older people, and previously issued car stickers encouraging people to check on older neighbours. The campaign went national in 1993 and now involves eighty voluntary organisations.

CareLocal

CareLocal was founded in 1975 as Care for Dublin Old Folk Living Alone in Dublin, by a couple who wished to develop a visiting service for lonely older people living alone. The visiting service was built up over the following years, the organisation attracting a growing number of volunteers. The organisation obtained a shared office desk in the Carmichael Centre for Voluntary Organisations in Richmond Street, and in the 1990s adopted a constitution, changed its name to CareLocal, took on a development officer, appointed staff under the Community Employment scheme, and, in 2000, attracted a health board grant for the first time.

About seventy volunteers visit several hundred older people, principally in city-centre flats throughout the Dublin City Council area. The criterion for visiting is loneliness rather than poverty, but in reality most of those visited tend to be in limited economic circumstances. Until recently, CareLocal used to provide Christmas hampers and focused much of its energies on the provision of clothes, bed linen, coal, shopping, help with electricity, telephone and gas bills and, in the case of disabled older people, through the provision of wheelchairs. The decrease in informal social contact and the fragmentation of communities, undermining traditional neighbourliness, has meant that older people are at greater risk of exclusion, with associated practical, physical and psychological difficulties. CareLocal emphasises the value of its one-to-one weekly contact with older people in their homes, contact which continues should an older person be hospitalised or go into long-term care. For some older people, the volunteer's visit may be the only companionship they have all week, and the importance of listening is explained to volunteers; many older people say that people no longer have the time to sit and listen. Volunteers also help with practical tasks such as shopping, bringing people to the doctor and collecting prescriptions from the chemist, simple but essential tasks that become more difficult with advancing age. The guarantee of a weekly volunteer visit greatly alleviates anxiety for people with diminished capacity and mobility.

Money is raised through carol singing, raffles, table quizzes and a summer sponsored walk. CareLocal has made a limited contribution to policy-making, documenting the situation of the residents visited by the service (Tansey, 2001) and subsequently, in 2002, contributing a submission to the health strand of the revision of the National Anti-Poverty Strategy.

Friends of the Elderly
Friends of the Elderly works with about 320 older people in Dublin, of whom about 170 are visited regularly. The association has one staff member who is part-time paid, part-time volunteer, and 160 volunteers, of whom thirty work in the shop and sixty to seventy visit older people. Friends of the Elderly has a large hall in Bolton Street, Dublin, which serves as an office, clothing store and sorting place, weekly club and function room for seasonal parties. The volunteers visit older people in their own homes, drive them to and from parties, fundraise and assist in organising events. Funding comes from the organisation's shop, Ritzy Rags, and from fundraising, the organisation receiving no state grants. Many of the shop's clothes are sent in twice a year on a truck from its sister organisation in Paris, so Ritzy Rags is known as the Dublin charity shop with the best French fashions (Boland, 2005). The shop also receives local donations of clothes, books, bric-a-brac and unwanted gifts.

Friends of the Elderly was established in 1980 in Dublin by the French charity, Les Petits Frères des Pauvres (Little Brothers of the Poor), and is now part of its international federation. Les Petits Frères des Pauvres was set up in France by Armand Marquiset after the war, to assist women, children and older people who were left in the most difficult situations. The organisation now works in seven continental European countries (also the United States, Canada and Mexico) and has a philosophy of providing both friendship and material help (in Marquiset's words, 'Flowers before bread'). The founder had a particular interest in Ireland (he retired to Ireland and is buried in Cruit Island, County Donegal). The Dublin Friends of the Elderly followed the model of Les Petits Frères des Pauvres, except that the club for old people was a distinctive feature here. The service expanded and by 1993 had five salaried staff. It had, in fact, overextended itself and found itself unable to pay bills. Friends of the Elderly almost collapsed, being rescued by the parent organisation in France and making a fresh start, but without full-time salaried staff.

The main work of Friends of the Elderly is visiting older people. Volunteers must have references and they are trained in the dos and don'ts of visiting. The club is for more mobile older people and often organises visits to the theatre, cinema or pantomime, and outings further afield.

There is an annual visit to France, and the French connection is firmly maintained. All the visiting is within the M50 ring. About a quarter of those visited are in nursing homes, hospitals or geriatric wards, either temporarily or permanently. Older people are referred to Friends of the Elderly by social workers, public health nurses or hospitals, the principal criteria being loneliness and the need for personal support. People visited range from those in residential homes in Dublin 4 to people living in city-centre flats. The association emphasises its ideal of friendship, an ongoing relationship and something much more than 'checking if you're still alive'. The association would love to be able to organise light services for older people, such as alarms, kitchen improvements, removing draughts and repairing electrical systems.

For volunteers, Friends of the Elderly runs an international full-time residential one-year internship volunteer programme. So far, thirty-eight have participated over the past ten years, with three participating at a time, at this moment from Spain, the United States and the Czech Republic. They apply either on foot of information provided in their colleges or through the Friends of the Elderly website. Some may be on placement on degree courses in social care. These are the only full-time volunteers who work for Friends of the Elderly and all the Irish volunteers are part-time. Part-time volunteers come by word of mouth; through the website, especially in the case of young people; and through exhibitions where the association mounts a stand. Volunteers are typically young people of student age and retired people. Generally, older people volunteer for daytime and students for night-time. At present, the association has sufficient volunteers to maintain its service.

Funding is raised by the shop (60 per cent of income), a Christmas appeal (bringing in about €10,000); runners in the city marathon (about €5,000), donations (for example, chairs from the health board), commercial gifts in kind (for example, Vodafone), company donations (typically €50 to €100) and special appeals (for example, leftover or forgotten money from the euro changeover). The administration is carried out by a volunteer committee and all its tasks are performed on a voluntary basis, including auditing and accounts. Volunteers have an annual meeting.

Friends of the Elderly does not apply for money from the Health Service Executive (or the health boards before that) because funds are available only for specific programmes or services (which do not match or fit in with Friends of the Elderly's current operations) and because the HSE's reporting and accounting requirements are too onerous for an organisation without full-time staff. The health services have never approached the organisation to suggest ways in which they could assist its work, taking the view that 'It's up to you to apply if you want to'.

Cork Friends of the Elderly started in 2005 on the initiative of sociology undergraduates and postgraduates in University College Cork. About twenty-five are now involved and they are currently planning, with nurses and social workers, a service in the city.

These are all Dublin organisations. The other regional services identified in the course of this research were those provided by social services councils, outstandingly Clare and Galway, the latter since renamed COPE. This now provides a meals-on-wheels service (100 daily), a day centre, the Sonas drop-in centre (information, advocacy, support, breakfast club, baking group, film show, laundry services, shopping service, visiting, tea dances, outings, holidays, internet and webcam training).

Few regional networks of older people yet exist. For a number of years, there was a Dublin Council for the Aged, which helped to promote the formation of the Carers Association, but it appears not to operate any longer. An interesting example of an ad hoc partnership is the Council for Services for Older People in the north-west inner city in Dublin, a coordinating network comprising the health service, Garda Síochána and community groups. More recently, there is some evidence of the formation of county-based associations, and two examples are given. For example, fourteen organisations came together in 2003, to form the Longford Older People's Network. The following year, it won representation on the county's Community and Voluntary Forum and, in 2005, organised a first annual conference, 'The Way Forward'.

In Waterford, the area partnership assisted in the formation of a Senior Citizens Action Forum (Power, 2005). Following a large conference, the Forum was formed with a view to promoting a better quality of life for older people and to enable people to be active in the decisions that affected them. The Forum has a strong focus on empowerment, the community development approach and rectifying the disadvantage experienced by many older people without educational qualifications. It has raised with the authorities such issues as road and street safety, transport to hospitals, bin charges, parking, and equality awareness, and participates in an active citizenship programme with other European countries within the Grundtvig programme. Some partnerships have clearly begun the process of building the capacity of older people's organisations at local level, but it is too early to judge whether this work will be sustained for the years sufficient to make a difference.

A.3

VOLUNTARY AND COMMUNITY ACTION FOR OLDER PEOPLE: PROFILES

This research made provision for a number of case studies or profiles illustrating the nature of voluntary action in the area of older people and, in particular, areas of good practice and innovation. Those interviewed in the course of the research were invited to nominate groups that, to them, demonstrated some of the key features of voluntary action with older people. Eight groups were selected and are illustrated here.

Senior Helpline
The Senior Helpline (1850 440 444) was an initiative of the Summerhill Active Retirement Association in County Meath. This was an innovative service, for it sought to offer telephone assistance to the age group in the country that was historically slowest to use telephone services, namely older people. The service was conceived in an initiative by Mary Nally of the association, who continues to be its full-time chief executive officer, with Dr Nazih Eldin of the North Eastern Health Board. It opened in 1998.

The idea of the service was Italian, coming from *Filo d'Argento* (literally, silver threads*)*, a listening service developed by a voluntary association of retired trade unionists in Italy. Irish older people expressed an interest in a service coming both from a nongovernmental source and from experienced people, one designed to respond to issues of loneliness, isolation and depression.

The service has a strong voluntary base, the telephone lines being staffed by 300 volunteers who provide a morning and evening service, six hours a day, seven days a week. It is designed as a service for older people run by older people (over fifties), who, it is felt, best understand the situations in which other older people may find themselves. The first telephone centre, called telecentre, was opened in Summerhill itself and was then followed by others in Ballincollig, Limerick, Cavan, Mullingar, Finglas, Tallaght, Sligo, Waterford, Arklow and Galway. The number of callers using the service has risen from 126 in the first year, 1998, to 2,127 in 2003, with duration of calls also lengthening (O'Shea, 2004), with over 5,000 callers in 2005. Loneliness is the main motivation for calling, accounting for 50 per cent of calls, with significant proportions of callers being anxious or depressed.

The cost of the service is about €200,000 a year (2006), kept down by low staffing costs (one part-time administrator, all other tasks being carried out by volunteers) and the lack of a publicity budget. The funding is spent on the physical plant (premises, telephone systems) and training. Evaluation (O'Shea, 2004) showed positive outcomes both for callers and participating volunteers and it was adjudged as providing a significant contribution to the welfare of older people at low cost. The service builds on the strong tradition of localism in the volunteering tradition in the country. Although it is a nationally accessible helpline, with one national number, the operation of the telephone service is rotated around twelve local centres according to the time of the day and the day of the week. The most recent local centres contributing to the national service are Ballyfermot and Wexford.

Positive Age, Cavan

Positive Age, subtitled 'Social gain for the older person', is an organisation for 2,000 older people in Cavan and Monaghan. Its activities embody the active-living ethos of modern health policy for older people, and the service provides a range of activities, such as computer training, creative writing, woodwork, arts and crafts, tai chi, dancing, library, computer suite, gym, arts and drama, learning programmes, and even educational trips to continental Europe (for example, Croatia, Rome). The aim of Positive Age is to 'promote social gain', 'challenge the negative attitude to ageing and combat the isolation of older people in society'. The centre is funded by Cavan and Monaghan companies and enterprises, as well as the Health Service Executive. The 2006 programme included a day on fashion design, history talks, cross-border exchange and visit, attendance at drama in Dublin, swimming lessons, walking groups, picnics and outings and parties. There is a strong emphasis on listening to the needs articulated by older people themselves. For example, the foreign holidays originated from older people who felt that they were 'a nuisance' holidaying with their children or grandchildren and lacked confidence to holiday on their own — but a group like this was different.

Positive Age was founded in 1988 by a number of volunteers, one of whom, Frances O'Callaghan, was the current administrator and manager. The purpose of the organisation was to provide a focal point and service for older people in Cavan and Monaghan, many of whom were isolated, were not listened to and suffered when some services went to some social classes more than others. Positive Age worked from a temporary office until 1997–98 when the health service provided rooms in an old hospital building. Now Positive Age has a large room able to take 300 people, offices, bowling and a computer suite. Funding of the service comes from the Health Service Executive or sponsorship (40 per cent) and own fundraising (60 per cent).

Community Employment made a significant difference in the expansion of Positive Age and there are now four FÁS places and one Rural Social Scheme post. The centre has about 140 volunteers, mainly older people over fifty and mainly women, who come through personal contact and some advertising. The loss rate is small, about 1 per cent a year, but it is difficult to attract young volunteers, who are perceived to see working with older people as unattractive and tend to volunteer for youth clubs instead. Positive Age has a board recruited by the manager, comprising people from professional and skilled backgrounds.

There appear to be few other services so focused on the 'social gain' model, although many other services for older people incorporate the concept. While the theory of social gain is well accepted within the health services, most find it difficult to put the ideal into practice or to see the health and other benefits from doing so.

Cavan and Monaghan are border counties and there is a high level of collaboration with groups in Northern Ireland — exchanges, functions and visits, for example the Apple Blossom Tour in Armagh. Positive Age belongs to the ACDM Old People's Forum, named after Armagh, Cavan, Dungannon and Monaghan, a twelve-person committee that promotes cooperation between senior citizen groups in the area. Positive Age also established a national organisation for older men in 1999, to address health and social needs specific to men.

Westgate Foundation

The Westgate Foundation is an example of a voluntary organisation working with older people that has expanded substantially in recent years. It is located in Ballincollig, an old garrison town 8km west of Cork city. The foundation grew from the Ballincollig Senior Citizens' Club, which in 1986 was very small and catered for only twenty-five people. Now it is a modern, self-contained complex of homes, day-care centre, relaxation rooms, restaurant, medical facilities and officers. The core is a day-care service for fifty people, supplemented by meals-on-wheels for twenty-five. It is nationally known and achieved the unusual distinction of being cited as a model in the *Programme for Government for 2007–2012* (Department of the Taoiseach, 2007).

The development of the foundation is associated with Noel Byrne who was a musician who played at the parties of the Ballincollig Old Folk's Association in the early 1980s. Disturbed by the paternalism evident in services provided for old people at the time, he resolved to establish a more modern, client-centred, progressive service, so he formed the Senior Citizens' Club, soon renamed the Westgate Foundation so as to move away from the image of 'old folks' and 'senior citizens'. He himself enlisted in

University College Cork to acquire the skills necessary to manage a progressive service. The core values in the Westgate Foundation were set as:

- Being a secular service, without the involvement of the religious
- Providing services for well older people and sick older people, together
- Providing services based on listening to older people and their having a say, based on respect, decency, care, equality and compassion
- Quality, professional management
- Concentrating services in one place, to maximise efficiency.

The foundation was built up over the following years. Nowadays, its key statistics are:

- Regular use of its services by 1,200 people
- Turnover of €1.6 million, assets valued at €30 million
- Fifty-one salaried staff (including fourteen managers), thirty FÁS staff
- Two hundred volunteers
- Thirty-six sheltered homes for forty-two people
- Eighty different social and recreational services provided.

The Westgate Foundation is a company recognised for charitable purposes, with 110 members (local people who pay €30 a year to join), an annual general meeting of forty to forty-five people, from which a board of thirty is elected, meeting monthly, with management exercised weekly by an executive committee of four. Most board members are over sixty years old and are encouraged to join because of their experience in the area of work, some not having had formal education. There is also a professional advisory panel of a medical doctor, a nurse, a psychologist, a legal expert and an accountant. Volunteers, mainly elderly, are recruited through local advertising and must go through an application and training process. There is a strong emphasis on professional quality of service, with an insistence on health and safety, environmental standards, security (for example, the 'wanderer' system of bracelets for patients with memory loss), weekly accounts and monthly management consultancy for each project. There are three-monthly meetings of the residents and many other opportunities for them to voice their needs, with a complaints system, although management is disappointed with the low level of complaints so far. The Westgate Foundation is funded through housing rental income, FÁS, project grants, service-level contracts and its own fundraising (23 per cent).

The foundation was built up by the chief executive officer over the past twenty years through relentless pressure on the Southern Health Board, the city and county councils, state agencies (for example, FÁS) and the church authorities, through a mixture of cash grants, land grants and service contracts. The process of dealing with the health services proved to be a difficult, frustrating, adversarial one and there still are ongoing difficulties as to the services to be provided, under what financial terms and the schedule of payments. The foundation has frequently found itself taking financial risks and attempting to provide services that are needed but unfunded (for example, elder abuse, Alzheimer, mental health, weekend care). The chief executive officer has worked closely with Dáil deputies and councillors to generate support for the foundation's projects and has run many media campaigns to publicise the needs of older people.

Although Ballincollig is a long distance from Northern Ireland, the Westgate Foundation has operated joint and exchange programmes with the north from the very start in 1986. The present programme is funded by the Community Bridges strand of the International Fund for Ireland and the Department of Foreign Affairs. This involves older people in Cork, Derry, Belfast, Donegal, Louth and Monaghan, averaging a thousand people a year, in a programme of exchange visits, seminars, workshops and joint training in counselling, education and awareness.

Carlow EQUAL

Carlow EQUAL is part of the European Union Community Initiative Programme, EQUAL, designed to support projects working for diversity, social inclusion and against discrimination. There are twenty-two such projects in Ireland for the period 2000–06 (round two), addressing the discrimination issues that fall within the competence of the European Union (such as gender, age, sexual orientation, membership of ethnic minority). Carlow EQUAL is of particular interest because if confronts directly the problem of discrimination against older workers, thereby addressing a much 'harder' issue than most service-providing issues.

Carlow EQUAL is one of two Irish EQUAL projects to work with older people.[39] Indeed, people over forty are designated as the target group of the project, be they employed, unemployed, at risk of unemployment, low-income farmers, engaged in home duties or with a disability. The aim of the project, which began work in the later stages of the 2000–06 period, is to promote an inclusive labour market employing older people, to promote the employability of older workers, to combat discriminatory practices and to disseminate and mainstream the lessons learned.

To begin its work, Carlow EQUAL carried out the study, *Analysis of the labour market in County Carlow — opportunities and trends, 2005–7*. This led to many positive findings about older workers, who were valued for

---

1   The other is Senior Select, a project of Age Action Ireland, the Chambers of Commerce in Ireland, the state training agency FÁS and the Irish Congress of Trade Unions, and aimed at recruiting and retraining older people in the workforce.

their loyalty, skills and work ethic, their main disadvantage being perceived unfamiliarity with new information technologies. The study examined many of the perceptions about older workers, such as their flexibility, wage expectations, and preparedness to work with and take guidance from younger people. With the research completed, Carlow EQUAL is now proceeding to:

- Provide a series of interventions for 150 workers to enable them to develop the skills necessary to integrate or reintegrate fully into the workplace. The project is not just a training programme, but is one that offers a range of services such as mentoring and job seeking
- Work with employers in the county on a no-fee basis to promote age-friendly recruitment, training, policies and procedures so that they may benefit from the participation of older workers.

Sligo Alzheimer

The Alzheimer Day Care Centre, Dunally, Sligo, is one of a number of new services developed by the Alzheimer Society in the past twenty years. The service began in 1992 when the national Alzheimer Society called a meeting in Sligo to explore what could be done to assist people suffering from dementia. A local committee of four founding members was duly formed, and the local geriatric hospital offered a meeting place for the committee. First, a carer's support service was provided and then, after a search for premises, a day centre was duly opened in an old school. From the start, the idea of a Sligo Alzheimer centre received good support from the health board, which welcomed the project and contributed a capital grant of £15,000. There were no special difficulties in developing the service, the main problem being around land acquisition. Dunally Day Centre now provides a day room and related accommodation, minibus transport, meals, an activities programme, respite and other services (hairdressing and chiropody), with a nurse manager and other trained staff four days a week. The society in Sligo provides a home support for those suffering from Alzheimer's and related dementias in their own homes, with respite, visitor and care worker.

The society is run by a committee of nine people, elected from an annual general meeting normally attended by about twenty-two or twenty-three supporters. Typically, committee members include retired people and people drawn from professions such as teaching and veterinary medicine. Slightly over two-thirds of funding (68 per cent) comes from the Health Service Executive, which is considered a fair arrangement, with the balance coming from fundraising, donations, flag days and other events, such as the Sligo Rose of Tralee contest. The society has about twenty–

thirty volunteers who fundraise for the society in Sligo and Leitrim. It employs sixteen staff, including the nurse manager, administrator, Community Employment supervisor, driver, care workers (three) and community care workers (two). For the future, the society hopes to develop a home-from-home scheme, whereby people take a person with dementia into their own home to mind them, for a fee, an idea developed from a scheme of this nature in Selkirk, Scotland. Although no work is formally carried out with groups in Northern Ireland, it is intended to undertake activities with groups in Fermanagh shortly.

Dublin Central Mission
The Dublin Central Mission is a pioneer in housing services for older people. The mission is a Methodist organisation dating its charitable work in Dublin to 1893, providing clothes and money to needy people, orga-nising holidays and even cutting turf in the Dublin mountains to heat the homes of the poor during the war (Booth, 1993). In 1960, the leaders of the Methodist congregations in Dublin, Rev. Hugh Allen of Belfast and Sister Margaret Hunter of Newtownards, defined the need for accommo-dation for older people, and this led to the construction of Margaretholme in Sandymount, a housing complex for thirty-eight older people (Cooney, 1999). The project was inspired by Methodist social housing in Britain and was the first of its kind in Ireland. Its aim was to provide all-in-one services where old people could obtain accommodation, food, and, if they needed it, medical care, all in one place. The main house included a residents' lounge where they were encouraged to mix and socialise. Individual men, women and married couples were encouraged to come, breaking the tradition of a service providing for either men or women separately. Although the service was best known to the Methodist community, in practice, it has operated in a nondenominational way. Nowadays, some aspects of its approach might be regarded as paternalist. Residents are still expected to take their meals in the complex, but this serves two important secondary functions of alerting the staff to anyone who might be unwell and providing social interaction.

The waiting list had grown to such an extent in the 1980s that a second social housing project was begun: Ailt an Óir, in Glenageary, with single and double units for fifty people. This had a central core where all-in-one services were again provided, but with accommodation in three satellite wings. The Methodist Church also developed similar projects in Cork and Limerick, again working on the concept of integrating accommodation, food and support services.

The Dublin Central Mission is now considering how to develop its future housing services, but the nature of housing for older people has changed (Silke, 1994). First, older people expect a higher standard than in the 1960s, with more space and better furnishings. Second, they expect to live more independently, making their own choices about their daily routines (for example, choosing their own food over the convenience of it being provided for them in the canteen). Third, older people are generally looking for sheltered accommodation at a much later age, in their eighties or even nineties, rather than in their seventies.

An ongoing problem with housing for older people is the persistent failure of the state's housing and health services to bridge the gap between a housing service and a health service. The mission is prevented from providing accommodation to anyone who might be considered in any way 'dependent' (although they may not require full nursing-home support) as this might jeopardise its housing status. However, if it operates only as a housing service, health services are slow to provide support. The problem is that not all older people are either clinically completely 'dependent' or 'independent'.

The Dublin Central Mission employs professional care support and catering staff but has a voluntary board of management drawn from experts in the areas of accountancy, personnel, the law and construction.

Sue Ryder Foundation
The Sue Ryder Foundation provides supported, affordable housing for older people who are in housing need or otherwise unable to cope on their own. Established in Ireland in the late 1970s, it was modelled on the principles of the late Sue Ryder, who emphasised the importance of independent living in security, peace and dignity.

The first project opened in Ballyroan, County Laois, in 1984, providing high-quality accommodation with twenty-four-hour support, a range of communal facilities including four-course lunch each day, laundry, maintenance and repairs, light, heat, hot water and a domiciliary nurse. Residents are also encouraged to use local and specialist health agencies.

Other projects were subsequently established for several hundred residents in Owning, County Kilkenny; Dalkey, County Dublin; Holycross, County Tipperary; and Portlaoise, County Laois. More are planned in Ferbane, County Offaly; Dromahair, County Leitrim; Carlow town; Granard, County Longford; Mountrath, County Laois; and Suncroft, County Kildare. Each project has a local management committee, works with the local statutory agencies, and is designed for wheelchair standards. Sue Ryder shops, staffed by volunteers, assist with fundraising, as well as provide shopping outlets for people on low incomes, the proceeds going to capital development and a subvention for some residents.

There is a growing need for social housing for older people, far greater than that represented on the local authority waiting list. For them, sheltered housing will be an increasingly valuable element in the housing picture, as well as catering for the needs of Irish people returning from abroad. The Sue Ryder Foundation quotes research showing that one in four favoured sheltered housing as a community-based option.

The Sue Ryder Foundation has an international dimension going back to 1947, when the founder established homes in Poland, East Germany and the Balkans, to assist survivors from the prison camps. As recently as 2003, new services were opened in Albania and Macedonia, with the help of funding from Ireland.

St Francis Hospice, Raheny

St Francis Hospice in Raheny is interesting for two main reasons: first, because it has been in the forefront of the development of hospice care; and second, because of its development of volunteer programmes in such a sensitive area of service. The service dates to the reorganisation of cancer services in Dublin in 1989, at which time the north side of the city did not have any hospice service. The idea of the service in Raheny was driven by the Daughters of Charity, the Irish Hospice Foundation, Dr Mary Redmond and the late Justice Mella Carroll.

The service started with a Portakabin on land donated by the Capuchin order, and formally opened in 1993. The present service comprises a nineteen-bed inpatient unit; hospice day care and a home-care service; and bereavement support and counselling services. Whilst some of the funding is provided by the health service, a large amount of fundraising is required for these services, about €135,000 a month, raised through donations, events, golf classics, church-gate collections, legacies, draws, mite boxes in shops, and sponsorships in the mini-marathon and other events. The hospice plans to develop in Blanchardstown in the near future, so as to provide a comprehensive hospice service for the expanding parts of north-west Dublin. Most patients are older people with cancer or motor neurone disease. The hospice is run by a board comprising representatives of the Daughters of Charity and professional people brought in for specific skills in medicine, nursing, the law, accounts and engineering.

St Francis Hospice has a volunteer programme with a full-time coordinator of volunteer services. Volunteers are recruited in a variety of ways, such as volunteer centres and parish newsletters. Some see the volunteer page of the St Francis Hospice website and subsequently tele-phone or apply on line. Some information is available on the motivation of volunteers. Many offer their help because a relative or friend has been cared for by the hospice; as a result, they may have come to admire the service or wish to give something back in return (those recently bereaved are asked to wait a year before volunteering). Other volunteers see the hospice as part of the local community and wish to 'give something back'. For some volunteers, the hospice can be seen as a social activity with other friends, and for younger people it can be seen as part of their career development.

At any one time, there are 200 volunteers on the books. Most volunteers will carry out one activity a week for not more than four or five hours, such as helping people at home, shopping for them, or in the hospice itself providing complementary therapy, hairdressing, running the coffee shop, visiting patients, driving, working at reception, bereavement support, assisting with fundraising or minding the garden. Applicants complete an application form, meet with the coordinator and the relevant department manager, make an agreement as to what work they will do according to their areas of interest and participate in subsequent training. The co-ordinator will steer unsuitable volunteers in the direction of other, more appropriate organisations or Volunteering Ireland. There is a *Volunteer handbook*, outlining policies and guidelines for volunteers.

The hospice maintains an up-to-date database of all volunteers, the profile of whom is becoming younger and more gender balanced: 64 per cent are over fifty-five years, and males now account for 25 per cent of volunteers. The drop-out rate for volunteers is very low, the reason for dropping out normally being a change in family circumstances, illness or work pressures. Volunteers, like staff, are invited to attend the annual foundation-day lecture and annual conference. International Volunteer Day is always celebrated, and social events are organised for volunteers during the year. There are long-service awards for volunteers who stay five, ten or fifteen years.

Bibliography and References

Acheson, N. (2003), 'Voluntary Action and Disability in Northern Ireland', unpublished PhD thesis, University of Ulster, Coleraine

Acheson, N., Harvey, B., Kearney, J. and Williamson, W. (2004), *Two Paths, One Purpose: Voluntary Action in Ireland, North and South*, Dublin: Institute of Public Administration

Acheson N. and Williamson, A. P. (2007), 'Civil Society in Multi-Level Public Policy: The Case of Ireland's two Jurisdictions', *Policy and Politics*, vol. 35, no. 1, pp. 25–44

Acheson, N., Cairns, E., Stringer, M. and Williamson, A. P. (2007), *Voluntary Action and Community Relations in Northern Ireland*, Coleraine: Centre for Voluntary Action Studies, University of Ulster

Age Action (1998), *Directory of Research on Ageing and Opportunity in Ireland*, Dublin: Age Action

Age Action (1998), *Directory of Services for Older People in Ireland*, 2nd edn, Dublin: Age Action

Age Action (1999), *Directory of Services for Older People in the West of Ireland*, Dublin: Age Action

Age Concern Northern Ireland (2006), *Annual Report, 2005/2006*

Age & Opportunity (2000), *A Review of the First 12 Years*, Dublin: Age & Opportunity

Age & Opportunity (2005), *Annual Report, 2004*, Dublin: Age & Opportunity

Almond, G. A. and Verba, S. (1963), *The Civic Culture: Political Attitudes and Democracy in Five Nations*, Newbury Park, CA: Sage Publications

ALONE (undated), *About ALONE*, Dublin: ALONE

Anheier, H. K. (2004), 'Third Sector — Third Way: Comparative Perspectives and Policy Reflections', in R. Surender and J. Lewis (eds), *Welfare State Change: Towards a Third Way?*, Oxford: Oxford University Press

Anheier, H. K. (2005), *Non-Profit Organisations: Theory, Management, Policy*, New York, Abingdon: Routledge

Athlone Social Services Council (1973), *A Survey of the Aged*, Athlone: Athlone Social Services Council

Audit Commission, Healthcare Commission and the Commission for Social Care Inspection (2006), *Living Well in Later Life: A Review of Progress Against the National Service Framework*, London: Audit Commission, Healthcare Commission and the Commission for Social Care Inspection

Bagguley, P. (1994), 'Prisoners of the Beveridge Dream? The Political Mobilization of the Poor Against Contemporary Welfare Regimes', in R. Burrows and B. Loader (eds), *Towards a Post-Fordist Welfare State*, London: Routledge

Baines, S., Lie, M. and Wheelock, J. (2004), 'Volunteering, Self-help and Citizenship in Later Life', Paper presented to the 10th Researching the Voluntary Sector Conference, Sheffield Hallam University, 1–2 September

Banting, K. and Kymlicka, W. (2006), 'Introduction: Multiculturalism and the Welfare State: Setting the Context', in K. Banting and W. Kymlicka (eds), *Multiculturalism and the Welfare State: Recognition and Redistribution in Contemporary Democracies*, Oxford: Oxford University Press

Barnes, M. (1997), *Care, Communities and Citizens*, London: Longman

Barrington, R. (2000), *Health, Medicine and Politics in Ireland, 1900–70*. Dublin: Institute of Public Administration

Batljan, I. (2005), *Care for the Elderly as an Investment in the Future*, Presentation to the National Economic and Social Forum

Bell, V. (2004), 'In Pursuit of Civic Participation: the early experiences of the Northern Ireland Civic Forum 2000–2002', *Political Studies*, vol. 52, pp. 565–84

Bermingham, W. and Ó Cunaigh, L. (1978), *Alone*, Dublin: ALONE

Bermingham, W. and Ó Cunaigh, L. (1982), *Alone Again*, Dublin: ALONE

Bermingham, W. and Ó Cunaigh, L. (1989), *Alone Once More*, Dublin: ALONE

Birrell, D. and Williamson, A. P. (2001), 'The Voluntary-Community Sector and Political Developments in Northern Ireland since 1972', *Voluntas*, vol. 12, no. 3, pp. 205–20

Boland, R. (2005), 'Helping the Elderly Not Just for Christmas' *The Irish Times*, 17 December

Boldt, S. (1998), *The Educational Needs of People Aged 55 and Over — A Study in the Midland and Western Health Board Regions*, Dublin: Age & Opportunity

Booth, L. (1993), *Dublin Central Mission, 1893–1993, A History*, Dublin: Dublin Central Mission

Boyle, G. (1997), 'Community care for older people in Ireland — a conceptual critique of the literature', *Administration*, vol. 45, no. 2

Boyle, R. and Butler, M. (2003), *Autonomy vs Accountability — Managing Government Funding of Voluntary and Community Organisations*, Dublin: Institute of Public Administration

Brandsen, T., Van Der Donk, W. and Putters, K. (2005), 'Griffins or Chameleons? Hybridity as a Permanent and Inevitable Characteristic of the Third Sector', *International Journal of Public Administration*, vol. 28, no. 9, pp. 749–65

Breda, J., Schoenmaekers, D., Van Landeghem, C., Claessens, D. and Geerts, J. (2006), 'When Informal Care becomes a Paid Job: The Case of Personal Assistance Budgets in Flanders', in C. Glendinning and P. Kemp (eds), *Cash and Care: Policy Challenges in the Welfare State*, Bristol: The Policy Press

Brown, S. (1996), 'Developments in community care for elderly people', in *Administration*, vol. 44, no. 3

Browne, M. (1992), *Swimming Against the Tide — Coordinating Services for the Elderly at Local Level. A report on two pilot projects*, Dublin: National Council for the Aged

Browne, M., O'Mahony, A., and Murray, E. (2002), *Elders in Irish Society — Beyond the Dismal Scenario. Issues for Policy and Practice in the 21st Century*, Dublin: O'Mahony-Browne Research Consultants for Social Innovations Ireland

Callan, T. and Nolan, B. (2000), 'Taxation and social welfare', in B. Nolan, P. J. O'Connell and C. Whelan (eds), *Bust to boom? The Irish Experience of Growth and Inequality*, Dublin: Economic and Social Research Institute and Institute of Public Administration

CareLocal (2001), *Submission by CareLocal to the National Anti Poverty Strategy*, Dublin: CareLocal

Carers Association (2005), *Toward a Family Carers Strategy*, Kilkenny: Carers Association

Carers UK (2007), *Valuing Carers — Calculating the Value of Unpaid Care*, www.carersuk.org/Newsandcampaigns/Valuingcarers/Fullreport/ValuingcarersFINAL.pdf (accessed 20 September 2007)

Carey, E. (2004), *A Brief History of Active Retirement, 1978–2004*, Dublin: Federation of Active Retirement Associations

Caul, B., Herron, S. (1992), *A Service for People: Origins and Development of the Personal Social Services of Northern Ireland*, Belfast: December Publications

Central Statistics Office (2005), *Census of Population, 2002*, Cork: CSO

Central Statistics Office (2005), *Population and Migration Estimates, April 2005*, Cork: CSO

Central Statistics Office (2005), *Regional Population Projections, 2006–2021*, Cork: CSO

Central Statistics Office (2007), *Census 2006 — Principal Demographic Results*, Cork, CSO

Charities Commission for England and Wales (2007), *Stand and Deliver: The Future for Charities Delivering Public Services*, London: Charities Commission for England and Wales

Charley, C. (2007), *Vision and Venture: A History of the Bryson Charitable Group, 1906–2006*, Belfast: Bryson Charitable Group

Clarke, J. and Newman, J. (1997), *The Managerial State: Power, Politics and Ideology in the Remaking of Social Welfare,* London: Sage Publications

Coakley, D. (1997), 'Out of the Shadow — developing services for the elderly'*,* in J. Robins (ed.), *Reflections on Health — Commemorating Fifty Years of the Department of Health, 1947–1997*, Dublin: Institute of Public Administration

Commission for Social Care Inspection (2006), *Annual Report*, London: Commission for Social Care Inspection

Commission on Social Welfare (1986), *Report of the Commission on Social Welfare*, Dublin: Department of Social Welfare

Connell, P. and Pringle, D. (2004), *Population Ageing in Ireland — Projections 2001–2021*, Dublin: National Council on Ageing and Older People, report 81

Connolly, E. (2007), 'The institutionalization of antipoverty and social exclusion policy in Irish social partnership'*,* Dublin: Combat Poverty Agency, research working paper

Convery, J. (1987), *Choices in Community Care — Day Centres for the Elderly in the Eastern Health Board*, Dublin: National Council for the Aged

Cooney, D. L. (1999), *From Mount Hulings to Margaretholme — A Short History of Margaretholme*, Dublin: Dublin Central Mission

Coordinating Committee of Social Problems (CCSP) (1980), *Tomorrow's Resource: A Review of Government Policy towards the Voluntary Sector in the Field of Social Welfare*, Belfast: Department of Health and Social Services

Cornerstone (2006), 'Assessment of housing need 2005', *Cornerstone*, magazine of the Homeless Agency, no. 28, October

Cousins, M. (2000), 'The 1986 report of the Commission on Social Welfare and recent developments', in A. Lavan (ed), *50 Years of Social Welfare Policy*, Dublin: Department of Social, Community and Family Affairs

Coxall, B. (2001), *Pressure Groups in Britain*, Harlow: Pearson Education

Crossley, N. (2002), *Making Sense of Social Movements*, Buckingham: Open University Press

Crowley, N. (2005), *An Ambition for Equality*, Dublin: Irish Academic Press

Cullen, P. (2007), 'Ireland Spending Relatively Less on Healthcare, *The Irish Times*, 19 May

Cullen, K., Delaney, S. and Duff, P. (2004), *Caring, Working and Public Policy*, Dublin: the Equality Authority

Cumming, E. and Henry, W. E. (1961), *Growing Old — The Process of Disengagement*, New York: Basic Books

Curry, J. (1993), *Irish Social Services*, Dublin: Institute of Public Administration

Dahl, R. A. (1961), *Democracy in the United States. Promise and Performance*, Boston: Houghton Mifflin

Delaney, S., Cullen, K. and Duff, P. (2005), *Social Inclusion of Older People at a Local Level*, Dublin: National Council on Ageing and Older People, report 90

Dempsey, A. (2002), *Opportunities in Retirement — New Challenges in Older Age*, Dublin: Age & Opportunity

Department of Health (1968), *Care of the Aged*, Dublin: Department of Health

Department of Health (1988), *The Years Ahead — A Policy for the Elderly*, Report of working party on services for the elderly, Dublin: Stationery Office

Department of Health (1994), *Shaping a Healthier Future*, Dublin, Stationery Office

Department of Health (1997), *A Plan for Women's Health 1997–99*, Dublin: Stationery Office

Department of Health (undated), *Widening the Partnership*, Dublin: Department of Health

Department of Health and Children (1998), *Adding Years to Life and Life to Years — A Health Promotion Strategy for Older People*, Dublin: Health Promotion Unit

Department of Health and Children (2000), *National Health Promotion Strategy 2000–5*, Dublin: Department of Health and Children

Department of Health and Children (undated), *Enhancing the Partnership*, Dublin: Department of Health and Children

Department of Health and Children (2001), *Report of the National Advisory Committee on Palliative Care*, Dublin: Department of Health and Children

Department of Health and Children (2001), *Quality and Fairness — A Health System for You*, Dublin: Department of Health and Children

Department of Health and Social Services (1993), *Strategy for the Support of the Voluntary Sector and for Community Development in Northern Ireland*, Belfast: HMSO

Department of Health, Social Services and Public Safety (2002a), *Review of Community Care: First Report*, Belfast: Department of Health, Social Services and Public Safety

Department of Health, Social Services and Public Safety (2002b), *Investing for Health*, Belfast: Department of Health, Social Services and Public Safety

Department of Social and Family Affairs (2002), *Study to Examine the Future Financing of Long-Term Care*, Dublin: Mercer Ltd and Government of Ireland (often referred to as the Mercer Report)

Department of the Environment (1991), *A Plan for Social Housing*, Dublin: Department of the Environment

Department of the Environment (1995), *Social Housing, The Way Ahead*, Dublin: Department of the Environment

Department of the Environment and Local Government (2002), *Local Authority Housing Needs Assessment, 2002*, Dublin: Stationery Office

Department of Social Development (2003), *Partners for Change: A Government Strategy for the Support of Voluntary and Community Organisations*, Belfast: Department of Social Development

Department of the Taoiseach (2002), *Sustaining Progress*, Dublin: Stationery Office

Department of the Taoiseach (2006), *Toward 2016*, Dublin: Stationery Office

Department of the Taoiseach (2007), *Programme for Government*, Dublin: Stationery Office

Department of Work and Pensions (DWP) (2005), *Opportunity Age: Meeting the Challenges of Ageing in the 21st Century*, London: Department of Work and Pensions

Dimas, S. and Almunia, J. (2004), *The Social Situation in the European Union, 2004*, Brussels: European Commission

Ditch, J. (1988), *Social Policy in Northern Ireland between 1939 and 1950*, Aldershot: Avebury

Donnellan, E. (2005), 'Percentage in Nursing Homes Same as Late 1960s', *The Irish Times*, 28 October

Donnelly-Cox, G. and Breathnach C. (ed.) (2006), *Differing Images: The Irish Nonprofit Sector and Comparative Perspectives*, Dublin: The Liffey Press

Donoghue, F. (1998), 'Defining the Nonprofit Sector: Ireland', in L. Salamon, A. K. Anheier (eds), *Working Papers of the Johns Hopkins Comparative Nonprofit Sector Project No. 28*, Baltimore: the Johns Hopkins Institute for Policy Studies

Donoghue, F. (undated a), *Reflecting the Relationships — An Exploration of Relationships between the Former Eastern Health Board and*

Voluntary Organisations in the Eastern Region, Dublin: Northern Area
Health Board, South Western Area Health Board and East Coast Area
Health Board

Donoghue, F. (undated b), 'Non-profit organisations as builders of social
capital and channels of expression — the case of Ireland', paper
presented to conference on 'Nonprofit impacts: evidence from around
the world'

Donoghue, F., Anheier, H. K. and Salamon, L. M. (1999), *Uncovering the
Nonprofit Sector in Ireland: Its Economic Value and Significance*,
National College of Ireland and the Johns Hopkins University Institute
for Policy Studies, Center for Civil Society Studies

Duignan, C. (1996), 'Day Care for Older People — A Rural Perspective',
unpublished MSc thesis, University College Dublin

Dunne, M. A. (2001), 'Champion of the Retired', *Garda Review*

East Coast Area Health Board (2001), *Annual Report, 2000*, Dublin: East
Coast Area Health Board

Eastern Health Board (1995), *Review of Services for the Elderly*, Dublin:
Eastern Health Board

Eastern Health Board (1999), *10-Year Action Plan for Services for Older
People, 1999–2008*, Dublin: Eastern Health Board

Eastern Health Board (2001), *Annual Report, 1999–2000*, Dublin: Eastern
Health Board

Ellison, N. and Pierson, C. (eds) (2003), *Developments in British Social
Policy*, Basingstoke: Palgrave Macmillan

Equality Authority (2002), *Implementing Equality for Older People*,
Dublin: Equality Authority

Esping-Andersen, G. (1990), *The Three Worlds of Welfare Capitalism*,
Cambridge: Polity Press

European Commission (1981), *Final Report from the Commission to the
Council on the First Programme of Pilot Schemes and Studies to
Combat Poverty*, COM 81/769, Brussels: European Commission

European Commission (1991), *Final Report on the Second European
Poverty Programme*, COM 91/29, Brussels: European Commission

European Commission (2003), *Adequate and Sustainable Pensions* —
joint report by the Commission and the Council, Employment and
Social Affairs, *Social Security and Social Integration* series, Brussels:
European Commission

European Commission (2005a), *Confronting Demographic Change: A
New Solidarity between the Generations — A Green Paper*, Brussels:
European Commission

European Commission (2005b), *Joint Report on Social Protection, Staff
Working Paper, Technical Annexe*, Brussels: European Commission

European Commission (2007a), *Reconciliation of Professional and Private Life — Exchange of Good Practices*, Brussels: European Commission

European Commission (2007b), *Adequate and Sustainable Pensions — Synthesis Report*, Luxembourg: Office of Official Publications

European Commission (2007c), *Growing Regions, Growing Europe — Fourth Report on Economic and Social Cohesion*, Brussels: European Commission

Eurostat (2001), *Key Data on Health, 2000*, Luxembourg: Eurostat

Eurostat (2005), 'Social protection expenditure in the EU25 accounted for 27.7 per cent of GDP', press release and table, 25 October, Luxembourg: Eurostat

Eurostat (2007), *Preliminary Vital Statistics for 2006*, Luxembourg: Eurostat

Evason, E. (2007), *Who Cares Now? Changes in Informal Caring 1994–2006*, ARK Research Update 51, Belfast: ARK <http:www.ark.ac.uk/publications/updates/update45.pdf>

Evason, E., Dowds, L. and Devine, P. (2004), *Ageism in Ireland*, Belfast: ARK Northern Ireland Social and Political Archive

Evason, E., Lloyd, K., McKee, P. and Devine, P. (2004a), *Older People in Northern Ireland: Report 1 — Setting the Scene*, Belfast: Institute of Governance, Public Policy and Social Research, Queen's University, Belfast

Evason, E., Lloyd, K., McKee, P. and Devine, P. (2004b), *Older People in Northern Ireland: Report 2 — Financial Circumstances*, Belfast: Institute of Governance, Public Policy and Social Research, Queen's University, Belfast

Evason, E., Lloyd, K. and McKee, P. (2005a), *Older People in Northern Ireland: Report 3 — Health and Social Wellbeing*, Belfast: Institute of Governance, Public Policy and Social Research, Queen's University, Belfast

Evason, E., Lloyd, K., McKee, P. and Devine, P. (2005b), *Older People in Northern Ireland: Report 4 — The Angry Generation*, Belfast: Institute of Governance, Public Policy and Social Research, Queen's University, Belfast

Evason, E., Lloyd, K., McKee, P. and Devine, P. (2005c), *Report 5: Older People in the Republic of Ireland*, Belfast: Institute of Governance, Public Policy and Social Research, Queen's University, Belfast

Evason, E., Lloyd, K., McKee, P. and Devine, P. (2005d), *Older People in Northern Ireland: Final Report*, Belfast: Institute of Governance, Public Policy and Social Research, Queen's University, Belfast

Evers, A. (2005), 'Mixed Welfare Systems and Hybrid Organisations:

Changes in the Governance and Provision of Social Services', *International Journal of Public Administration*, vol. 28, no. 9, pp. 737–48

Evers, A. and Laville, J.-L. (2004), 'Defining the Third Sector in Europe', in J.-L. Laville and A. Evers (eds), *The Third Sector in Europe*, Cheltenham, UK, and Northampton, MA: Edward Elgar

Fahey, T. (1995), *Health and Social Care Implications for Population Ageing in Ireland, 1991–2011*, Dublin: National Council for the Elderly, report 42

Fahey, T. (ed) (1999), *Social Housing in Ireland — A Study of Success, Failure and Lessons Learned*, Dublin: Combat Poverty Agency and Katherine Howard Foundation

Fahey, T. and Russell, H. (2001), *Older People's Preferences for Employment and Retirement in Ireland*, Dublin: National Council on Ageing and Older People, report 67

Faughnan, P. (1997), 'A healthy voluntary sector — rhetoric or reality?' in J. Robins (ed.), *Reflections on Health — Commemorating Fifty Years of the Department of Health, 1947–1997*, Dublin: Institute of Public Administration

Fisher, L. R. and Schaffer, K. Bannister (1993), *Older Volunteers — A Guide to Research and Practice*, London: Sage

FitzGerald, E. (2000), 'Community service for independence in old age, rhetoric and reality', *Administration*, vol. 48, no. 3

FitzGerald, G. (2005), 'Population ageing', in E. O'Shea, and P. Conboy (eds), *Planning for an Ageing Population*, Dublin: National Council on Ageing and Older People, report 87

FitzGerald, J. (2000), 'The story of Ireland's failure — and belated success', in B. Nolan, P. J. O'Connell and C. Whelan (eds), *Bust to boom? The Irish Experience of Growth and Inequality*, Dublin: Economic and Social Research Institute and Institute of Public Administration

Fogarty, M. J. (1986), *Social Cohesion and Time Available for Assistance to the Elderly*, Dublin: European Foundation for the Improvement of Living and Working Conditions

Garavan, R., Winder, R. and McGree, H. (2001), *Health and Social Services for Older People in Ireland*, Dublin: National Council on Ageing and Older People

Gartland, F. (2006), 'Home Helpers Protest on Pay and Conditions', *The Irish Times*, 14 March

Giddens, A. (1998), *The Third Way: The Renewal of Social Democracy*, Cambridge: Cambridge University Press

Government of Ireland (1997), *Sharing in Progress — the National Anti Poverty Strategy*, Dublin: Stationery Office

Government of Ireland (2002), *Building an Inclusive Society*. Dublin: Stationery Office

Government of Ireland (2003), *National Action Plan Against Poverty and Social Exclusion*, Dublin: Government of Ireland

Grant, W. (2000), *Pressure Groups and British Politics*, London: Macmillan Press

Griffiths, H., Nic Ghiolla Choille, T., and Robinson, J. (1978), *Yesterday's Heritage, Tomorrow's Resource*, Coleraine: New University of Ulster

Haase, T. (2005), *Early Onset Dementia — A Needs Analysis of Younger People with Dementia in Ireland*, Dún Laoghaire: Alzheimer Society

Harvey, B. (2002), *Rights and Justice Work in Ireland — A New Base Line*, York: Joseph Rowntree Charitable Trust

Haslett, D. (undated), *The Role and Future Development of Day Services for Older People in Ireland*, Dublin: National Council on Ageing and Older People

Haslett, D., Ruddle, H. and Hennessy, G. (1998), *Future of the Home Help Service in Ireland*, Dublin: National Council on Ageing and Older People, report 55

Hayes, I. (2006), 'Charity Buries 13 Elderly People who Died Alone', *Sunday Tribune*, 6 August

Health Service Executive: *National Service Plan, 2005*, Dublin: HSE

Healy, A. (2007), 'Census Shows Radical Change in Way Modern Ireland Operates', *The Irish Times*, 29 June

Help the Aged (2003), *The Age Sector Infrastructure*, Belfast: Help the Aged

Help the Aged (2007), *Spotlight on Older People in the UK*, London: Help the Aged

Hennessy, M. (2005), 'Government Considers Option to Defer State Pension until 70', *The Irish Times*, 17 November

Hillyard, P., Kelly, G., McLaughlin, E., Patsios, D. and Tomlinson, M. (2003), *Bare Necessities: Poverty and Social Exclusion in Northern Ireland, Key Findings*, Belfast: Democratic Dialogue

Hodgins, M. and Greve, J. (2004a), 'Ageism in health policy', *Administration*, vol. 52, no. 2

Hodgins, M. and Greve, J. (2004b), *Attitudes to Ageing and Older People*, Galway: Centre for Health Promotion Studies, National University of Ireland, Galway

Home Office (1979), *The Government and the Voluntary Sector*, London: the Home Office

Home Office (1993), *The Efficiency Scrutiny,* London: HMSO

Homeless Agency (2006), *Counted in*, Dublin: Homeless Agency

Hospice Foundation (2004), *List of Voluntary and Community Hospice Groups in Ireland*, Dublin: Hospice Foundation

Hospice Foundation (2006), *Baseline Study on the Provision of Hospice/ Specialist Palliative Care Services in Ireland*, Dublin: Hospice Foundation

Hughes, J., Knox, C., Murray, M. and Greer, J. (1998), *Partnership Governance in Northern Ireland: The Path to Peace*, Dublin: Oak Tree Press

Hurley, M., Scallan, E., Johnson, H. and De La Harpe, D. (1997), 'Survey of eccentric vulnerable adults living in the greater Dublin area', unpublished, Dublin Council for the Aged and Eastern Health Board

Institute of Public Administration (2007), *Yearbook & Diary*, Dublin: IPA

Irish Association of Older People (1999), 'Older people in Ireland', staff briefing for the Equality Authority, 15 July

Irish Association of Older People (2000–05), *Getting on*, newsletter, various

Irish Council for Social Housing (2005), *An Overlooked Option in Caring for the Elderly — A Report on Sheltered and Group Housing Provided by Housing Associations in Ireland*, Dublin: Irish Council for Social Housing

Johnson, N. (1998), *Mixed Economies of Welfare: A Comparative Perspective*, Hemel Hempstead: Harvester Wheatsheaf

Jordan, A. (1989), 'Voluntary Societies in Victorian and Edwardian Belfast', unpublished PhD thesis, Queen's University, Belfast

Kearney, J. (1995), 'The Development of Government Policy and its Strategy towards the Voluntary and Community Sectors', in N. Acheson and A. P. Williamson (eds), *Voluntary Action and Social Policy in Northern Ireland*, Aldershot: Avebury

Kearney, J. and Williamson, A. P. (2001), 'Northern Ireland – the Delayed Devolution', in *Next Steps in Voluntary Action: An Analysis of Five Years of Developments in the Voluntary Sector in England, Northern Ireland, Scotland and Wales*, London: Centre for Civil Society, LSE and NCVO

Kemp, P. and Glendinning, C. (2006), 'Introduction', in C. Glendinning, and P. Kemp (ed), *Cash and Care: Policy Challenges in the Welfare State*, Bristol: The Policy Press

Kendall, J. (2003), *The Voluntary Sector: Comparative Perspectives in the UK,* London and New York: Routledge

Kendall, J., Knapp, M. and Forder, J. (2006), 'Social Care and the Nonprofit Sector in the Western Developed World', in W. W. Powell and R. Steinberg (eds), *The Non-Profit Sector: A Research Handbook*, 2nd edn, New Haven and London: Yale University Press

Kenway, P., MacInnis, T., Kelly, A. and Palmer, G. (2006), *Monitoring Poverty and Social Exclusion in Northern Ireland*, York: Joseph Rowntree Foundation

Knox, C. (2003) 'Democratic Renewal in Fragmented Communities: the Northern Ireland Case', *Local Governance,* vol. 29, no. 1, pp.14–37.

Knox, C. and Carmichael, P. (2007), 'The Review of Public Administration' in P. Carmichael, C. Knox and R. Osborne (eds), *Devolution and Constitutional Change in Northern Ireland,* Manchester: Manchester University Press

Koopmans, R. and Statham, P. (1999), 'Ethnic and Civic Conceptions of Nationhood and the Differential Success of the Extreme Right in Germany and Italy' in M. Giugni, D. McAdam, C. Tilly (eds), *How Social Movements Matter,* Minneapolis, MN: University of Minnesota Press

Land, H. (2006), 'Securing the Dignity and Quality of Life of Older Citizens', in C. Glendinning and P. Kemp (eds), *Cash and Care: Policy Challenges in the Welfare State,* Bristol: The Policy Press

Larragy, J. (2006), 'Origins and Significance of the Community and Voluntary Pillar in Irish Social Partnerships', *The Economic and Social Review,* vol. 37, no. 3, pp. 375–98

Lavan, A. (ed.) *50 Years of Social Welfare Policy,* Dublin: Department of Social, Community and Family Affairs

Layte, R. (2005), *Reflections,* remarks made to the National Council of Ageing and Older People, north–south conference, Dublin, 28 November

Layte, R., Fahey, T. and Whelan, C. T. (1999), *Income, Deprivation and Wellbeing among Older Irish People,* Dublin: National Council on Ageing and Older People, report 55

Layte, R., Nolan, B. and Whelan, C. T. (2000), 'Trends in Poverty', in B. Nolan, P. J. O'Connell and C. Whelan (eds), *Bust to Boom? The Irish Experience of Growth and Inequality,* Dublin: Economic and Social Research Institute and Institute of Public Administration

Lee, J. (1985), *Ireland, 1912–85,* Cambridge: Cambridge University Press

Lewis, J. (1999), 'Reviewing the Relationship between the Voluntary Sector and the State in Britain', *Voluntas,* vol. 10, no. 3, pp. 255–70

Lewis, J. (2004), 'The State and the Third Sector in Modern Welfare States: Independence, Instrumentality, Partnership', in A. Evers and J.-L. Laville (eds), *The Third Sector in Europe,* Cheltenham and Northampton, MA: Edward Elgar.

Lowe, R. (2005), *The Welfare State in Britain Since 1945,* Basingstoke: Palgrave Macmillan

Lukes, S. S. (1974), *Power: A Radical View,* London: Macmillan Press

Lundström, F. and McKeown, K. (1994), *Home Help Services for Elderly People in Ireland,* Dublin: National Council for the Elderly

Lynch, B. (2005), 'Community development with older people', *Inclusion through Local Development,* autumn, Dublin: Pobal

Lynch, B. (2005), *Age and Change,* Dublin: ADM

McAdam, D. (1996), 'Political Opportunities: Conceptual Origins, Current Problems, Future Directions', in D. McAdam, J. McCarthy and M. Zald (eds), *Comparative Perspectives in Social Movements*, Cambridge, New York and Melbourne: Cambridge University Press

McAdam, D., Tarrow, S., Tilly, C. (2001), *Dynamics of Contention*, Cambridge: Polity Press

McCall, C. and Williamson, A. P. (2001), 'Governance and Democracy in Northern Ireland: The Role of the Voluntary and Community Sector after the Agreement', *Governance*, vol. 14, no. 3, pp. 363–83

McCashin, A. (2005), 'The state pension — toward a basic income for the elderly', in J. Stewart (ed), *For Richer, For Poorer — An Investigation of the Irish Pension System*, Dublin: TASC

McCashin, A., O'Sullivan, E. and Brennan, C. (2002), 'The National Economic and Social Forum, social partnership and policy formulation in the Republic of Ireland', *Policy and Politics*, vol. 30, no. 2, pp. 263–79

McCrumm, J. (2002), *The Face of Older Homelessness*, Northern Ireland: Simon Community Northern Ireland

McGiven, Y. (ed.) (2004), *The Role and Future Development of Day Services for Older People in Ireland*, Dublin: National Council on Ageing and Older People

McKeown, K. (2004), 'A Review of Family Support Services in ClareCare', unpublished report, Dublin.

Maloney, W., Jordan, G. and McLaughlin, A. (1994), 'Interest Groups and Public Policy: the Insider/Outsider Model Revisited', *Journal of Public Policy*, vol. 14, no. 1

Mangan, I. (2005), 'The challenge of implementing equality for older people', *Inclusion through Local Development*, autumn, Dublin: Pobal

Midland Health Board (2001), *Annual Report, 2000*, Tullamore: Midland Health Board

Mid Western Health Board (2001), *Annual Report, 2000*, Limerick: Mid Western Health Board

Mid Western Health Board, *Service Plan, 2000*, Limerick: Mid Western Health Board

Milne, K. (1986), *Protestant Aid, 1836–1986 — A History of the Association for the Relief of Distressed Protestants*, Dublin: Protestant Aid

Mullins, D., Rhodes, M. L. and Williamson, A. (2003), *Non-profit Housing Organisations in Ireland, North and South: Changing Forms and Challenging Futures*, Belfast: Northern Ireland Housing Executive

Mulvihill, R. (1993), *Voluntary–Statutory Partnership in Community Care of the Elderly*, Dublin: National Council for the Elderly, report 25

Murphy, G. (2005), 'Interest groups in the policy-making process', in J. Coakley and M. Gallagher, *Politics in the Republic of Ireland*, 4th edn,

London and New York: Routledge and PSAI Press

Murray, P. (2005), 'Corralling the vulnerable', *Living it,* November

Murray, P. (2006), 'It is Time for us to Finally Say Goodbye to Ageism', *The Irish Times*, 15 February

Murray, P. K. (2004), 'This is no country for old men? Older people in the Republic of Ireland', presentation to Centre for Cross Border Studies seminar, 'Improving the Lives of Older People on the Island of Ireland', 2 June

National Committee on Volunteering (2002), *Tipping the Balance — Report and Recommendations to Government on Supporting and Developing Volunteering in Ireland*, Dublin: National Committee on Volunteering

National Council for the Elderly (1994), *Strengthening the Links — Coordination of Statutory and Voluntary Services for the Elderly at Local Level*, Dublin: National Council for the Elderly

National Council on Ageing and Older People (2000), *Annual Report*, Dublin: National Council on Ageing and Older People

National Council on Ageing and Older People (2005a), *An Age-Friendly Society — A Position Statement*, Dublin: National Council on Ageing and Older People; and *A Resource Document,* supplement

National Council on Ageing and Older People (2005b), 'New report points to evidence of ageing in Irish health and social services', Dublin: National Council on Ageing and Older People

National Council on Ageing and Older People (2005c), *Loneliness and Social Isolation among Older Irish People*, Dublin: National Council on Ageing and Older People, report 84

National Council on Ageing and Older People (undated a), *Community Care Services*, fact file 6, Dublin: National Council on Ageing and Older People

National Council on Ageing and Older People (undated b), *Voluntary Sector Services*, fact file 10. Dublin: National Council on Ageing and Older People

National Economic and Social Council (2005), *The Developmental Welfare State*, Dublin: NESC

National Economic and Social Forum (NESF) (2003a), *Equality Policies for Older People — Implementation Issues*, Dublin: NESF and Government Publications, forum report 29

National Economic and Social Forum (NESF) (2003b), *The Policy Implications of Social Capital*, Dublin: NESF and Government Publications, forum report 23

National Economic and Social Forum (NESF) (2006), *Care for Older People*, Dublin: NESF

NCB (2006), *2020 Vision — Ireland's Demographic Dividend*, Dublin: NCB

Newman, J. (2001), *Modernising Governance: New Labour, Policy and Society*, London, Thousand Oaks, CA: Sage Publications

North Eastern Health Board (2001a), *Healthy Ageing — A Secure Future: A Five Year Strategy for the Delivery of Services to Older People*, Strategic Reference Framework, Kells: North Eastern Health Board

North Eastern Health Board (2001b), *Service Plan, 2000*, Kells: North Eastern Health Board

North Western Health Board (2001), *Annual Report, 2000*, Manorhamilton: North Western Health Board [draft]

North Western Health Board (2001a), *Financial Statement and Service Plan 2000*, Manorhamilton: North Western Health Board

Northern Area Health Board (2001b), *Annual Report, 2000*, Dublin: Northern Area Health Board

Northern Ireland Council for Voluntary Action (NICVA) (2002), *The State of the Sector III*, Belfast: NICVA

Northern Ireland Council for Voluntary Action (NICVA) (2005), *State of the Sector IV*, Belfast: NICVA

Northern Ireland Housing Executive (NIHE) (2006), *Annual Report 2005/2006*, Belfast: NIHE

Northern Ireland Statistics and Research Agency (NISRA) (2003), *A Statistical Profile of Older People in Northern Ireland*, Belfast: NISRA

O'Brien, C. (2006a), 'Charities Regulator Included in New Bill', *The Irish Times*, 10 March

O'Brien, C. (2006b), 'Call for Mandatory Retirement at 65 to be Abolished', *The Irish Times*, 21 June

O'Brien, C. (2006c), 'Over 50, Happy and a Challenge to the Stereotype', *The Irish Times*, 7–8 September

O'Brien, C. (2007), 'Irish More Likely to Work into Old Age — Report', *The Irish Times*, 22 May

Ó Cinnéide, S. (2000), 'The 1949 white paper and its impact on social welfare policy', in A. Lavan (ed.), *50 Years of Social Welfare Policy*, Dublin: Department of Social, Community and Family Affairs

O'Connell, C. (1994), 'Housing in the Republic of Ireland — a review of trends and recent policy measures', *Administration*, vol. 42, no. 2

O'Ferrall, F. (2000), *Citizenship and Public Service — Voluntary and Statutory Relationships in Irish Healthcare*, Dublin and Dundalk: Adelaide Hospital Society and Dundalgan Press

O'Hanlon, A., McGee, H., Barker, M., Garavan, R., Hickey, A., Ronroy, R. and O'Neill, D. (2005), *Health and Social Services for Older People II (HeSSOP II) — Changing Profiles from 2000–4*, Dublin: National Council on Ageing and Older People, report 91

O'Loughlin, A. (2005) 'Social Policy and Older People', in S. Quin, P. Kennedy, A. Matthews and G. Kiely (eds), *Contemporary Irish Social Policy*, Dublin: University College, Dublin

Ó Riain, S. and O'Connell, P. (2000), 'The role of the state in growth and welfare', in B. Nolan, P. J. O'Connell and C. Whelan (eds), *Bust to Boom? The Irish Experience of Growth and Inequality*, Dublin: Economic and Social Research Institute and Institute of Public Administration

O'Shea, E. (1993), *The Impact of Social and Economic Policies on Older People in Ireland*, Dublin: National Council for the Elderly, report 24

O'Shea, E. (2004), *Evaluation of the Senior Help Line*, Summerhill, County Meath: Senior Help Line

O'Shea, E. (2006), 'Older People Must Not Be Last in the Queue', *The Irish Times*, 24 July

O'Sullivan, T. (1994), 'The voluntary statutory relationship in the health services', *Administration*, vol. 42, no. 1

Office of First Minister and Deputy First Minister (2005a), *Ageing in an Inclusive Society*, Belfast: Office of First Minister and Deputy First Minister

Office of First Minister and Deputy First Minister (2005b), *A Shared Future: Policy and Strategic Framework for Good Relations in Northern Ireland*, Belfast: Office of First Minister and Deputy First Minister

Office of First Minister and Deputy First Minister (2006), *Lifetime Opportunities: Government's Anti-Poverty and Social Exclusion Strategy for Northern Ireland*, Belfast: Office of First Minister and Deputy First Minister

Osborne, S.P. and McLaughlin, K. (2004), 'The cross-cutting review of the voluntary sector. Where next for local government — voluntary sector relationships?' *Regional Studies*, vol. 38, no. 5, pp. 571–80

Our Lady's Hospice (2003), *Annual Report, 2002*, Dublin: Sisters of Charity

Phillipson, C. and Scharf, T. (2004), *The Impact of Government Policy on the Social Exclusion of Older People, A Review of the Literature*, London: the Cabinet Office

Pierson, C. (1998), *Beyond the Welfare State: The New Political Economy of Welfare*, Cambridge: Polity Press

Pierson, P. (2001), *The New Politics of the Welfare State*, Oxford: Oxford University Press

Power, B. (1978), *Old and Alone in Ireland — A Survey of Old People Living Alone*, Dublin: Society of St Vincent de Paul

Power, C. (2005), 'Promoting active citizenship across the EU', *Inclusion through Local Development*, autumn, Dublin: Pobal

Pratt, H. J. (1995) 'Seniors' organisations and seniors' empowerment — an international perspective', in D. Thursz, C. Nusberg and J. Prather, *Empowering Older People — An International Approach*, London: Cassell

Prendergast, D. (2006), 'Non-profit sector: Role in providing home care', in V. Timonen, M. Doyle and D. Prendergast (2006), *No Place Like Home: Domiciliary Care Services for Older People in Ireland*, Dublin: The Liffey Press

Prospectus (2003), *Audit of Functions and Structures in the Health System*, Dublin: Department of Health and Children

Protestant Aid (2005), *Annual Report, 2004*, Dublin: Protestant Aid

Prunty, Martina (2007), *Older People in Poverty in Ireland*, Dublin: Combat Poverty Agency

Putnam, R. D. (1993), *Making Democracy Work: Civic Traditions in Modern Italy.* Princeton, NJ: Princeton University Press

Putnam, R. D. (2000), *Bowling Alone: The Collapse and Revival of American Community*, New York: Simon and Schuster

Respond! (2005), 'Interim report on Baldoyle', unpublished report, Dublin

Rhodes, R. A. W. (1994), 'The hollowing out of the state', *Political Quarterly*, no. 21, pp. 181–205

Robins, J. (ed.) (1997), *Reflections on Health — Commemorating Fifty Years of the Department of Health, 1947–1997*, Dublin: Institute of Public Administration

Rottman, D. B. (1999), 'Problems of, and Prospects for, Comparing the Two Irelands', in A. F. Heath, R. Breen, C. T. Whelan (eds), *Ireland, North and South: Perspectives from the Social Sciences*, Proceedings of the British Academy, Oxford: Oxford University Press

Rourke, S. (2005), *Research Project on Older People Living in Stoneybatter*, Dublin: An Siol

Ruddle, H., Donoghue, F. and Mulvihill, R. (1997), *The Years Ahead Report — A Review of the Implementation of its Recommendations*, Dublin: National Council on Ageing and Older People, report 48

Salamon, L. and Anheier, H. (1994), *The Emerging Sector: The Nonprofit Sector in Comparative Perspective — An Overview*, Baltimore: The Johns Hopkins University Institute for Policy Studies

Salamon, L. and Anheier, H. (1998), 'Social Origins of Civil Society: Explaining the Nonprofit Sector Cross-Nationally', *Voluntas*, vol. 9, no. 3, pp. 213–48

Scharf, T., Phillipson, C. and Smith, A. (2005), *Multiple Exclusion and Quality of Life amongst Excluded Older People in Disadvantaged Neighbourhoods*, London: Cabinet Office

Scott, D. and Russell, L. (2001), 'Contracting: the Experience of Service Delivery Organisations' in M. Harris and C. Rochester (eds), *Voluntary*

Organisations and Social Policy in Britain: Perspectives on Change and Choice, Basingstoke: Palgrave Macmillan

Silke, D. (1994), *Older People's Attitudes to their Accommodation — What We Want*, Dublin: Dublin Central Mission with Dublin University (Trinity College)

Silke, D. (1996), 'Older people's attitudes to their accommodation', *Administration,* vol. 44, no. 3

Simpson, D. (1999), *Pressure Groups*, London: Hodder & Stoughton

Smelser, N. (1962), *Theory of Collective Behaviour,* London: Routledge & Kegan Paul

Smith, S. R. and Gronbjerg, K. (2006), 'Scope and Theory of Government-Nonprofit Relations', in W. W. Powell, and R. Steinberg (eds), *The Non-Profit Sector: A Research Handbook*, 2nd edn, New Haven and London: Yale University Press

Smyth, D. (2005), 'Policy perspectives', remarks made to National Council on Ageing and Older People north–south conference, Dublin, 28 November

Society of St Vincent de Paul (2005), *Making a Difference — Annual Report of the Society of St Vincent de Paul, 2005*, Dublin: Society of St Vincent de Paul

South Eastern Health Board (2000), *Annual Report, 1999*, Kilkenny: South Eastern Health Board

Southern Health Board (2001a), *Annual Report, 2000*, Cork: Southern Health Board

Southern Health Board (2001b), *Service Plan, 2000*, Cork: Southern Health Board

Southside Partnership (1999), *Directory of Older Persons' Organisations*, Dún Laoghaire: Southside Partnership

Stewart, J. (ed) (2005), *For Richer, For Poorer — An Investigation of the Irish Pension System*, Dublin: TASC

Stratton, D. (2004), *The Housing Needs of Older People*, Dublin: Age Action Ireland

Stratton, D. (2005), 'Looking after our ageing population — the case for pension reform', *Action on Poverty Today*, vol. 11, winter.

Surender, R. (2004), 'Modern Challenges to the Welfare State and the Antecedents of the Third Way', in R. Surender and J. Lewis (eds), *Welfare State Change: Towards a Third Way?*, Oxford: Oxford University Press

Tansey, J. (2001), *CareLocal Clients — Where They Live and Related Issues*, Dublin: J. Tansey

Tarrow, S. (1994), *Power in Movement: Social Movements, Collective Action and Mass Politics in the Modern State*, Cambridge: Cambridge University Press

Taylor, M. (2000), 'Communities in the lead: Power, Organisational Capacity and Social Capital', *Urban Studies*, vol. 37, no. 5–6, pp. 1019–35

Taylor, M. (2003), *Public Policy in the Community*, Basingstoke: Palgrave Macmillan

Timonen, V., Doyle, M. and Prendergast, D. (2006), *No Place Like Home: Domiciliary Care Services for Older People in Ireland*, Dublin: The Liffey Press

Walker, A. (1998), 'Speaking for themselves — the new politics of old age in Europe', *Education and Ageing*, vol. 13, no. 1

Walker, A. (1999), *Attitudes to Population Ageing in Europe — A Comparison of the 1992 and 1999 Eurobarometer Surveys*, Sheffield: University of Sheffield

Walker, A. (2003), 'Social Exclusion and Growing Older', paper given at the 'Ageing in an Inclusive Society' conference, Belfast, 28 March

Walker, A. and Naegele, G. (1993), *The Politics of Old Age in Europe*, Buckingham: Open University Press

Wanless, D. (2006), *Securing Good Care for Older People: Taking a Long Term View*, London: the King's Fund

Watson, D. and Williams, J. (2003), *Irish National Survey of Housing Quality*, Dublin: Economic and Social Research Institute

Western Health Board (1998), *An Information Guide to Western Health Board Services*, Galway: Western Health Board

Western Health Board (1999), *Directory of Health and Voluntary Services*, Galway: Western Health Board

Western Health Board (2001a), *Annual Report, 2000*, Galway: Western Health Board

Western Health Board (2001b), *Service Plan, 2000*, Galway: Western Health Board

Whelan, C. T., Nolan, B. and Maitre, B. (2005), *Trends in Welfare for Vulnerable Groups, Ireland, 1994–2001*, Dublin: Economic and Social Research Institute

Wolfenden, Lord (1978), *The Future of Voluntary Organisations: Report of the Wolfenden Committee*, London: Croom Helm

Young, I. M. (2000), *Inclusion and Democracy*, Oxford: Oxford University Press

Zaidi, A. (2006a), *Pension Policy in EU25 and its Possible Impact on Elderly Poverty*, Vienna: European Centre for Social Welfare Policy and Research

Zaidi, A. (2006b), *Poverty of Elderly People in EU25*, Vienna: European Centre for Social Welfare Policy and Research

Index

Abbeyfield Societies in NI 87, 192–193
Acheson, N. 2, 31, 67, 68, 69, 70, 71,
    74, 87, 97, 175, 177, 181
active ageing 50, 88
Age & Opportunity (Ireland) 50–51,
    120, 164, 167, 201
Age Action Ireland 111, 128, 179, 197–
    199
    Department of Health and Children,
        role of 169
    directory 124, 130
    funding 197–198
    National Economic and Social Forum
        166, 167, 198
    networks 97, 136, 197, 198, 208
    social partnership 166
    style/perception of 168, 169–170, 171,
        175, 198–199
Age Concern Northern Ireland 87–88,
    102, 105, 175, 179
    Atlantic Philanthropies 102–103
    Equality Commission 156
    funding 81, 87
    Help the Aged and 89
    networks 84, 87, 88, 93, 94, 198
        Age Sector Reference Group 90, 91
        Engage with Age 98
        Older People's Forum 92
    policy-making 159, 161
    set up 68, 69, 87–88
    trading company 88
age discrimination *see* discrimination
Age Sector Reference Group (NI) 89–
    91, 101–102, 103, 156, 180–181
    Assembly 90, 153–154
    Civic Forum 90, 157
Albania 228
Allen, Hugh 226
Almond, G.A. 2
ALONE 111, 120, 141, 175, 214–216

    funding 214, 215
Alzheimer Society
    Ireland 111, 124, 140–141, 211–212
        funding 117, 124, 212
        Sligo Day Care Centre 225–226
    Northern Ireland
        funding 81
Amsterdam Treaty (1997) 8, 10, 181
Anheier, H.K. 2, 5
Arthritis Care Northern Ireland 81
arts festival 50–51
Atlantic Philanthropies 182
    Ireland 119–120, 161, 182
    Northern Ireland 102–103
Austria 11, 13

Bagguley, P. 184
Baines, S. 127
Banting, K. 74, 104
Barnes, M. 26
'Barnett' process 29, 149
Barrington, R. 121
Batljan, I. 13
Belfast Central Mission (BCM) 191–192
Belgium 2, 13
Bell, V. 157
Bermingham, W. 43, 56–57, 214, 215
Birrell, D. 145
Blair, Tony 104
Boland, R. 217
Boldt, S. 50
Booth, L. 226
Boyle, G. 47
Boyle, R. 110
Breda, J. 27
Brown, S. 60, 123, 127–128
Browne, M. 44, 54, 60–61, 113
Bryson House Charitable Group, Belfast
    87, 193–194
Byrne, Noel 141, 222–223

Callan, T. 41
Callely, Ivor 162–163
CareLocal 47, 216–217
carers
    allowances 27, 54, 178
    Ireland 54, 114, 124, 129, 140–141
        Care Alliance 208
        Carers Association 111, 141, 163,
            170, 208–209
    Northern Ireland 21–22, 27, 33, 154,
        157, 173
        Carers Northern Ireland 81, 87, 160,
            195–196
        legislation 196
Carey, E. 50, 120, 205
Carlow EQUAL 224–225
Carroll, Mella 228
Caul, B. 30
charities, legal basis in Ireland of 108, 109
Charles, Iris 208
churches *see* religious groups
Churchill, Winston 51
Citizens' Information Board (Ireland) 108
Civic Forum (NI) 90, 157–158
Clare Social Services Council (now
    Clarecare) 108
Clarke, J. 104
Coakley, D. 45, 52
Comfort Keepers 49
community action *see* voluntary action
Community Foundation for NI 78
comparison between Ireland and NI
    conclusions 181–186
    differences 177–178, 180–181
    similarities 178–180
Connolly, E. 143
Convery, J. 121–122
Cooney, D.L. 226
Cornerstone 57
corporatist
    approach 146, 147, 167, 168, 172, 174
    regimes 5
Council for Services for Older People
    (Dublin) 219
councils, local
    Northern Ireland 99–100, 150–151
Cousins, M. 41

Cowley, Jerry 167
Coxall, B. 147
cross-border networks 86, 97–98, 136–
    137, 198, 222
Crossley, N. 183
Crowley, N. 58
Cullen, K. 54
Cullen, P. 41
Cumming, E. 12
Curry, J. 47, 54, 55, 56

Dahl, R.A. 2
Darby, J.J. 45
definitions xiv–xvi
Delaney, S. 44, 165
Delors, Jacques 9
Democratic Unionist Party (DUP) 157
demographic trends 6–8
    Ireland 38–40
    Northern Ireland 17–18
Dempsey, A. 50
Denmark 12, 13, 41
Department for Health and Children
    (Ireland) 14, 45, 116
    funding of voluntary sector 117, 120
        individual bodies 117, 198, 199,
            204, 205, 208, 210
    health policy 45–51, 114–115
    policy-making 161–164, 168–169,
        172–173
    voluntary housing and social care 213
    see also Health Service Executive
Department of Health, Social Services
    and Public Safety (DHSSPS) (NI)
    151, 152, 153, 157, 160–161
    funding from 80–81, 152
    Investing for Health 33–34, 95, 98, 99,
        104, 154–155
Department for Social Development
    (DSD) (NI) 29, 72, 152, 158
dependency ratio 8, 23, 39
Dimas, S. 40, 42, 106
disability or illness, long-term
    Ireland 166, 176
    Northern Ireland 20–21, 105, 154, 175
        Disability Action 84
    see also discrimination

discrimination
    Ireland 58–60
        Carlow EQUAL 224–225
        Northern Ireland 34, 105, 156, 181
        group rights 73, 74, 90, 101, 104–
            105, 153, 154, 155, 156, 171,
            196
    United Kingdom 28, 34
disengagement paradigm 12
Ditch, J. 68
domiciliary care
    Ireland 46, 47, 48, 49, 50, 51, 112,
        113, 124, 131
    Northern Ireland 26–27, 46
Donnellan, E. 47
Donoghue, F. 2, 123, 127
Down Lisburn Health and Social
    Services Trust 81–82
Dublin Central Mission 139, 226–227
Duignan, C. 122
Dunne, M.A. 203

Eldin, Nazih 220
Ellison, N. 23, 69
Engage with Age (NI) 94, 98–100, 155
England 104
    charities and public services 74
    fuel poverty 20
    independent service providers 70
    social care 25, 26, 27
equality *see* discrimination
Equality Authority (Ireland) xv, 50, 58,
    59, 65, 128, 164
Equality Commission (NI) 90, 105, 156
Esping-Andersen, G. 2, 5, 22
European Court of Justice 10
European Parliament 199
European Union xv, 50, 181–182
    Community Initiative Programme,
        EQUAL 224
    demographic trends 6–8
    funding from 78, 96, 97, 181–182
    National Action Plans on poverty 36
    policies 8–9
    social spending 41
    voluntary action 9–10
        historical development 10–14

Evason, E. 18, 19, 20, 21, 22, 102, 183,
    184
Evers, A. 3, 6, 185
ExtraCare Northern Ireland 73, 161,
    189–190
    funding 190

Fahey, T. 40, 56, 127
Faughnan, P. 107, 108
Federation of Active Retirement
    Associations (FARA) (Ireland) 136,
        138, 204–206
Fianna Fáil 61–62
FitzGerald, E. 39, 47, 61
FitzGerald, G. 39, 41
Fogarty, M.J. 123
Fold Housing Association 160, 194–195
    Telecare 190, 195
France 13
Francis Hospice, St (Raheny) 139, 228–
    229
Friends of the Elderly 111
    Cork 219
    Dublin 217–218
fuel poverty 20, 44
funding of voluntary sector
    comparison of Ireland and NI 179,
        180
    European Union 78, 96, 97, 181–182
    Ireland 109, 112, 116–120, 124, 125,
        135–136, 172
        Atlantic Philanthropies 119–120,
            182
        Department of Health and Children
            117, 120
        Departments, other 58, 119, 120
        health boards 107, 111, 117, 170
        Health Service Executive 117–119,
            120, 136
        lottery 117, 180
        section 39 grants 117
        section 65 grants 107, 116, 117, 170
    Northern Ireland 72–73, 78–82, 93,
        96, 99
        Atlantic Philanthropies 102–103,
            161, 182
        DHSSPS 80–81, 152

health and social services trusts 78,
    79–80, 81–82, 96
Help the Aged, grants from 89
Housing Executive 190, 191–192
lottery 78, 93, 95, 99
    see also individual organisations

Gallagher, Eric 192
Gartland, F. 50
Germany 5, 11, 12, 13, 14, 178
'Good Friday' agreement 71, 73, 89
Grant, W. 147, 172, 201
Green Party (Ireland) 61
Griffiths, H. 68
group rights, NI 73, 74, 90, 101, 104–
    105, 153, 154, 155, 156, 171
    carers 196

Harney, Mary 49
Harvey, B. 117
Haslett, D. 46, 113, 123
Hayes, I. 216
Health Service Executive (Ireland) 50,
    51, 111, 167
    funding of voluntary sector 117–119,
        120, 136
        individual bodies 198, 208, 210,
            212, 218, 221, 225
    National Service Plan 2005 51, 114,
        162
    policy, execution of 162, 163, 170
health and social care, public policy on
    Ireland 45–51, 114–115
    Northern Ireland 24–27, 29–34
Healy, A. 54
Help the Aged Northern Ireland 86, 88–
    89, 102, 105, 179, 198
    Age Concern Northern Ireland and 89
    Age Sector Reference Group and 90,
        91
    Atlantic Philanthropies 102–103
    Engage with Age 98
    funding from DHSSPS 81
    Older People's Forum 92
    review of age sector 92–93
Hennessy, M. 53
Hillyard, P. 18, 19

Hodgins, M. 12, 60, 175, 176
homelessness 43, 62
hospice care 129
    Hospice Foundation 115–116, 130,
        209–211
    St Francis Hospice, Raheny 228–229
housing 41
    Ireland 41, 42, 43–44, 48, 56–58, 115,
        126
        Dublin Central Mission 139, 226–
            227
        funding 119, 120, 126
        Irish Council for Social Housing
            (ICSH) 126, 136, 213–214
        Respond! 213–214
        social care 213
        Society of St Vincent de Paul 126,
            206
        Sue Ryder Foundation 140, 141,
            227–228
    Northern Ireland 19–20, 41, 126, 152
        Fold Housing Association 160, 194–
            195
Hughes, J. 150
Hunter, Margaret 226
Hurley, M. 43

income distribution 5, 19
income poverty rates 18–19, 40, 41–42
inflation 19
insider/outsider groups 73, 74, 147–148,
    169, 170
institutional approach 2–3
International Fund for Ireland
    Community Bridges 224
Investing for Health initiative (NI) 33–
    34, 95, 98, 99, 104, 154–155
Irish Association of Older People 164,
    166, 202–203
Irish Council for Social Housing (ICSH)
    126, 136, 213–214
Irish Countrywomen's Association 201,
    205
Irish Hospice Foundation 115–116, 130,
    209–211
Irish Senior Citizens Parliament 128,
    136, 166, 170, 171, 179, 199–201

funding 117, 199
Italy 11, 13

Johnson, N. 3
Jordan, A. 67

Kearney, J. 68, 69, 71, 145
Kemp, P. 24
Kenway, P. 18, 178
Knox, C. 72, 150, 152
Koopmans, R. 183

Land, H. 22, 25, 26, 27
Larragy, J. 171
Law Centre, Northern Ireland 84, 160
Layte, R. 40, 42, 43–44, 55–56
Lee, J. 14, 51
Lewis, J. 4, 5, 104
liberal regimes 5
life expectancy
    European Union 7, 38
    Ireland 38, 48–49
    Northern Ireland
        Investing for Health initiative 33,
            155
        UK antipoverty strategy 35
Lions Clubs 210
local government
    Ireland 45, 46, 165
    Northern Ireland 99–100, 150–151
loneliness *see* social
        exclusion/isolation
Longford Older People's Network 219
lottery funding
    Ireland 117, 180
    Northern Ireland 78, 93, 95, 99, 180
Lowe, R. 23, 69
Lukes, S.S. 148, 175
Lundström, F. 46
Luxembourg 13
Lynch, B. 112

Maastricht Treaty (1992) 8, 9
McAdam, D. 183, 184
McCall, C. 157
McCashin, A. 51
McCrumm, J. 43

McDonald, Charles 141
Macedonia 228
McGiven, Y. 114
McKeown, K. 108
Maloney, W. 147, 148
managerialism, rational scientific 146,
    159, 173, 174
Mangan, I. 63
men
    life expectancy 38
    pensioners, number of
        Northern Ireland 18
methods, research xiv
Milne, K. 120, 121, 126
Mullins, D. 126
Mulvihill, R. 113, 120, 125, 136
Murphy, G. 145
Murray, P. 9, 49, 58–59, 169, 199
Murray, P.K. 43, 61

Nally, Mary 220
National Council for the Aged (Ireland)
    (June 1981–Jan 1990) 50, 113, 163,
    164
National Council for the Elderly
    (Ireland) (Jan 1990–Mar 1997) 113,
    163
National Council on Ageing and Older
    People (Ireland) 59, 65, 125, 143,
    163–164, 166, 173
    criticism of public policy/
        implementation 43, 60, 61, 62
    over eighties 39
    perception of community services 47
    pluralist model 168
    policy community 169
    social situation of older people 43, 44
    volunteering 127
National Economic and Social Council
    (Ireland) 52, 53, 61, 63, 110, 164
National Economic and Social Forum
    (Ireland) 63, 65, 109, 110, 164
    Care for Older People (2005) 39, 41,
        59–60, 115, 128, 166–167, 169
    social capital 109, 127
National Federation of Pensioners'
    Associations (Ireland) 172, 203–204

National Social Service Council
(Ireland) 108, 177
Netherlands 11, 12, 13, 178
Newman, J. 104, 147
Newry and Mourne Senior Citizens'
Consortium 96–97, 100
Newry University of the Third Age 101
Nice Treaty (2001) 8–9, 181
Northern Ireland Act 1998 34, 74, 90,
104–105, 156, 161, 171, 181, 196
Northern Ireland Council on Ageing *see*
Age Concern Northern Ireland
Northern Ireland Council for Social
Services (NICSS) 68, 69, 87, 177,
178
Northern Ireland Council for Voluntary
Action (NICVA) 69, 70, 87, 92,
177–178
Northern Ireland Social Care Council
(NISCC) 154
Northern Ireland Voluntary Trust 69
Norton, William 51
nursing and residential homes
Ireland 47, 48, 49, 121, 124–125, 126
UK 25, 26, 27
Northern Ireland 26, 32–33

O'Brien, C. 40, 44, 59, 108, 127
O'Callaghan, Frances 221
Ó Cinnéide, S. 52
O'Connell, C. 56
O'Ferrall, F. 121
Office of First Minister and Deputy First
Minister (OFMDFM) 34, 36, 151–
152, 156–157, 160, 161
O'Halloran, Michael 199
O'Hanlon, A. 123
Older Women's Network (OWN) 201–
202
O'Loughlin, A. 121
Ó Riain, S. 41, 43
Osborne, S.P. 72, 176
O'Shea, E. 124, 220, 221
O'Sullivan, T. 107, 123
outsider/insider groups 73, 74, 147–148,
169, 170

palliative care services, Ireland 47–48,
49, 62
hospice care 129
Hospice Foundation 115–116, 130,
209–211
St Francis Hospice, Raheny 228–229
Pensioners' Convention, UK National/NI
90, 92, 105, 159, 179
pensions 13
comparison between Ireland and NI
178
European Union 8–9
introduction of 10, 11
Ireland 41, 42, 43, 51–53, 65
commitments on 165
nineteenth century 121
United Kingdom 23–24
Phillipson, C. 29, 35
Pierson, C. 5
Pierson, P. 5
pluralist model 146, 167–168
policy community approach 146, 147,
159–160, 168, 172, 173, 174
policy-making: Ireland
conclusions 171–176
Department of Finance 169, 173, 175
Department for Health and Children
161–164, 168–169, 172–173
electoral cycle 165
experience of participation in 168–171
generally on policy-making 145–148
health board system (1970–2004) 162,
170
Health Service Executive 162, 163,
170
local authorities 165
National Council on Ageing and Older
People 163–164, 166, 169, 173
National Economic and Social Council
164
National Economic and Social Forum
164, 166–167, 169
national partnership agreements 165–
166
Oireachtas 167
typology of engagement 146–147,
167–168, 174

policy-making: Northern Ireland
  1998 devolution settlement 150, 151–152
  2005 Review 150–151, 152–153
  Age Sector Reference Group 90, 91, 153–154, 156, 157, 181
  'Barnett' process 149
  Central Personal Social Services Advisory Committee 153
  Civic Forum 90, 157–158
  conclusions 171–172, 173–175, 176
  Department of Health, Social Services and Public Safety (DHSSPS) 151, 152, 153, 154–155, 157, 160–161
  Department for Social Development 72, 152, 158
  direct rule 149–150
  experience of participation in 158–161
  generally on policy-making 145–148
  government/voluntary-sector forum 158, 161
  introduction 148–149
  Office of First Minister and Deputy First Minister (OFMDFM) 151–152, 156–157, 160, 161
  social care, regulation of 154
  typology of engagement 146–147, 159–160, 174
population trends 6–8
  Ireland 38–40
  Northern Ireland 17–18
Portugal 12
Positive Age, Cavan 139, 221–222
poverty 178
  Ireland 40, 41–42
    antipoverty policy 54–56
    fuel 44
  Northern Ireland 18–19
    antipoverty policy 34–36, 156–157, 160
    fuel 20
Power, B. 41, 122–123, 127, 169, 175, 207
Power, C. 219
power relations and policy-making 148, 175
Pratt, H.J. 10–11

Prendergast, D. 46
Presbyterian Board of Social Witness 81
Protestant Aid (previously Association for the Relief of Distressed Protestants) 120, 121, 126
Prunty, M. 42, 58, 178
public policy in Ireland 45
  care packages 49–50
  conclusions 63–65
  critique of 60–63
  demographic trends 38–40
  equality 58–60
  health 45–51
  housing 56–58
  landmarks in development of 64
  medical cards 47, 54
  poverty and social inclusion 54–56
  social situation of older people 40–44
    average age of retirement 44
    health 41, 44
    housing and fuel poverty 41, 42, 43–44
    social spending 40–41
  voluntary sector 106–116
    funding 107, 109, 111, 112, 116–120
    welfare and income support 51–54
public policy in Northern Ireland 22–24
  conclusions 36–37
  demographic trends 17–18
  differences between NI and rest of UK 29–33
    equality and strategic policy 34–36
    Investing for Health initiative 33–34, 95, 98, 99, 104, 154–155
  introduction 16
  social care 24–27
  social situation of older people 18
    health and social care 20–22
    housing and fuel poverty 19–20
    incomes 18–19
  strategy for ageing society 27–29
  voluntary sector and 67–74, 103–105
Putnam, R.D. 2

Queen's University, Belfast 102–103

rational scientific managerialism 146,
    159, 173, 174
Red Cross 121–122
Redmond, Mary 228
Relatives Association NI 81
religious groups 10
    Ireland 121, 122, 123
        Catholic orders 121, 125, 129, 210,
            228
        Protestant Aid (previously
            Association for the Relief of
            Distressed Protestants) 120,
            121, 126
        Northern Ireland 100, 101
    residential and nursing homes
        Ireland 47, 48, 49, 121, 124–125,
            126
        UK 25, 26, 27
            Northern Ireland 26, 32–33
Respond! 126, 132, 213–214
Rhodes, R.A.W. 5
Rottman, D.B. 2
Rourke, S. 44, 46, 59
Ruddle, H. 56, 57, 62
Rural Community Network (NI) 84
Ryan, Tom 203

St Francis Hospice, Raheny 139, 228–
    229
Salamon, L. 2
Saunders, Cicely 209
Scotland 25, 29
Scott, D. 70
Senior Citizens Action Forum
    (Waterford) 219
Senior Helpline (Summerhill Active
    Retirement Association, Co Meath)
    139, 140, 220–221
Silke, D. 125, 227
Sinn Féin 151
Sligo Alzheimer Day Care Centre 225–
    226
Smelser, N. 183
Smith, S.R. 2
Smyth, D. 14

social democratic regimes 5
social exclusion/isolation 22, 28–29, 34–
    36, 44, 101, 179
social movement theory 183–184
social security benefits
    Ireland 54, 178
    UK 24, 27, 29, 178
        Northern Ireland 18, 19, 20–21, 29,
            152
social situation of older people
    Ireland 40–44
    Northern Ireland 18–22
social work service
    Ireland 46–47
Society of St Vincent de Paul (SVP) 111,
    123, 124, 166, 206–207
    funding 81, 207
    housing 126, 206
Spain 13, 41
Sperrin Lakeland
    Health and Social Services Trust 81,
        82
    Senior Citizens' Consortium 94–95,
        97, 102
Stewart, J. 53
Stratton, D. 53
Sue Ryder Foundation 140, 141, 227–
    228
Surender, R. 4
Sweden 5, 13, 46, 178

Tansey, J. 47, 56, 57, 127, 217
tax credits, pension 24
taxation
    Ireland
        tax relief for pension contributions
            53
    Northern Ireland 29, 159
Taylor, M. 73, 147, 148
travel on public transport, free 54, 178
Travellers 43, 47

United Kingdom 12, 13, 14, 185
    antipoverty strategy 35–36
    carers 22, 27
    comparison with Ireland 178
    England 20, 25, 26, 27, 70, 74, 104

income poverty rates 18–19
National Pensioners' Convention 92
Northern Ireland *see* comparison
  between Ireland and NI;
  individual bodies/organisations;
  policy-making: Northern Ireland;
  public policy in Northern Ireland;
  voluntary action in Northern
  Ireland
public policies for older people 22–24
  differences in NI 29–36
  social care 24–27
  strategy for ageing society 27–29
  voluntary sector 103–104, 105, 176
social isolation 22
social spending 41
Wales 25, 70, 74
University of the Third Age 101

Vincent de Paul, Society of St (SVP)
  111, 123, 124, 166, 206–207
  funding 81, 207
  housing 126, 206
voluntary action in Ireland
  case studies 138–141
    Carlow EQUAL 224–225
    Dublin Central Mission 139, 226–
      227
    Positive Age, Cavan 139, 221–222
    St Francis Hospice, Raheny 139,
      228–229
    Senior Helpline (Summerhill) 139,
      140, 220–221
    Sligo Alzheimer Day Care Centre
      225–226
    Sue Ryder Foundation 140, 141,
      227–228
    Westgate Foundation 139, 141,
      222–224
  conclusions 141–144
  cross-border contacts 86, 97–98, 136–
    137, 198, 222
  current position 123, 125, 128–130
    campaigning voice 127–128, 181
    housing 126
    information, sources of 124, 130
    nursing homes 121, 124–125, 126

    role of older people in
      planning/service delivery 128
    volunteering 121, 126–127
  definition xv–xvi
  emergence of 120–123, 126
  features of 132–133, 138
    age profile 133–134
    federation and co-operation 136–
      137
    funding 135–136
    future work 137
    old people served 134
    policy-making, involvement in
      137
    staffing and volunteers 134–135
  mapping of 130–131
    local organisations 131–132
    public policy and 106–116
      1988 *The Years Ahead* 112, 113
      2000 *Supporting Voluntary Activity*
        108–109
      charities, legal basis of 108, 109
      funding 107, 109, 111, 112, 116–
        120
      service-level agreements 110–111
      social partnership 109–110, 111–112
      social service councils 107–108
      volunteering 109
    see also individual organisations
voluntary action in Northern Ireland
  advocacy record 181
  conclusions 103–105
  definition xv–xvi
  features of
    activities 83–84
    age profile 75–76
    funding 78–82
    membership 77–78
    paid staff and volunteers 82–83
    policy process, engagement in 84–
      86
    types of organisation 77, 78
  independent voice of older people
    101–103
  introduction 66–67
  local organisations
    strengths and weaknesses 100–101

public policy and 67–74
  1920–1949 67–68, 69
  1950–1980 68–69
  2003 *Partners for Change* 71–72
  civic development and social
    cohesion 71–72
  group rights 73, 74, 101, 104–105,
    153, 154, 155, 156, 171, 196
  split between purchase and
    provision of services 69–70
  uncertainty over role 72, 73–74
regional bodies 86–87
  Age Concern *see* Age Concern
  Age Sector Reference Group 89–91,
    101–102, 103, 153–154, 156,
    157, 180–181
  Help the Aged *see* Help the Aged
  Older People's Policy Forum 92
  Pensioners' Convention 90, 92, 105,
    159, 179
  subregional network organisations 87,
    92–94, 180
  cross-border contacts 86, 97–98,
    136–137, 198, 222
  Engage with Age 94, 98–100, 155
  Newry and Mourne Senior Citizens'
    Consortium 96–97, 100
  Sperrin Lakeland Senior Citizens'
    Consortium 94–95, 97, 102
  see also individual organisations

Wales 25
  charities and public services 74
  independent service providers 70
Walker, A. 8, 11, 12, 35, 128

Wanless, D. 25
water charges (NI) 91, 181
Watson, D. 43
Webster, Robin 197
welfare regimes 4–6, 22–23
Welfare Services Act (Northern Ireland)
  1949 67
Westgate Foundation 139, 141, 222–224
Whelan, C.T. 42
White, Mary 62
Wolfenden, Lord 68
women
  Association for the Relief of
    Distressed Protestants 121
  carers 54
  health 48
  income poverty 178
    Ireland 40, 42
    Northern Ireland 19
  life expectancy 38
  Older Women's Network (OWN) 201–
    202
  pensioners, number of
    Northern Ireland 18
  screening services
    Ireland 59
Women's Coalition 157
Workers' Educational Association 102–
  103
World Health Organisation 33, 50, 154

Young, I.M. 3, 185

Zaidi, A. 42, 53